CW01678011

The Renaissance of the Nottinghamshire Market Town

The Renaissance of the Nottinghamshire Market Town 1680–1840

Catherine A. Smith

MERTON

First published 2007

Published by
Merton Priory Press Ltd
9 Owen Falls Avenue
Chesterfield S41 0FR

ISBN 978 1 898937 46 3

Dedication

For my mother and in loving memory of Mabel Grimwood

Printed by
Dinefwr Press Ltd
Rawlings Road, Llandybie
Carmarthenshire SA18 3YD

Contents

	List of Tables	vi
	List of Figures	viii
	Acknowledgements	ix
	Abbreviations used in the Footnotes	x
1	Introduction	1
2	Sources and Methods	20
3	Urban Space	39
4	Population Growth and Economic Change	58
5	Wealth, Status and Association	86
6	Improvement and Refashioning	131
7	Conclusion	166
	Bibliography	173
	Index	187

List of Tables

2.1	Hearth tax assessments and probate inventories	29
2.2	Numbers of hearths and inventory values	30
2.3	Numbers of hearths and occupations and statuses	31
3.1	Households in hearth tax assessments	41
3.2	Archbishop Herring's visitation returns	42
3.3	Census house data, 1801–41	44
3.4	Courts and alleys of Stockwell Gate in Mansfield in 1824	56
4.1	Regional distribution of the English population, 1701–1851	60
4.2	Population estimates, 1664–1801	61
4.3	Occupations recorded in probate documents	66
4.4	Tradesmen and professionals, 1721–1841	68
4.5	Inventories and inventory declarations for maltsters	75
4.6	Weekly coach destinations in 1832	81
4.7	Inns, taverns and beerhouses	82
5.1	Distribution of hearths in 1674	93
5.2	Distribution of inventories by value	98
5.3	Distribution of higher value inventories	99
5.4	Inventories valued at over £1,000	100

5.5 Inventories valued at between £500 and £999 101

5.6 Frequency of ittems recorded in inventories 106

5.7 Occupation or status of those possessing consumer goods 107

5.8 Average value of household goods in inventories 109

5.9 Clubs and societies in Nottinghamshire market towns 115

5.10 Distribution of hearths by street in Newark and Mansfield 122

5.11 Distribution of hearths by street in Newark 123

5.12 Distribution of hearths by street in Mansfield 124

5.13 Gentry residence in 1841 128

6.1 Public buildings erected, 1752–1840 143

List of Figures

1	Nottinghamshire market towns in the eighteenth century	10
2	The medieval borough of Newark	43
3	Urban development of Newark 1790–1841	45
4	Worksop: urban expansion, 1774–1851	48
5	Bingham in 1841	49
6	Newark market place, *c.*1790	51
7	Castle Gate Wharves, Newark, in 1836	52
8	Stanton's Mill, Mansfield	53
9	Plans of proposed houses off Appleton Gate, Newark	54
10	Plans of proposed houses on the Norfolk estate at Westgate, Worksop	55
11	Residential segregation in Newark in 1841	126
12	A seventeenth-century house in Mansfield	133
13	Handley House, Newark	134
14	Waverley House, Mansfield	136
15	Georgian Terrace, Worksop	138
16	The new Mansfield Town Hall of 1752	139
17	The later Mansfield Town Hall of 1836	141

Acknowledgements

My first thanks must go to my former Ph.D. supervisors, Professor John V. Beckett and Dr Catherine Delano-Smith. I have learnt so much from John and Catherine and I will always remember their support and guidance during the research and writing of the thesis which has formed the basis of this book. I have been equally fortunate in working at the University of Northampton with colleagues who have given so much academic support and friendship. In particular, I would like to say thank you to Professor Peter King. Family and friends have played an equally important role in helping with the completion of this book and I would like to say thank you to my mother for all her love and patience. Finally, thanks to all the staff of the Nottinghamshire Archives Office, without whose help and flexibility my research would have been much more difficult.

Figure 10 is reproduced by kind permission of His Grace the Duke of Norfolk KG. For permission to publish other illustrations I am grateful to Newark and Sherwood District Council Museum Service (front cover and Fig. 6), Nottingham University Department of Manuscripts (Fig. 7) and Nottinghamshire Archives (Fig. 9).

While this book could not have been completed without the support of others, I myself must accept responsibility for any errors that arise within it.

University of Northampton Catherine Smith
2007

Abbreviations used in the Footnotes

The abbreviation NAO has been used throughout the footnotes to refer to Nottinghamshire Archives and NUMD to refer to the Department of Manuscripts and Special Collections of Nottingham University Library. For an explanation of abbreviated references to collections in these and other repositories see the Bibliography.

ONE

Introduction

This book explores the development of six Nottinghamshire market towns from *c.*1680 to 1840, a period long recognised and partially characterised by its growing urbanisation. Contemporaries and latter-day historians have documented this process from the demographic, physical, cultural, social and political perspectives. Of particular note in this period is the fact that this growing urban presence was not solely a reflection of the fortunes of London. While London continued to grow and develop, much more noticeable was the rise of the provincial towns. These included ports like Newcastle, Bristol and Liverpool, manufacturing towns like Birmingham and Sheffield, towns with an increasing industrial presence like Manchester and Leeds, and a rising number of resort and spa towns like Bath and Tunbridge Wells. The impact and dynamism of towns like these, as Penny Corfield rightly highlighted, 'exercised a profound gravitational force' on eighteenth-century society.[1] Most academic focus has concentrated on those towns at the forefront of this growing urban dynamic, towns whose populations had grown to over 20,000, towns which developed a specialised economic or cultural base and those that developed into the industrial centres of the Victorian era. The development of these places, and the problems and possibilities such growth incurred, is hard to underestimate, but one of the interesting and perhaps most distinctive elements of the urban picture of the long eighteenth century is the range of towns that continued to survive and prosper, demographically and economically. This book, based on the fortunes of market towns in Nottinghamshire, aims to demonstrate that the urban story of the long eighteenth century has much greater depth and complexity than has been fully appreciated.

Six Nottinghamshire market towns were chosen for this purpose. Only one, Newark, had a population that exceeded 10,000 in 1841. Two of them, Bingham and Ollerton, had populations that remained under 2,000 in 1841. How does the experience of these places fit into the urban historiography of the long eighteenth century and what explains their varying fortunes? Fortunately, the story that emerges from the Nottinghamshire examples can be compared and contrasted with the experience

[1] P.J. Corfield, *The Impact of English Towns 1700-1800* (Oxford, 1982), p. 188.

of other market towns and the national picture that has emerged from two important publications, which have presented a much healthier picture of English small town experience in the long eighteenth century. This is not to say that all English smaller towns enjoyed the growth and development common to their larger provincial neighbours, but many did. We are inevitably looking at different timescales and a different pace of change. Equally there were special problems and challenges, but what is striking is how well most English small towns did, particularly in comparison with their European counterparts. It is, however, impossible neatly to present a synthesis of the *one* small town English experience. Clark and Langton have highlighted the importance of the region as a key determining factor in the fortunes of smaller towns.[1] As Pat Hudson has argued, differences in the social, cultural and geographical make-up of regions was important in moulding economic development,[2] and this in turn had a major impact on the fortunes of local towns. As Alan Dyer points out, in regions such as East Anglia the decline in cloth-making had a negative effect on the development of small towns, but equally, as Clark has illustrated, the growth experienced in the Midlands and North West brought significant benefits to these settlements.[3]

Measuring exactly how a regional dynamic affected urban growth is difficult, perhaps especially in a period where national and international markets were of growing importance. Nevertheless, Jon Stobart and Neil Raven's recent publication on *Towns, Regions and Industries* in the Midlands has attempted to address the geography of historical change.[4] The Midlands region offered great potential for smaller towns well situated to benefit from its central position and good communication routes. Existing communication and transport links saw regular and sustained improvement through turnpike trusts, river navigation schemes and waggon- and coach-building technology in the eighteenth and

[1] P. Clark (ed.), *Small Towns in Early Modern Europe* (Cambridge, 1995); idem, *The Cambridge Urban History of Britain, vol. 2: 1540–1840* (Cambridge, 2000).

[2] P. Hudson (ed.), *Regions and Industries: A Perspective on the Industrial Revolution in Britain* (Cambridge, 1989), p. 30.

[3] A. Dyer, 'Small towns in England, 1600–1800' in P. Borsay and L. Proudfoot, *Provincial Towns in Early Modern England and Ireland. Change, Convergence and Divergence* (Proceedings of the British Academy, 108, 2002) p. 55; Clark, *Small Towns*, pp. 103–8.

[4] J. Stobart and N. Raven, *Towns, Regions and Industries. Urban and industrial change in the Midlands, c.1700–1840* (Manchester, 2005).

nineteenth centuries.[1] At the same time, canal building opened up new communication routes, particularly for landlocked areas. In Nottinghamshire the Great North Road, the Fosse Way, the river Trent and later locally developed canal links ensured the processes of urban change commonly identified with larger provincial and county centres, port, spa and industrial towns did not by-pass the smaller Nottinghamshire market towns. This can be seen economically in terms of the range of products and shops available in these towns and in the growth of manufacturing interests; physically and demographically in terms of their growth and expansion; culturally in terms of new town halls, theatres, libraries and coffee rooms, and houses fashionably styled and furnished.

As noted above, the timescale and pace of change was different for the smaller towns. There seem to have been two chronological phases to the urban development of the Nottinghamshire market towns and this pattern seems to be consistent with findings for other similar towns. The first, from *c.*1680 to 1770, saw a relatively modest expansion of the physical size of the towns and their populations, but some diversification of the economy. By contrast, from *c.*1770 to 1840 the pace of change quickens. Demographically and spatially all but the smallest towns, Bingham and Ollerton, experience an increased rate of growth and development. Culturally, the towns were transformed. Economically we see the establishment of large-scale production aimed at the growing national and international markets in malt, brewing and cotton manufactures. Collectively, these changes contributed to a growing sense of urban pride reflected in new architectural styles and public buildings, and a zest for urban improvement, but perhaps ultimately in the publishing of town histories using the past to establish and celebrate the present. In many respects the Nottinghamshire market towns were following a fashion, with all these trends found earlier in the larger provincial centres. For Peter Borsay, in the century after the Restoration English provincial towns experienced a cultural renaissance. Based on economic prosperity, the urban landscape and urban leisure were transformed.[2] This book will argue that the notion of an 'urban renaissance' can be extended beyond the county towns where it gained an early foothold. There was a time lag between the renaissance of larger and smaller towns and of course there was a difference in the scale of change

[1] N. Raven and J. Stobart, 'Networks and hinterlands: transport in the Midlands' in *Towns, Regions and Industries*, pp. 80–101.

[2] P. Borsay, *The English urban renaissance. Culture and society in the provincial towns, 1660–1770* (Oxford, 1989).

experienced. This can be explained by the more moderate economic development of smaller towns in Nottinghamshire and elsewhere, particularly in the period from 1680 to 1770; nonetheless, there is little doubt that many market towns enjoyed their own renaissance, which gained momentum in the late eighteenth century.

The renaissance of the smaller town has implications that extend beyond the urban history of the long eighteenth century. There is little doubt that the growth of towns generally contributed to and stimulated broader economic, cultural and social change.[1] But in order to evaluate their full impact, we need to embrace the full range of towns and we need to be clear what constituted a town in the long eighteenth century. While the 1851 census counted as urban all who lived in 'towns of some 2,000 or more inhabitants, without any organisation other than a parish vestry', many historians have not been so generous, even for an earlier period.[2] Corfield, Law and Wrigley exclude towns with populations either below 2,500 or 5,000.[3] More recently Ellis has argued that while the 2,500 threshold is useful for comparative purposes, in relation to the process of urbanisation, smaller settlements had demonstrable 'urban' functions and features.[4] This is important when we consider the number of towns that fell below the 5,000 and 2,500 population thresholds. Although Everitt has estimated that by 1770 'perhaps as many as one third of the 800 market towns in England and Wales had become extinct', there were in fact still over 500 market or small towns in existence in the early nineteenth century.[5] Chalklin suggests that in 1700 there were 500 towns of between 500 and 1,800 people; 40 to 50 had a population of between 2,000 and 5,000, 24 had between 5,000 and 10,000, seven regional capitals had in excess of 10,000, and London and Norwich each had over 25,000.[6] By these estimates over four-fifths of England's towns had a population of less than 2,000.[7] In 1700, Langton

[1] Corfield, *Towns,* Preface and Conclusion.

[2] F.M.L. Thompson, *The Cambridge Social History of Britain 1750-1950. 1. Regions and Communities* (Cambridge, 1990), p. 3.

[3] Corfield excludes towns with populations of less than 2,500 (*Towns*, p. 7); C.M. Law, 'Some notes on the urban population of England and Wales in the eighteenth century', *Local Historian*, 10 (1) (1972), p. 18; E.A. Wrigley, 'Urban growth and agricultural change: England and the Continent in the early modern period', *Journal of Interdisciplinary History*, 15 (4) (1985), pp. 684–90.

[4] J.M. Ellis, *The Georgian Town* (2001), pp. 12–13.

[5] A. Everitt, 'Urban Growth 1550–1770', *Local Historian*, 8 (4) (1968), p. 120.

[6] C.W. Chalklin, *The Provincial Towns of Georgian England: a study of the building process, 1740–1820* (London, 1974), pp. 4-5.

[7] Ibid., p. 5.

argues, small towns comprised about 90 per cent of the English urban system.[1] In 1758 some 681 markets were recorded and in 1772 no fewer than 550 places held regular markets.[2] Together these smaller towns may have housed no less than half the urban population of England and Wales over the eighteenth and early nineteenth centuries and thus their impact could be crucial.[3]

Corfield estimates that the proportion of the urban population living in towns of between 2,500 and 5,000 remained at 12 per cent in 1701, 1750 and 1801. This is despite the number of towns in this category increasing from 37 in 1700 to 104 in 1750 and 188 in 1801, with their average population ranging between 3,000 and 3,500.[4] Langton's figures, which cover towns with populations below 2,500, show a decline in number from 927 in the sixteenth century to 708 in 1801 and 487 by 1841, with the proportion of the urban population living in these places falling from 21 in 1801 to only 8 per cent by 1841.[5] While these figures show the demographic importance of small towns was declining over the eighteenth century and particularly in the early nineteenth century, they do not necessarily mean that small towns individually fell into decline. Often, as a result of growth, they moved up a level in the league table of town size.

But as Ellis points out, late eighteenth- and early nineteenth-century writers often demonstrated the 'urbanity' of a community by more than simply 'crude population growth'.[6] Towns can be, and have been, defined in a variety of terms. These include population size, but also focus on function, occupational structure, housing density and legal status. As Everitt remarked in relation to Charlbury, it was 'as small a place as can properly be called a town, but during most of its history it has born the essential characteristics that distinguish every town, however small—namely the possession of trading rights and functions independent of farming activities'.[7] This is further emphasised in Ellis's discussion of new settlements surrounding Nottingham which developed

[1] J. Langton, 'Urban growth and economic change: from the seventeenth century to 1841', in Clark, *Cambridge Urban History*, pp. 463, 466.

[2] J. Brown, *The English Market Town* (Marlborough, 1986), p. 14.

[3] M. Noble, 'Growth and development in a regional urban system: the country towns of eastern Yorkshire', *Urban History Yearbook* (1987).

[4] Corfield, *Towns*, p. 8.

[5] Langton, 'Urban growth', Tables 14.1 and 14.3, pp. 462, 471.

[6] J. Ellis, 'Industrial and urban growth in Nottingham, 1680–1840' in Stobart and Raven, *Towns, Regions and Industries*, p. 156.

[7] A. Everitt, 'The Banburys of England', *Urban History Yearbook* (1974), pp. 28–9.

a distinctly 'suburban' character and other settlements within the orbit of Nottingham that developed demonstrable urban functions, a difference often highlighted in the language of contemporary commentators.[1]

Nonetheless, by sheer weight of number alone, there is a strong case for including the experience of smaller towns in the broader historiography of eighteenth- and nineteenth-century urban development. Where this work has been undertaken we are seeing a very different picture emerge from that presented in the 1960s. Thus, in 1962 Finberg argued that whereas 'down to the era of stage coaches [market towns] flourished more or less vigorously, then [they] … became backwaters and sank into a deathlike trance'.[2] Corfield presented a more balanced analysis in 1982, highlighting the uneven nature of urban growth between 1700 and 1800 with the decline of minor markets situated away from major communication networks. As a result of this, she argued, the possession of a market grant could no longer be equated with urban status.[3] While Corfield's assessment allows for the growth of market towns well positioned in terms of resources, traffic routes and established urban networks, the role of such towns is underplayed in her broader consideration of the impact of towns.

Moreover, the evidence of functioning markets and population growth supports a more positive view of small town development. A growing number of more detailed studies of small towns directly contradict any general notion of stagnation or decline.[4] This results in a less tidy but more accurate picture of urban development in the long eighteenth century. Small towns did not simply decline as larger provincial centres increased their sphere of influence. Nor did they merely continue as basic service centres for their rural hinterlands. Slowly from 1680 and more noticeably from *c.*1770 many small towns developed a distinct identity increasingly at odds with their size. Undoubtedly, the eighteenth century hastened and concluded the nemesis of some market towns. As Clark argues, the specialisation and rationalisation of the market network that came with improved communications had a negative effect on some towns. He draws a parallel between the decline of the small landowner

[1] Ellis, 'Nottingham, 1680–1840', p. 156.

[2] H.P.R. Finberg, *Approaches to History* (London, 1962), p. 119.

[3] Corfield, *Towns*, pp. 11, 21.

[4] See for example J.D. Marshall, 'The rise and transformation of the Cumbrian market town 1660–1900', *Northern History*, 19 (1983); R.W. Unwin, 'Tradition and transition: market towns of the Vale of York, 1660–1830', Idem, 7 (1981); Noble, 'The county towns of eastern Yorkshire'; N. Powell, 'Do numbers count? Towns in early modern Wales', *Urban History*, 32 (1) (2005), 46–67; Dyer, 'Small towns'.

and that of the smaller urban communities, but at the same time the point is made that there were many exceptions to this picture. One small town could be favoured by the same developments that led to the eclipse of another and we need to think carefully about when this specialisation and rationalisation of the market network came about.[1] It is also clear, as Leonard Schwarz has demonstrated for Lichfield, that some market towns could manage 'marginalisation very well'.[2]

This book on the Nottinghamshire market towns, together with similar work done for Cumbria, the Vale of York and Derbyshire, alongside the national and international picture outlined by Clark and Langton, points to a more positive interpretation of the fate of the Georgian small town. Marshall has argued that the period from 1660 to 1900 saw the rise and transformation of the Cumbrian market town, Unwin has described that of 1660 to 1830 as a 'formative' one in the history of market towns, and Noble has shown that the larger market towns of eastern Yorkshire saw growth and expansion in this period. Collectively this body of evidence supports Dyer's idea of a 'Golden Age' for small towns between *c.*1660 and 1800.[3] The eighteenth century, it would seem, provided a window of opportunity open to small and larger towns alike. Key to this was economic development at the regional, national and international level. In the provincial towns this growth encouraged cultural renewal and an expansion in leisure facilities that was mirrored lower down the urban hierarchy. As Marshall suggests, it was at this time between 1760 and 1830 that 'the smallish market centre, of perhaps a few hundred people in the urban settlement proper, reached a high noon of importance and activity. It was both economic outlet and social foregathering place, with elaborate trade connections and growing institutions ... '.[4] To Marshall's list we can add 'industrial producer' and 'manufacturer' especially from the late eighteenth century, roles not normally associated with a market town. Given that there were some 500 small towns to which some of these developments may apply, in aggregate this raises some interesting questions not just for urban historians but also for those more generally interested in the long eighteenth century. Why were small towns able to prosper and what does this say about the nature of change in this period?

First and foremost, we must remember that improvements in transport

[1] P. Clark (ed.), *The Transformation of English.Provincial Towns* (London, 1984), p. 20; a similar point is made by Corfield, *Towns*, pp. .19–20.

[2] L. Schwarz, 'On the margins of industrialisation: Litchfield', in Stobart and Raven, *Towns, Regions and Industries*, p. 176.

[3] Dyer, 'Small towns', pp. 54–6.

[4] Marshall, 'Cumbrian market town', pp. 152–3.

and communications, and changes in the organisation of industry, did not occur at a revolutionary pace. Transport improvements were often initiated at the local level. Thus, there could be considerable variation in, for example, the turnpiking of roads. This may partially explain the differing regional dynamic emphasised by Clark and Langton. Similarly, the research of Berg and Hudson has revised our interpretation of the industrial revolution, with greater emphasis being placed on, amongst other factors, regional diversity and a more varied form of large-scale production and specialisation of employment beyond the physical walls of the factories and mills that loom so large in traditional accounts.[1] It is also clear that having a local industrialist or entrepreneur pushing and often financing improvements in transport or business connections could make a significant difference to the fortunes of a place. In other words, the dynamics of rationalisation and specialisation so often employed in the broader analyses of the national urban picture could be disrupted by very specific local factors.

The case for Nottinghamshire market towns

The decision to choose Nottinghamshire market towns for study was made for two main reasons. First, more work is still needed on the market towns which numerically figure so large on the urban map of eighteenth- and nineteenth-century Britain. While a national picture has emerged, largely from statistical accounts of population growth, towns represent more than simply a mass of population, and given their importance in this period, we need to understand more about how these towns developed and under what influences. Second, there is still relatively little research on Nottinghamshire as a county and the east midlands as a region. Stobart and Raven's recent publication on urban and industrial change in the Midlands is a welcome step forward but relatively little focus is given to Nottinghamshire and where it is the focus is predominantly on Nottingham itself.

For most of the period between 1680 and 1840, and particularly from the late eighteenth century onwards, Nottinghamshire balanced a successful agricultural economy with a growing industrial and manufacturing sector. Cotton spinning, lace making and framework knitting formed the basis of the local textile industry, and the county also

[1] M. Berg and P. Hudson, 'Rehabilitating the Industrial Revolution', *Economic History Review*, 45 (1992), pp. 24–50.

developed an extensive trade in malt and beer and, from the early nineteenth century, coal.[1] Nottinghamshire's mixed economy benefitted from its central location and its situation between the growing industrial towns and villages of northern England and the West Midlands, the rich agricultural county of Lincolnshire, and the extractive industries of Derbyshire. Lying between these mixed economies, Nottinghamshire had long functioned as a focal point for trade and exchange.

Natural advantages encouraged the county's economic prosperity. The county lies within the basin of the river Trent, which flows through its southern parts before turning northwards to form the boundary with Lincolnshire. The Trent had always been navigable at least as far as Nottingham but, until an improvement Act was passed in 1772, the section from Shardlow to Gainsborough was unsatisfactory.[2] Good river communication was enhanced by long-established major roads. The Roman Fosse Way crosses the county from east to west, while the Great North Road runs north to south. The county's roads and rivers were to see slow but continuous improvement during the eighteenth and early nineteenth centuries (see Chapter 4).

Between 1680 and 1840 Nottinghamshire had ten market towns, including the county town itself. As in other parts of England, this represented a decline from earlier periods but the number remained stable into the nineteenth century.[3] The six towns chosen for this study are Newark, Mansfield, Worksop, East Retford, Bingham and Ollerton (Fig. 1). These towns were selected for three main reasons. First, the towns varied greatly in size. In 1841 the parish of Newark had a population of 10,195, whereas Ollerton chapelry had only 777, barely sufficient in even the broadest sense to qualify as a town. Three of the towns, East Retford, Bingham and Ollerton, had populations below 5,000 until 1851 and beyond. This would have excluded their consideration from several previous studies. Yet taking Ellis's point, all three performed, albeit to different degrees, what we might consider to be urban, central place functions, and all certainly possessed an occupational structure more complex than that of surrounding villages. Moreover, all three were classified as towns by contemporaries throughout the period and size did not always dictate how the towns were seen. Thus White's *Directory* (1832) described Bingham as a 'straggling and inconsiderable market

[1] J.D. Chambers, *Nottinghamshire in the Eighteenth Century* (2nd edn, 1966).

[2] A.C. Wood, 'The history of trade and transport on the river Trent', *Trans. Thoroton Soc.* (1950), p. 26.

[3] A. Everitt, 'The marketing of agricultural produce' in J. Thirsk (ed.), *The Agrarian History of England and Wales. IV. 1500–1640* (Cambridge, 1967), pp. 466–592.

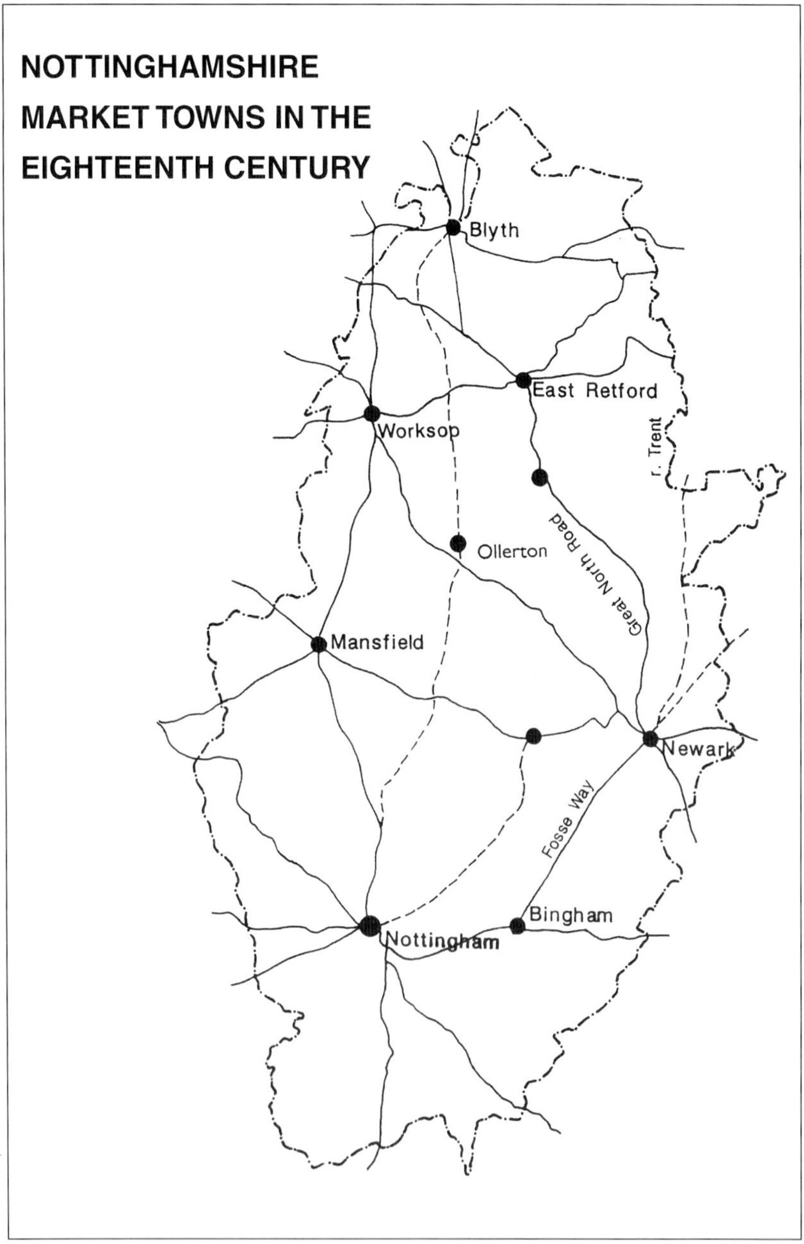

Figure 1 Nottinghamshire market towns in the eighteenth century.

town', yet Ollerton, smaller and more straggling, was simply described as a 'small market town'.[1] What constituted a town was as unclear in the eighteenth and nineteenth centuries as it is looking back on that period today, especially when we are discussing small settlements. As Dyer highlights, the growth of industry in the eighteenth century makes the distinction between urban and rural settlements more problematic. Rural industry could encourage population growth in settlements that possessed few other urban characteristics, and thus population in itself is a limited indicator of urban status.[2] Irrespective of whether we focus on population size, market functions, housing density or legal status we are always going to face problems in drawing an all-encompassing threshold to determine urban from rural, town from village.

Size is, however, a more accurate reflection of prosperity and the diversity of the six towns clearly reflects their differing fortunes between 1680 and 1840. Location may have been key to this, and so the second reason for choosing them was that they were geographically dispersed. Worksop and East Retford lie to the north of the county, Newark, Mansfield and Ollerton are more centrally placed on an east–west axis, while Bingham is close to Nottingham in the south. This dispersal means the towns could have quite different local agrarian economies, largely reflecting differences in geology and soil. Like Nottingham itself, Newark lies in the Trent valley on the Keuper marls. Bingham, to the east of Nottingham and the Trent, is in the arable region of the Vale of Belvoir. East Retford lies in a narrow belt of Keuper waterstones and enjoys a rich loamy soil. In contrast, Mansfield, Worksop and Ollerton lie on the poorer Bunter sandstone.[3]

The towns were not only geographically and demographically diverse but also had differing administrative status. East Retford and Newark were both boroughs. East Retford was granted a charter in 1225 and Newark was incorporated in 1549.[4] The other four towns stayed under manorial control throughout this period. We might suppose that East Retford and Newark had a greater degree of self-government and independence because of their status, but this was far from the case. Their right to return two members of Parliament actually militated against this, as they were often caught up in the political battles of the

[1] Loc. cit., pp. 418, 480.

[2] Dyer, 'Small Towns', p. 54.

[3] K.C. Edwards, *Land of Britain: Nottinghamshire* (1944), p. 507.

[4] M.W. Bishop, 'The origins of East Retford', *Trans. Thoroton Soc.*, 82 (1978); M.W. Barley, 'Newark in the sixteenth century', Ibid., 53 (1949).

local aristocracy. For example, the dukes of Newcastle increased their influence and control in Newark, largely by purchasing land and property in the town, for political ends.[1]

For all this diversity, the six towns shared one thing in common: all were regarded as market towns by contemporaries for most of the period. Bingham and Ollerton markets seem to have failed for short periods in the eighteenth century but were revived by the nineteenth century. All six supported trades and services that distinguished them from surrounding villages and justifies their inclusion here.

A range of wider questions can be raised in relation to the six towns. How did population growth, economic development, industrialisation, agricultural change, consumerism, the rise of the 'middling ranks', commercialisation, and an urban renaissance affect them? Do we see in the period from 1680 to 1840 the emergence of a more 'distinctly modern market town' and, if so, how representative is this development of other small towns in England? And, finally, how does the development of the Nottinghamshire market towns contribute to current interpretations of the 'long eighteenth century'?

Interpretations of the 'Long Eighteenth Century'

Seen as falling somewhere between 1660 and 1820, the 'long eighteenth century' has become the subject of renewed interest. While it is obvious that England was very different in the late seventeenth century as compared with the early nineteenth, such a simple antithesis does not help to characterise the intervening period, although there seems to be an underlying consensus that the years from 1660 to 1820 saw the emergence of a more distinctly 'modern' society. Earle suggests that the period from 1660 to 1730 'defined and created the society and economy which ushered in the modern world'.[2] George described the middle years of the eighteenth century as 'a watershed dividing old England from the modern world as we know it', while Porter called the eighteenth century as a whole 'a distinctive moment in the making of modern England'.[3] More recently Rule has described the period from 1714 to 1815 as the 'vital century'; to him it was vital 'in terms of direction, changing

[1] M.J. Smith, 'Politics in Newark in the 1790s', *Trans. Thoroton Soc.*, 84 (1980).

[2] P. Earle, *The Making of the English Middle Classes: Business, Society and Family Life in London, 1660–1730* (1989), p. xi.

[3] D. George, *England in Transition* (1964 edn), p. 9; R. Porter, *English Society in the Eighteenth Century* (1982), p. 16.

structures and the revelation of a transforming potential for the output of material goods and the harnessing of resources for that end, the recognisable beginnings of the modern economy'.[1]

There is no consensus as to how transformative a period the 'long eighteenth century' was. Both Crafts and Wrigley, in their studies of selected aspects of the economy, have argued that earlier optimism should be modified. National output figures tend to flatten the rate of both agricultural and manufacturing growth in the eighteenth century.[2] Their challenge to the perception of the eighteenth century as a period of significant change has been extended to constitutional and social history. Clark, for example, has argued that between 1688 and 1832 English society remained firmly embedded in the *ancien régime*.[3] While few would deny that the landed élite enjoyed political hegemony, and that the ownership of land remained the currency of power from parliament to parish, others have pointed to the increasing role played by the urban, commercial and bourgeois elements in eighteenth-century society.[4]

For those who emphasise change rather than continuity, this 'modernising' society was characterised by certain key developments. First and foremost was the almost continuous population growth of the eighteenth and early nineteenth centuries.[5] A number of factors underpinned this expansion: economic growth (both in terms of industrial and agricultural output), urbanisation, the 'birth of a consumer society', the beginnings of industrialisation, the growth of the middle classes, the rise of polite society, and perhaps even the beginnings of a working class consciousness. Eighteenth-century society, it has been argued, became more 'capitalist, materialist, market-orientated; worldly, pragmatic, responsive

[1] J. Rule, *The Vital Century: England's Developing Economy, 1714–1815* (1992), p. 317

[2] N.F.R. Crafts, 'British Economic Growth, 1700–1831: a review of the evidence', *Economic History Review*, 2nd ser. 26 (1983); idem, *British Economic Growth during the Industrial Revolution* (Oxford, 1985); E.A. Wrigley, *Continuity, Chance and Change: The Character of the Industrial Revolution in England* (Cambridge, 1988).

[3] J.C.D. Clark, *English Society, 1688–1832: Ideology, Social Structure and Political Practice during the Ancien Regime* (Cambridge, 1985).

[4] Corfield, *Towns*; Borsay (ed.), *Eighteenth-century Town*; idem, *Urban Renaissance*; Porter, *English Society*; P. Langford, *A Polite and Commercial People: England 1727–1783* (Oxford, 1989); Earle, *Middle Classes*.

[5] There is clear evidence that from 1680 the only period to witness absolute population decline was from the late 1720s to 1730. For the rest of the period population grew, though at varying rates. E.A. Wrigley and R.S. Schofield, *The Population History of England 1541–1871. A Reconstruction* (Cambridge, 1989 edn), p. 208.

to economic pressures'.[1] At the same time, it also became more introspective, measuring, documenting and debating these signs of change, a characteristic which also brings it closer to our own society.

Some of these developments are easier to measure than others. Between 1714 and 1815 the population of England is estimated to have doubled from about 5.25 million to 10.5 million.[2] Over the 'long eighteenth century' population grew by perhaps 130 per cent, and between 1680 and 1840 the figure is thought to have been nearer 200 per cent.[3] This increase was without precedent and was unequalled anywhere else in Europe.[4] Furthermore, it was achieved without the subsistence crisis that Malthus had predicted. Estimates of English agricultural output suggest that by the end of the eighteenth century England was virtually self-sustaining, notwithstanding a fall of about a third in the numbers engaged in agriculture.[5]

Much of this demographic increase was to be found in towns. The urban proportion of the population rose from an estimated 18 per cent in 1700 to 22 per cent in 1750 and 30 per cent by 1801.[6] Besides London, only Norwich and Bristol had populations of over 20,000 in 1670, but by 1750 Bristol had a population of 50,000, Norwich 36,000, Newcastle, Birmingham and Liverpool over 22,000. By 1801, Manchester and Liverpool had passed 80,000, and another fifteen towns had 20,000 or more inhabitants.[7] Not only did each town's population grow but so too did its sphere of economic, social and political influence. It is generally agreed that this expansion of the provincial and commercial centres of Georgian England was crucial to the transformation of the country as a whole, simply because the sheer number of individuals living within towns encouraged agricultural and industrial development to meet the demand for food and services.[8]

[1] Porter, *English Society,* p. 16.

[2] Rule, *Vital Century,* p. 5.

[3] Wrigley and Schofield, *Population History,* p. 208.

[4] Rule, *Vital Century,* p. 5.

[5] Ibid., p. 308.

[6] Corfield, *Towns,* p. 9. The proportion would be larger if towns with populations below 2,500 were included.

[7] E.A. Wrigley, 'Urban Growth and Agricultural Change: England and the Continent in the Early Modern Period', in Borsay (ed.), *Eighteenth-century Town,* p. 42.

[8] Wrigley, 'Model of London'; for a contemporary analysis of the impact of towns see 'How the Commerce of towns contributed to the Improvement of the Country' in A. Smith, *Enquiry into the Nature and Causes of the Wealth of Nations* (Everyman Ed.), i (1964), pp. 264–74.

Towns served as centres of exchange and distribution, not only of goods, but also of ideas, news and fashions. They were often the location of early large-scale industrial development and, as Corfield has argued, 'accumulators and circulators of investment capital' and 'purveyors of the new consumer ethos', centres of sociability and polite society and the base from which many of the rising middle classes were to make their living.[1] It was also the growth of towns like Birmingham, grossly under-represented in Parliament, which eventually forced political reform in 1832.

The notion of England as the scene of rapidly expanding provincial towns oversimplifies the paradoxes so evident in the long eighteenth century.[2] Much of the urban population lived in smaller market towns, and only in 1851 was a majority of the entire population recorded as town-dwellers.[3] Much industry was also still based in the countryside.[4] Thus to try to integrate those aspects of eighteenth-century society which seem 'modern' with those that seem alien into a single vision is particularly difficult.[5] The result has often been a balancing act, with historians pointing out the contrast between those aspects of eighteenth-century society which seem 'modern' and those which appear more traditional. This applies especially to urban history, and also economic history, where Berg and Hudson have argued that the division between modern and traditional sectors is an 'analytical device which hides more than it reveals'.[6] Many years ago Dorothy Marshall highlighted the distinction between an old and new urban England which grew up from the late eighteenth century:

> English towns can be divided into those that look forward to the future and those that look back to the past. Foremost in the first category were the great industrial towns ... Representative of the past were such cities as Bristol and Norwich ... and the host of

[1] Corfield, *Towns,* p. 97.

[2] J. Rule, *Albion's Society. English Society 1714–1815* (1992), p. 251.

[3] R.J. Morris and R. Rodger (ed.), *The Victorian City. A Reader in Urban History, 1820–1914* (1993), p. 3.

[4] E.A. Wrigley, 'Men on the land and men in the countryside. Employment in agriculture in early nineteenth-century England', in R. Bonfield, R. Smith and K. Wrightson, *The World we have gained. Histories of Population and Social Structure* (1986), pp. 295–336.

[5] J. Innes, 'Not so Strange? New Views of Eighteenth-century England', *History Workshop*, 29 (1990), p. 179.

[6] Berg and Hudson, 'Rehabilitating', p. 32.

> small market towns, which were little more than the surrounding countryside.[1]

Such a comment illustrates how the history of eighteenth-century society has tended to be written with reference to London and the rapidly expanding provincial centres. The bias can be justified in terms of the growing number of towns with populations of over 20,000 in the period 1750 to 1801, since the phenomenon was indeed something new and specific to the period, and by no means typical of contemporary European experience.[2] Moreover, the mere existence of towns of this size can be taken as an indicator of significant social and economic change. However, it can also be argued that by concentrating on the larger towns we are underestimating the scale of change across eighteenth-century society as a whole. The impression 'still obtains that the Victorian market town was usually a mere backwater, a stagnant place necessarily living on its past and out of touch with the realities of the contemporary world'.[3] It may be much easier to trace 'modernisation' in larger towns, but this does not mean that the process was limited to these places. By asking how far the signs of modernity and development can be traced in 'traditional backwaters' such as market towns, and by reviewing the contemporary situation according to a local and regional, rather than a national, perspective, we may begin to discover how pertinent these broad concepts of change are to the local experience, assuming that they are applicable at all.

This approach lends itself to another revision of views of the eighteenth century. Berg and Hudson have reopened the debate on the concept and significance of an 'Industrial Revolution' from the 1780s. Supporting the case for regional and local studies, they have rehabilitated the term through broadening its definition.[4] They argue that by taking too strict a definition of what is considered to be 'industrial' and by focusing too much on the term 'revolution', historians have undervalued the degree of economic and perhaps social change evident in this period. Likewise, looking for the roots of modern society in six Nottinghamshire towns (none of which would strike some historians as a source of evidence for the transformation to modern society) I find ample evidence

[1] D. Marshall, *Industrial England 1776–1851* (1973 edn), pp. 28–9.

[2] Corfield, *Towns*, p. 8; J. de Vries, *European Urbanisation 1500–1800* (1984) pp. 95–101.

[3] Everitt, 'The Banburys of England', pp. 36–7.

[4] Berg and Hudson, 'Rehabilitating'.

of growth, change and development. Perhaps our definition of 'urban' for the long eighteenth century is also in need of review.

'The *Longer* Eighteenth Century'

A starting point of 1680 for this study was chosen for two reasons. First, it is the date from which it is generally agreed that we begin to see the origins of a more modern society. A starting-point of 1660 was impractical for lack of sources, especially probate inventories, which for Nottinghamshire are available in quantity only from 1680. In addition, the hearth tax assessments of 1662 and 1674 provide the first reasonably accurate estimate of population size. A terminal date of 1840 was selected partly because this provides a benchmark in the history of the smaller town, and perhaps more generally in English society as a whole. In addiition, the fate of the market town can be linked to the growth of the railway network, to changes in local agrarian economies and also to the decline in domestic industry experienced in some regions. In many industries the dominant place occupied by small- and medium-scale producers was giving way by the 1830s to large-scale production.[1]

The coming of the railways fundamentally altered the pattern of communications. Towns situated away from main railway routes faced an uncertain future, since many market towns were heavily dependent on the carriage of goods by road, which contracted sharply as the railway network grew. Their impact varied between regions and between towns but overall the railways brought a halt to the building of canals and new main roads.[2] In the eighteenth century most turnpike roads had followed traditional routes and canals were never sufficiently widespread to alter established transport networks fundamentally. Thus many small towns on routes between larger centres benefitted considerably from increased road, river and canal traffic and were less adversely affected by improvements than is sometimes suggested.

Nor was domestic industry everywhere in the decline, at least not until the 1840s. Since this was often the lifeblood of the smaller towns, we would not expect places heavily dependent on them to be adversely affected before then. Marshall has shown how the decline of handloom

[1] M. Berg, *The Age of Manufactures 1700–1820. Industry, Innovation and Work in Britain* (2nd ed., 1994), p. 205.

[2] A. Moyes, 'Transport 1730-1900' in R.A. Dodgshon and R.A. Butlin, *An Historical Geography of England and Wales* (1987 ed.), p. 403.

weaving in Cumbria, with the concentration of power looms in Carlisle, had a detrimental effect on the smaller towns of Wigton, Brampton and Longtown from the 1830s.[1] In general, it was not until the Victorian age that the centralisation of trade and manufacture in the larger provincial towns occurred and the smaller centres did not lose their domestic industry until then.[2] This is, perhaps, why a number of studies have a terminal date of 1830. For example, Unwin and Marshall have suggested the period 1660–1830 and 1760–1830 were formative ones for market towns in the Vale of York and Cumbria respectively.[3]

The period from 1760 to 1830 does appear to have been a prosperous one for the more substantial market town, particularly in the north of England and probably in the country as a whole.[4] Unwin notes that the population of a number of Vale of York townships fell between 1821 and 1831, which he attributes to a depression in agriculture, although these towns had not been severely affected by the depression after 1815.[5] In Nottinghamshire there was no sign of decline amongst the small towns in the 1830s. In April 1840, however, the *Nottingham & Newark Mercury,* in anticipation of the arrival of the railway, warned that:

> No town will be more seriously affected than Newark by the establishment of railways. This is shown by the circumstance that, though advertised to be let for months, the Clinton Arms, one of the most commodious and eligible posting houses on the Great North Road, cannot obtain a tenant.[6]

Later the same year the *Mercury* reported that 'the railway has had a very great affect on travelling through Newark to Doncaster ... The Great North Road has been entirely deserted; scarcely a carriage passing through Newark where hundreds were want to be seen'.[7] Road and river transport had underpinned Newark's prosperity in the eighteenth century and earlier, and contemporaries were well aware that the railways would undermine this. Not all Nottinghamshire towns faced such an uncertain

1 Marshall, 'Cumbrian market town', p. 198.

2 Ibid., p. 131.

3 Unwin, 'Tradition and transition'; Marshall 'Cumbrian Market Town'.

4 Marshall 'Cumbrian Market Town', p. 131.

5 Unwin, 'Tradition and transition', p. 80.

6 *Nottingham & Newark Mercury*, 17 April 1840.

7 Ibid., 2 Oct. 1840.

future. From 1840 the exploitation of coal around Mansfield marked the beginning of new growth in the town's economy. For this reason also this study ends at this turning point.

The 1840s also marked a profound change in the urban consciousness of the intellectual and political classes. This is seen in public discourse and in the civic policy proposals put forward in the 1830s and 1840s concerning not only such matters as health and housing, but also education, religion and policing, all of which were now seen as distinctly urban problems. These years marked the onset of a new era in the perception of the town, beyond the scope of this enquiry.

For all these reasons, the period from 1680 to 1840 is seen as having a special coherence. For about a century and a half most Nottinghamshire market towns prospered, albeit not continuously. Indeed, this seems to be true of many other towns.[1]

The chapters that follow explore the economic, social and cultural experiences of the six towns, prefaced (in Chapter 2) by a discussion of the main sources used to see how far and in what ways these may influence both the methodology employed and the conclusions drawn. In Chapter 3 the changing urban landscape of market towns is considered, together with the morphology of the built environment and the pattern of expansion. It is quite clear that the towns saw considerable physical development from 1770 to 1840. Population growth and economic expansion are examined in Chapter 4 and comparisons drawn between the national experience and that of both larger and smaller towns. In Chapter 5 the focus is narrowed to look more closely at how the economic and demographic development of the towns affected different social groups and the distribution of wealth. Chapter 6 explores town improvement, particularly from the 1770s onwards. The evidence here points to a renaissance of the market town along the lines identified in Borsay's work. Finally, Chapter 7 concludes by suggesting that between 1680 and 1840 we see the emergence of a more distinctly modern market town for all but the smallest of the six places studied. Whether the focus is on the home, the workplace or a broader consideration of the local economy, this was a period of significant change.

[1] P. Clark, 'Small towns in England 1550–1850: national and regional population trends' and M. Reed, 'The cultural role of small towns in England 1600–1800', both in P. Clark (ed.), *Small Towns*; Marshall, 'Cumbrian Market Town'; Unwin, 'Tradition and transition'; Noble, 'Country towns'.

TWO

Sources and Methods

This chapter discusses the main sources used in this study and their limitations in relation to the bearing they may have had on the overall conclusions reached. In particular, there is a general lack of reliable sources from which long-term trends in population and economic and social development can be traced. This is a special problem for the period from 1680 to 1770, given the aim of going beyond a mere local study to consider the the major themes discussed in the mainstream literature, with no census returns and only limited and indirect information on the economies and social structure of the towns. Because of the lack of continuous records, the series of snapshots that can be created for each town during the long eighteenth century are not always sufficient to allow one to feel confident about the interpretations. Questions are easier to raise than to answer. However, it does seem clear that the small-scale, piecemeal change found in late seventeenth- and early eighteenth-century Nottinghamshire towns was part of a national process.

Linked to the general paucity of material, particularly for the first ninety years of this study, is the imbalance of sources between the larger and smaller towns. Larger towns generate much more source material than smaller ones. There is, therefore, a greater quantity and range of sources for Newark and Mansfield than for Bingham and Ollerton. Consequently, a variety of sources have been used here, many of which, such as family papers, the minutes of corporation and vestry meetings and newspaper reports, do not lend themselves to systematic analysis. Wherever possible, such sources were used in conjunction with probate inventories and wills (available from 1680 to 1840), the hearth tax assessments of 1674, land tax assessments from 1780 to 1832, and records arising from the commutation of tithe between 1841 and 1853, which are not only available for each of the towns but in some cases for a number of years. They could therefore be used on a comparative basis both between the towns and over time. On the other hand, these sources are not without their problems: the Newark land tax assessments, for example, are missing for the years 1788 to 1810 and 1812 to 1817.

Population estimates

Aggregative analysis of the population of the six towns was not attempted for this study. The parish registers for some of the towns are incomplete and there is also the problem that urban parishes and market towns generally had a greater incidence of nonconformity, which affects the number of baptisms more than the number of burials.[1] Instead it was decided to use a number of sources to obtain snapshot estimates between 1662 and the census of 1801, a common procedure for studies of more than one town over a long period.[2]

A familiar standard source used to estimate the population of small towns in the late seventeenth century are hearth tax assessments.[3] The hearth tax was introduced in 1662 to alleviate some of Charles II's financial difficulties. Occupiers were to pay 2s. for each fire hearth and stove in their property in two instalments at Lady Day and Michaelmas. Individuals too poor to be liable for church and poor rates were exempt. Initially, so too were those who occupied properties worth 20s. a year or less and those whose real or personal property did not exceed the value of £10, although by 1674 this provision had been amended and anyone with two or more hearths was liable to pay.[4] The best known legacy of the hearth tax are the duplicate assessments returned to the Exchequer containing lists of those who were liable to pay the tax, arranged by constablery (for larger places the names of streets or wards may also be included), together with the number of hearths on which they were assessed and, in some cases, whether they were chargeable or not.

Several studies have used hearth tax assessments as a basis for

[1] E.A. Wrigley and R.S. Schofield, *The Population History of England 1541–1871. A reconstruction* (Cambridge, 1989 edn), p. 165.

[2] S.A. Lewis, 'An Historical and Geographical Study of the Small Towns of Shropshire, 1600–1830' (Unpublished Ph.D. thesis, University of Leicester, 1990); G.O. Cowley, 'Sussex Market Towns 1550–1750' (Unpublished M.A. thesis, University of London, 1965), pp. 56-97; J. Patten, *English Towns 1500–1700* (Folkestone, 1978); P. Clark, 'Small towns in England 1550–1850: national and regional population trends' in P. Clark (ed.), *Small Towns in Early Modern Europe* (Cambridge, 1995), pp. 90–120; J. Stobart, 'An eighteenth-century revolution? Investigating urban growth in North West England, 1664–1801', *Urban History*, 23 (1) (1996).

[3] National Archives, E 179. All the surviving Nottinghamshire assessents for 1664 and 1674 have been published in W.F. Webster (ed.), *Nottinghamshire Hearth Tax 1664–1674* (Thoroton Soc. Record Series, 37, 1988), although the original documents were also used here.

[4] Webster (ed.), *Nottinghamshire Hearth Tax*, pp. vii–viii.

population estimates, despite their undoubted limitations.[1] The unpopularity of the tax and the rigorous attempts to exact it by the government suggest that under-counting may have been a problem, although the 1674 assessments may be more complete than those for 1662, since an Act of 1663 required that both chargeable and not chargeable hearths should be included in the assessments, and another Act of 1664 saw a further tightening of the administration.[2] The main objection to the tax was that it was levied at a single rate regardless of income. This should mean that all properties in an area were included, but this was clearly not the case. The 1674 assessments for Newark, East Retford and Worksop, for example, omit not-chargeable households altogether, despite the provisions of the 1663 Act, which could imply a 35 per cent under-counting of households.[3] In Mansfield one of the main streets appears to have been omitted. Even if we can be reasonably sure of household numbers, the assessments do not give household size. To convert the lists of taxpayers into population estimates various multipliers between four and five have been used in other studies.[4] The decision to use a multiplier of 4.25 for this study was largely based on the arguments forwarded by other historians working on seventeenth-century Nottinghamshire and on small towns.[5]

The hearth tax assessments suffer from evasion, exemption and general incompleteness and any population estimates based on them must be subject to error, especially if used to obtain absolute, rather than comparative figures.[6] Similar problems apply to the Compton Census (1676), taken at a time of political concern at the extent of nonconformity. In

[1] Webster (ed.), *Nottinghamshire Hearth Tax*; J. Patten, 'The Hearth Taxes, 1662–1689', *Local Population Studies*, 1 (1971), pp. 14–25; R.W. Unwin, 'Tradition and transition in the market towns of the Vale of York, 1660–1830', *Northern History*, 17 (1981), pp. 72–116.

[2] T. Unwin, *Late Seventeenth-century Taxation and Population: the Nottinghamshire Hearth Taxes and Compton Census* (Historical Geography Research Series, 16, 1985), p. 12.

[3] See T. Arkell, 'Multiplying factors for estimating population totals from the Hearth Tax', *Local Population Studies*, 28 (1982), pp. 51–7; P. Clark and J. Hosking, *Population Estimates of English Small Towns 1550–1851* (Centre for Urban History, University of Leicester, Working Paper No 5, 1993), p. vi.

[4] Patten, 'Hearth Taxes', p. 23; P. Laslett, 'Mean household size in England since the sixteenth century' in P. Laslett and R. Wall (ed.), *Household and Family in Past Times,* (Cambridge, 1972), p. 139.

[5] Webster, *Nottinghamshire Hearth Tax*; Unwin, *Late Seventeenth-century Taxation and Population*, esp. p. 36.

[6] Webster, *Nottinghamshire Hearth Tax*; Patten 'Hearth Taxes'.

principle the census should give for each parish the number of persons, whether communicant, nonconforming or recusant, over the age of 16.[1] However, the guidelines sent out to bishops and incumbents were often unclear: for instance, no indication was given of the age or sex of those to be counted.[2] As a result some returns include only adult males, others the number of householders or the total number of parishioners, which could include children.[3] Various multipliers have been used according to the criteria being applied locally, where this information is available. In Nottinghamshire the clergy counted both male and female communicants and therefore, as in other similar studies, a multiplier of 1.5 has been applied.[4]

After 1676 the next available source is another ecclesiastical survey, Archbishop Herring's returns of 1743.[5] This lists households or families and therefore, as with the hearth tax assessments, a multiplier of 4.25 was used. After 1743 there is no similar source for Nottinghamshire until the census of 1801. Instead, from the 1790s onwards, there are various contemporary population estimates for individual towns in directories or local histories, which all tend to produce figures higher than those of the census.

For the period from 1801 the official census figures have been used. The first census taken was merely a head count with overseers of the poor asked to distinguish between families engaged in 'agriculture', 'manufacturing and handicraft' or neither. The censuses for 1811, 1821 and 1831 were compiled in the same way, although instead of the number of families in each of the three categories, the number of individuals had to be given. No original returns compiled by the overseers for the first four censuses have survived for Nottinghamshire and therefore all that is available are the published totals. In 1841, for the first time, each householder was provided with a form to complete, on which everyone who spent the night of the census in his house had to be named. Thus, right at the end of the period of study, we can establish a more complete picture of the population of each of the towns.

All estimates of population prior to 1801 must be regarded with

1 Wrigley and Schofield, *Population History*, p. 34.

2 Clark and Hosking, *Population Estimates*, p. vi.

3 Wrigley and Schofield, *Population History*, p. 34.

4 Clark and Hosking, *Population Estimates,* p. v; T. Arkell, 'A method for estimating population totals from the Compton Census returns' in K. Schurer and V.T.J. Arkell (ed.), *Surveying the People* (Oxford, 1992).

5 S.L. Ollard and P.C. Walker, *Archbishop Herring's Visitation Returns, 1743. Vol. 4* (Wakefield, 1930).

caution. The use of multipliers does not properly take into account different household sizes or allow for more than one family living together. Nevertheless, even rough population estimates provide some indication of the changing fortunes of each town.

Sources for the economic structure of the towns

Perhaps the most important sources giving some indication of the changing economic structure of the towns between 1680 and 1770 are wills and probate inventories. These are particularly useful where details of an individual's occupation are recorded and also where shop goods and lists of debts can throw light on trading practices. Although estimates suggest as many as two million inventories were made between the mid sixteenth and mid eighteenth centuries, one of the key issues for any study using them is the question of how representative these surviving inventories are of the population as a whole.[1] The work that has been done at local level to estimate numbers of inventories as a proportion of all deaths has produced, as Overton argues, 'wide variations from place to place, reflecting contrasting levels of wealth between different areas but also variations in the customs of probate courts'.[2] Despite doubts about how representative inventories are as a source, the occupational information they give is very useful for charting the range of trades in towns in the late seventeenth century and throughout most of the eighteenth.[3] The fact that inventories predominantly survive for the wealthy and middling town inhabitants is in itself revealing of what types of trade, occupation or profession were profitable and from which a good living had been made.

While the mere existence of an inventory may indicate a level of economic success their value as a source for the study of individual wealth and general occupational structures is still limited. First, they do not always reveal occupations fully. As Spufford has argued 'we are becoming more and more conscious of the importance both of dual

[1] J.S. Moore, 'Probate inventories: problems and prospects' in P. Riden (ed.), *Probate Inventories and the Local Community* (Gloucester, 1984), 16–17; M. Overton, J. Whittle, D. Dean and A. Hann, *Production and Consumption in English Households, 1600–1750* (2004), 22).

[2] M. Overton, 'Probate inventories and the reconstruction of agrarian landscapes' in M. Reed (ed.), *Discovering Past Landscapes* (1984), pp. 173–4.

[3] J. Patten, *English Towns 1500–1700* (Folkestone, 1978), ch. 4.

occupations and of the family budget'.[1] Few inventories record a second occupation or by-employment, although inferences can be made from lists of tools or, where an individual both followed a trade and had some agricultural interest, by reference to crops or animals, but, as Overton and his co-authors have demonstrated, women's contribution to the household economy is probably understated in many inventories.[2] Second, the items and values given in inventories cannot be taken as truly indicative of the total wealth of the deceased because real property (freehold and copyhold estates) is not included, although leases (which are personal property) may be.[3] While we have to proceed with caution in any analysis based on inventories, they remain an invaluable source for occupational diversity in a period in which few alternative sources are generally available.

The occupational information gleaned from probate records was supplemented where possible by freemen's lists for 1739 and for 1780 to 1824. These usually record the names of those granted the freedom of a town, their occupation, and often their birthplace. If the birthplace was omitted, it may be assumed that the freeman was born in the town. Given that substantial fees were often paid for this privilege, it may be surmised that these individuals represented some of the wealthier town members. From the late eighteenth century freemen's lists can be compared with lists of occupations culled from directories and poll books, before the census enumerators' books become available from 1841.

Local and national directories cannot be used for detailed analysis of the economic structure of towns because they do not record all occupations. The smaller the town, the less effort seems to have been made to include the full range of trades. For this reason, directories have been used here only in support of other sources to help reveal the diversity of trades and services and the growth of more specialised activities. Provincial directories did not become common until the late eighteenth century, by which time many national directories were also being

[1] M. Spufford, 'The limitations of the probate inventory' in J. Chartres and D. Hey (ed.), *English Rural Society: Essays in honour of Joan Thirsk* (Cambridge, 1990), p. 144.

[2] Overton, 'By employment, women's work and "unproductive households"' in idem, *Production and Consumption*, pp. 65–86.

[3] Spufford, 'Probate inventory', p. 142.

compiled.[1] The first directory used here is the *Universal British Directory of Trade, Commerce and Manufactures* (*c*.1790–8), which includes entries for Nottingham and Newark. In the early nineteenth century three directories become available, Pigot's *National Commercial Directory* (1828–9), White's *History, Gazetteer and Directory of Nottinghamshire* (1832) and Pigot's *National Commercial Directory* (1842), each of which was part of a national series. Publishers like White and Pigot employed full-time agents to collect information, which might suggest that their publications are both reliable and relatively complete.[2] Even so, a comparison of Pigot's directory of 1842 with the 1841 census enumerator's books for Newark showed that the directory omitted over eighty occupations recorded in the census, mostly the labouring and more menial ones. In Worksop only 25 per cent of occupations are recorded (excluding independents and the gentry) and this figure falls to 15 per cent in Bingham.

The 1841 census thus provides a far more reliable and comprehensive list of each town's occupations than contemporary directories. Yet it would be wrong to assume that even this source provides a complete survey of the working population. The instructions given with each householder's schedule advised that the 'profession &c. of Wives, or of sons or daughters living with and assisting their parents but not apprenticed or receiving wages need not be inserted'.[3] This could lead to a serious underestimate of the role of women and children in the working household, especially since there is evidence of outwork being conducted in the towns, with whole families involved in weaving or spinning at home. The role of women and children in the pre-industrial family economy is thus understated by the census, although other sources reveal its importance.[4] Even if the census seems to provide a comprehensive survey of the working population it is important to remember that it is not necessarily complete.

[1] G. Shaw, *British Directories as Sources in Historical Geography* (Historical Geography Research Series, 8, 1982); G. Shaw and A. Tipper, *British Directories: A Bibliography and Guide to Directories published in England and Wales (1850–1950) and Scotland (1773–1950)* (Leicester, 1989).

[2] Shaw, *British Directories*, p. 30.

[3] E. Higgs, 'Women, occupations and work in the nineteenth-century censuses', *History Workshop*, 23 (1987), p. 63.

[4] M. Berg, *The Age of Manufactures 1700–1820: Industry, Innovation and Work in Britain* (1994 edn); B. Hill, *Women, Work and Sexual Politics in Eighteenth-century England* (Oxford, 1993); P. Lane, N. Raven and K. Snell, *Women, Work and Wages* (Woodbridge, 2004).

Wealth and social structure

Social change, and in particular the growth of what is sometimes called the 'middling sort', is crucial to the argument that the eighteenth century saw the 'modernisation' of English society. Nowhere was this 'middling' group more evident than in the growing towns of Georgian England. In the towns such people could include 'some of the smallest self-employed businessmen, shopkeepers, tradesmen, craftsmen, even artisans [who] would for some purposes be counted with their more august mercantile and professional superiors'. Three criteria can be used to deduce an individual's status—title, occupation or information as to their level of wealth. Most of the sources, however, are selective, socially biased and only indirectly shed light on the social structure of a market town. There is also the problem of classifying different social groups. What criteria should be used to separate one from another? Even contemporaries, who thought the growing wealth and importance of the middle orders of society one of the most striking developments of the eighteenth century, felt an ambivalence as to how they should classify such individuals. Terms such as 'gentleman', 'esquire', or even Mr and Mrs, were used with increasing indiscrimination as the period progressed.[1]

Despite such problems, some attempt has been made here to recreate the social structure and distribution of wealth in each town. The main source used for the late seventeenth century was the hearth tax assessments of 1674, on the assumption that numbers of hearths equate to house size and house size to the occupants' wealth. In 1688 Gregory King compiled his social structure of England and Wales based on the hearth tax.[2] Unwin has argued that, because they concentrate mainly on chargeable taxpayers, the assessments are a valuable indicator of the distribution of wealth and social structure.[3] From the complete lists, including the non-chargeable entries, it should be possible to estimate both levels of poverty and the distribution of wealth.[4] Here, this assumption was tested by comparing the names of householders listed in the hearth tax assessments with those recovered from probate records, which enabled numbers of hearths to be linked to information on

[1] P. Langford, *A Polite and Commercial People: England 1727–1783* (Oxford, 1992 ed.), p. 62.

[2] P. Mathias, 'The social structure in the eighteenth century: a calculation by Joseph Massie', *Economic History Review*, 2nd ser. 10 (1957), p. 32.

[3] Unwin, 'Nottinghamshire Hearth Taxes', p. 41.

[4] Webster (ed.), *Nottinghamshire Hearth Tax*; Patten, 'Hearth Taxes'; Unwin, *Nottinghamshire Hearth Taxes*.

occupation (or status, such as 'gentleman', 'yeoman' etc.), house size and the value of moveable property.[1] The results are summarised in Table 2.1.

Table 2.1 shows that the link between numbers of hearths and average inventory value is not straightforward. While the lowest average inventory values were found among households with only one hearth and the highest among those with eight or more, the picture for households lying between is not clear-cut and to some extent questions any general assumption of a link between numbers of hearths and wealth. To test further the relationship between hearths and wealth, numbers of hearths were compared with average inventory values. Table 2.2 shows that the link between numbers of hearths and average inventory value is also not straightforward. While the lowest average inventory values were found among households with only one hearth and the highest among those with eight or more hearths, the picture for households lying between is again not clear-cut.

One final comparison was made between numbers of hearths and the occupations or status accorded an individual in the inventories and wills. Although most tradesmen, farmers, yeomen and husbandmen lived in houses with between one and five hearths, no clear relationship could be discovered between different types of trade or craft and the number of hearths each category was likely to possess. A more significant correlation emerges in the case of 'gentlemen', since individuals given this title were much more likely to have six or more hearths than anyone else (Table 2.3), although gentlemen also had houses with only two or three hearths.[2] In this instance, we can attach some significance to contemporary descriptions of status, and this is reflected in the assessments. These simple exercises do suggest that hearth tax records can be persuaded to yield a fair indicator of wealth and status, at least for the upper echelons of society, a conclusion similar to that found for Cambridgeshire by Margaret Spufford.[3]

Levels and types of wealth among the inhabitants of the six towns were further examined using wills and probate inventories. Marshall

[1] For a similar exercise see N. Goose, 'How accurately do the Hearth Tax returns reflect wealth? A local discussion of some urban evidence', *Local Population Studies*, 67 (2001).

[2] In Derbyshire many lesser gentry could be found in houses with fewer than eight hearths: D.G. Edwards (ed.), *Derbyshire Hearth Tax Assessments 1662–1670* (Derbyshire Record Society, 6, 1982).

[3] M. Spufford, 'The scope of local history and the potential of the Hearth Tax returns', *The Local Historian*, 30 (2000).

Table 2.1

A comparison of hearth tax assessments (1674) and probate inventories (1680–1710) for six Nottinghamshire towns

No. of Hearths	*No. of households in the Hearth Tax assessments*	*No. of house-holders for whom inventories were made*	*Percentage of householders listed in the Hearth Tax for whom inventories were made*
1	328	14	4.3
2	276	30	10.9
3	229	28	12.2
4	128	28	12.2
5	60	12	20.0
6	35	7	20.0
7	11	4	36.4
8	16	2	12.5
9	12	3	25.0
10+	22	5	22.7

Sources: TNA, E 179/254/30; NAO, PRNW and PRMW.

suggested some years ago that 'the examination and analysis of inventories' at local and regional level 'will eventually produce working estimates of changing wealth levels ... [and that] inventories used with care [will] yield considerable information relative to social aspiration and status'.[1] Over 2,000 inventories and inventory declarations relating to the six towns were examined for this study. One of the great advantages of inventories is that they cover a wide spectrum of the urban population, from labourers to skilled craftsmen, retailers and urban gentry. In principle, only for individuals with personal estate worth £5 or more did an inventory have to be made after death. The main problem raised is what proportion of a town's population met this criterion, since estimates from other studies vary considerably. Barley's comparison of numbers of burials with numbers of surviving inventories showed that inventories were made for 20 per cent of adult males in one Nottinghamshire village

[1] J.D. Marshall, 'Agrarian wealth and social structure in pre-industrial Cumbria', *Economic History Review*, 2nd ser. 33 (1980), p. 503.

Table 2.2

Numbers of hearths and inventory values

No. of Hearths	*No. of Households*	*Average Inventory Value (£)*
8+	7	518
6–7	6	246
5	6	299
4	18	254
3	21	257
2	17	126
1	6	84

Sources: TNA, E 179/254/30; NAO, PRNW and PRMW.

between 1660 and 1725, whereas Marshall calculated a figure as high as 40 per cent for Hawkshead in Cumbria.[1] A comparison of wills and inventories with numbers of burials in Nottingham between 1690 and 1750 suggests that on average inventories were compiled for one in three individuals in this period.[2] A recent study of wills and inventories for Kent and Cornwall found that while inventories were 'likely to have been made for those of higher status', inventories often excluded 'the richest 10 per cent and poorest 40 per cent of the population'.[3] Clearly, inventories are representative of only a minority of the urban population, a proportion that varies according to the wealth of a particular town or locality.

In a period when property ownership was the prime currency of political and social influence, a record of land ownership has multiple uses. In an attempt to compile a still more complete record of individual wealth, the names of individuals for whom inventories or inventory declarations survive were compared with names listed in the duplicate land tax assessments retained by the clerk of the peace for the period

[1] M.W. Barley, 'Farmhouses and cottages, 1550-1725', *Economic History Review*, 2nd ser. 7 (1955); J.D. Marshall, 'Social structure and wealth in pre-industrial England', Ibid., 33 (1980).

[2] J.V. Beckett and C.A. Smith, 'Urban renaissance and consumer revolution in Nottingham 1690–1750', *Urban History*, 27 (1), (2000).

[3] Overton, 'Probate inventories', in idem, *Production and Consumption*, pp. 22–6.

Table 2.3

Numbers of hearths and occupations and status as recorded in probate records, 1680–1700

No. of Hearths	*Status and Occupations*
8+	4 gentlemen, 1 innkeeper.
6-7	2 gentlemen.
5	2 maltsters, 1 gentleman, 1 yeoman, 1 husbandman, 1 blacksmith.
4	2 gentlemen, 2 mercers, 2 cordwainers, 1 butcher, 1 tanner, 1 glover, 1 maltster, 1 blacksmith, 1 widow.
3	2 yeomen, 2 maltsters, 1 chandler, 2 farmers, 2 butchers, 2 tanners, 1 gentleman, 1 framework knitter, 1 clerk, 1 blacksmith, 1 widow.
2	1 husbandmen, 2 carpenters, 1 maltster, 1 gentleman, 1 joiner, 1 no trade given.
1	2 cordwainers, 1 labourer, 1 widow.

1780–1832, as has been done occasionally elsewhere.[1]

All major, and many minor, landowners in the six towns were identified by comparing the names given in the land tax assessments with those recorded in probate records, directories, poll books and any other source which gave a name and occupation. Ginter has warned against nominal record linkage using the assessments, but Henstock has shown that it is possible to use them for house repopulation exercises providing other sources exist from which to test their accuracy.[2] Where this comparison could be made, it was possible not only to identify the principal landowners but also to discover how the pattern of landownership changed in a period of rapid development for at least four of the six towns studied here. Where possible, the assessments were sampled every five years. The decision to take a sample was made for two reasons. First, the assessments were not kept up-to-date and did not

[1] A. Henstock, 'House repopulation from the land tax assessments in a Derbyshire market town, 1780–1825', in M. Turner and D. Mills (ed.), *Land and Property: The English Land Tax 1692–1832* (Cambridge, 1986); M. Noble, 'Land tax returns and urban development', *Local Historian*, 15 (1982), pp. 86-92; A. Henstock (ed.), *A Georgian Country Town. Ashbourne 1725–1825* (Nottingham, 1989).

[2] D.E. Ginter, *A Measure of Wealth. The English Land Tax in Historical Analysis* (London, 1992), pp. 16-18; Henstock, 'House repopulation'.

always reflect recent conveyances of property.[1] Second, the sheer number of entries for the larger towns prohibited more detailed analysis. For instance, for Newark in 1780 there are 886 separate entries, rising to 905 for 1785; in contrast, the numbers for Ollerton in the same years are 74 and 138. Even so, 90 per cent of entries could be linked over each five-year gap. Those that disappeared were fairly easy to identify by reference to the records for a previous year (providing the arrangement of the list was consistent, which was not always the case). Some landowners (and indeed some plots of land) seem to have disappeared completely, possibly because, as occurred from 1798, the owner redeemed the tax,[2] or because the land had been bought by someone else and amalgamated with another entry.

Prior to 1800 each assessment was recorded individually, showing the name of each owner and occupier,[3] and the lists appear to have been compiled street by street. Although Ginter warns that spatial distribution should not be inferred from the layout of assessments,[4] the use of street names in Mansfield and Newark suggest that here such an assumption is valid. After 1800 the arrangement changed and proprietors were listed alphabetically, with properties amalgamated and assessed as a single unit. Although this makes it increasingly difficult to trace the history of individual plots, the change of format does not affect the use of the assessments as a record of landownership. On the other hand, the fact that Noble has shown that, for four out of six Yorkshire market towns, less than half the number of buildings reported in the 1831 census can be identified in the 1832 land tax assessment does question the comprehensiveness of this source.[5]

The Tithe Commutation Act of 1836 gave rise to the next major survey of land use and landownership. The Act provided for the commutation of all remaining tithes paid in cash or kind into a fluctuating rent-charge, adjusted according to the seven-year average of the price of wheat, barley and oats. A Tithe Commission was appointed either to confirm voluntary agreements or to impose awards where agreements

[1] D.E. Ginter, 'A wealth of problems with the land tax', *Economic History Review*, 35 (1982); idem, *English Land Tax*.

[2] Turner and Mills, *Land Tax*, p. 2. The names of those who redeemed were omitted from the Nottinghamshire assessments between 1805 and 1810.

[3] Ginter, *English Land Tax*, p. 15.

[4] Ibid., p. 32.

[5] M. Noble, 'The land tax assessments in the study of the physical development of country towns' in Turner and Mills, *Land Tax*, Table 3 and p. 116.

could not be reached.[1] The tithe apportionments produced as a result of this process proved to be the most useful for this study. Each contains the agreement for commutation and details of the tithe district, including the area of arable, grass and other lands subject to tithes, followed by a schedule (keyed to a large-scale map) which lists for each plot the owner, the occupier, a description of the property, its state of cultivation, its area and the rent-charge to be apportioned on it. Tithe maps are considered to be highly accurate: a proportion (the 'First-class maps', sealed by the commission) were admissible as evidence concerning boundaries.[2] Of the towns studied here, only the tithe map for Bingham fell into this category, but the second-class maps, available for the other five towns, are not necessarily inferior for present purposes. All the maps include an enlarged town plan which proved particularly valuable. In examining the wealth and social structure of the towns, the apportionments proved a useful guide to property ownership at the end of the period of study. Using census enumerators' books or directories, it is possible to find occupations or status titles for most of those who appear in the apportionment and thus compile a social register for each town.

The task of extracting information for different forms of wealth was fairly straightforward given the range of sources available for the six towns. In the end, the main problem, having compiled the data, was the classification of the different occupational and status groups in order to summarise the changing social structure of the towns in the long term. Any model or classification is inevitably a generalisation or simplification but is useful to elucidate or illustrate long-term structural change. In the process, however, local idiosyncrasies are masked and the complexity of change distorted. Six socio-economic groups were identified for the towns: the urban poor (1), unskilled workers (2), artisans and tradesmen (or women) (3), retailers and manufacturers (4), professionals (5), and the urban gentry (6). These six groups are distinguished in relation to the way they earned their living and the relative wealth they accrued from working.

Some historians have classified occupations in terms of the type of market or consumer they served, for example, whether they were involved in provisioning of food and drink, textiles or leather ware.[3] This approach is much more useful for highlighting economic rather than

[1] R.J.P. Kain and H.C. Prince, *The Tithe Surveys of England and Wales* (Cambridge, 1985), pp. 32, 34; J.V. Beckett, 'Tithe commutation in Nottinghamshire in the 1830s and 1840s', *Trans. Thoroton Soc.*, 96 (1992).

[2] Kain and Prince, *Tithe Surveys*, p. 81.

[3] Patten, *English Towns 1500–1700*, pp. 170–1.

social change and was not, therefore, adopted here. One major problem concerns the way different sources record some occupations. Particularly critical for Nottinghamshire, where framework knitting and brewing were important, is the confusion as to the status of framework knitters and maltsters. Individuals recorded with either of these occupations in the probate records were usually involved in more than just domestic production. In most of the Nottinghamshire towns, those described as 'maltsters', rather than as 'maltster labourers', and those described as framework knitters, usually ran businesses. They were either employers, albeit on a small scale, or they rented out frames for domestic production, and they themselves may not have been directly involved in the physical production of goods. For this reason they are classified here in Group 4 (retailers and manufacturers). However, in an analysis of occupations based on the 1841 census, framework knitters and maltsters are classified in Group 3 (artisans and tradesmen), since the enumerators employed a wider and more accurate vocabulary to describe employment, with the term 'manufacturer' or 'dealer' used for individuals who were operating on a larger scale. Another aspect of the same problem involves the classification of those in agricultural employment. Labourers were classified in Group 2 (unskilled workers), husbandmen in Group 3 (artisans and tradesmen), and farmers and yeomen in Group 4 (retailers and manufacturers). Yeomen and farmers were placed in Group 4 on the ground that they are usually considered to be the wealthier or élite members of the agricultural community.

Wealth and material culture

One of the ways differentials in wealth and status are reinforced is through the acquisition and display of fashionable or luxury consumer items. The late seventeenth century, it has been argued, saw a major increase in the numbers of people in England and America able to purchase such goods.[1] Thus the third element in the analysis of the six towns has focused on the rise of consumption.

The continuing spread of consumer goods, not just among the rich but increasingly in all but the poorest sectors of eighteenth-century society, is generally accepted as evidence of a more modern society. McKendrick

[1] N. McKendrick, J. Brewer and J.H. Plumb, *The Birth of a Consumer Society: The Commercialisation of Eighteenth-century England* (London, 1982), L. Weatherill, *Consumer Behaviour and Material Culture in Britain 1660–1760* (London, 1988); J. Brewer and R. Porter (ed.), *Consumption and the World of Goods* (London, 1993).

and others have made a strong case for a 'consumer revolution' in this period, albeit, as Glennie points out, this is one of many such claims made in English history from 1500 onwards.[1] Instead of revolutionary change, most historians now argue for important evolutionary changes in consumption patterns between 1550 and 1750.[2] McKendrick's thesis rests chiefly on the evidence of contemporary commentators, and also used the growth of often ingenious advertising gimmicks for the sale of consumer goods. However, while the great outpouring of contemporary comment on fashion and consumption, and the great effort of entrepreneurs like Josiah Wedgwood to sell their goods, must be indicative of something along these lines, little hard evidence is offered as to the precise nature of the goods finding their way into homes. As Shammas and Weatherill have pointed out, the evidence for a 'consumer revolution' largely rests on the supply of goods, rather than on the demand. Thus, studies such as Weatherill's and Overton's have traced the increasing commonplace character of certain items, such as clocks, pictures and curtains, conclusions reinforced by Mukerji and McCracken, who have demonstrated that such goods were mostly to be found in the homes of the urban trading and leisured sectors of society.[3]

Because the idea of increasing levels of consumption was uppermost in the minds of contemporaries, and among historians today, this study includes a detailed analysis of probate inventories. For all their limitations, inventories allow a peep inside individual Nottinghamshire homes between about 1680 and 1832, although the number of fully itemised inventories drastically declines from the mid eighteenth century. Inventories continued to be compiled for a much longer period in Nottinghamshire than in other counties. This may be due to the fact the archdeaconries of Nottingham, like Richmond, were also consistory courts and so operated, according to Arkell, more independently.[4] It is

[1] P. Glennie, 'Consumption within historical studies' in D. Miller (ed.), *Acknowledging Consumption: a review of new studies* (1995), p. 164.

[2] C. Shammas, *The Pre-industrial Consumer in England and America* (Oxford, 1990), pp. 291, 294; J. de Vries, 'Between purchasing power and the world of goods: understanding the household economy in early modern Europe' in Brewer and Porter, *Consumption and the World of Goods*, p. 107.

[3] C. Mukerji, *From Graven Images: Patterns of Modern Materialism* (New York, 1983); G. McCracken, *Culture and Consumption: New Approaches to the Symbolic Character of Consumer Goods and Activities* (Indiana, 1988); Overton, 'The material culture of consumption' in idem *Production and Consumption*, pp. 87–120.

[4] T. Arkell, 'The probate process' in T. Arkell, N. Evans and N. Goose, *When Death Do Us Part. Understanding and Interpreting the Probate Records of Early Modern England* (Oxford, 2000), p. 6.

also the case than in peculiars like Mansfield there was a tendency for inventories to be compiled later.[1]

Probate inventories were made under the terms of an Act of 1529. They list and value only personal estate for which the executor or administrator of an estate was responsible.[2] Personalty normally included clothes, money, households goods (often listed individually on a room by room basis), trade and farm stock and equipment, bonds, other securities, debts and leases. There might, however, be omissions. Bequests stipulated in a will were sometimes excluded and, since these were often the testator's most precious items, an important element of an individual's wealth may be overlooked. Watches, for example, were commonly bequeathed in wills but not mentioned in inventories; hence it is important to study a will alongside the inventory. Creating heirlooms was a way to avoid personal property appearing in an inventory.[3] Items of low value were not always listed in detail by the late seventeenth century; they might simply be put under the heading of 'other lumber' or omitted altogether. The more household goods became widespread, the less likely they were to be described individually, the appraisers paying most attention to 'new', 'novel' or 'rare' possessions of the deceased. It could be argued that the fact that an item is recorded less frequently in inventories suggests not a decline in its use but, on the contrary, that it had become commonplace. Thus, as Overton argues, 'inventories should never be used in a negative way to claim that a particular item is not present because it is not recorded'.[4]

Because of the wealth of data in probate inventories, the most appropriate method of analysis was to enter selected information onto a spreadsheet. A file was compiled for each room (if it was listed), agricultural and shop goods, debts, bonds or securities, and the deceased's purse and apparel. The names and the occupation or status of the deceased were also noted, together with the date of probate and the town in which the deceased had lived. From this data it was possible to analyse the distribution of each item or class of item over time, space and social class. The frequency of each consumer item was noted for three periods (1680 to 1720, 1721 to 1760 and 1761 to 1832) to see whether certain possessions were becoming more common. The first reference to a new item was also noted. Mahogany furniture, for

[1] J. and N. Cox, 'Probate 1500–1800: a system in transition' in ibid., p. 27.

[2] Spufford, 'Probate inventory', p. 142.

[3] Cox, 'Probate 1500–1800', p. 25.

[4] Overton, *Production and Consumption*, p.18.

example, is first encountered in an inventory for 1740 in East Retford. The chronological and geographical analysis was complemented by a social analysis. Once certain items had been traced in one household, their occurrence in the houses of those of different social standing was measured, again comparing different periods and towns, since it was in the towns that such goods were sometimes made, often marketed, and frequently distributed. Furthermore, it might be expected that members of middling families would have been amongst the first to have enjoyed a growing range of new and fashionable products.

Detailed probate inventories were largely replaced by inventory declarations from the mid eighteenth century. These give only a total estimate of the value of an individual's personal estate at a time when the Nottinghamshire market towns were expanding most rapidly, both economically and demographically (from the 1770s in particular). Thus, in precisely the period in which we might hope to identify significant developments, this becomes more difficult. To compensate for this loss, inventories compiled for auctions and lists of furniture advertised for sale in local newspapers were examined. However, since this information was often patchy, selective and on the whole covered only the wealthier inhabitants, it could only be used for example rather than detailed analysis.

Townscape

The other main aspect of structural change considered here was the physical growth of the six towns. Whereas attempts at estimating the total population or an analysis of economic and social structure involved the use of debatable tools such as multipliers or arbitrary social and economic classifications, the problems faced in trying to reconstruct the appearance of the towns were more straightforward.

The main problem is a general lack of source material, particularly for the early years. Detailed plans for small towns are not usually found until the late eighteenth century and the earliest tend to have been produced as part of an estate survey. For later times these manuscript plans can be supplemented by the locally published town maps, enclosure awards and tithe maps. For the earliest period, when no visual images could be found, the physical extent of each town has had to be reconstructed from any source yielding a street name. In Newark and Mansfield, these can be found in the hearth tax assessments of 1674. Street names can also be found in other tax assessments, poll books, directories and, of course, the 1841 census enumerators' books. From these sources it has proved possible to piece together the morphology of each town for the late seventeenth century and early eighteenth; a clearer picture then becomes available for the late eighteenth century, when the towns begin to grow most rapidly.

Expansion of the built-up area was only one of the ways in which a market town changed over the eighteenth century. New building materials and styles also contributed to an altered appearance. Information on these came from building plans, the minutes of corporation meetings (or those of the improvement commissioners set up in Mansfield in 1823), deeds, newspapers and contemporary descriptions.

The one context in which social classifications were used together with the town plan was in connection with residential patterns. In order to test whether the sample towns were more socially segregated in 1841 than they had been in 1674, the occupation or status of heads of households recorded in the 1841 census were ranked according to the six socio-economic categories defined earlier. This enabled an average value to be calculated for each street according to the status of the residents. Thus, Bridge Street in Mansfield had three labourers, ten artisans or tradesmen, four retailers or manufacturers, and one professional. Two points were awarded for each labourer, three for each artisan, four for each retailer and five for the professional (each point reflecting the social group in which each head of household has been classified). The total value for the street was 57 and the average value of the 18 households was 3.2. This rather crude analysis relies on occupational or status titles and the main problem with this exercise was how to classify heads of households described as ‘independent’. While some of these individuals were clearly of gentry status, others were not, as the term seems to have been used rather loosely by the enumerators. In an attempt to identify the real status of these individuals, they were, where possible, located in other sources. As a result, not all those accorded the title of independent in the census were classified as gentry in group six.

The lack of documentation for most of the period under study has resulted in the extraction of information from a variety of sources. Some of the tools used, particularly multipliers, will always be open to question. Notwithstanding these difficulties it has been possible to trace the demographic, physical, social and cultural development of the six towns.

THREE

Urban Space

This chapter examines the development of the urban landscape of each of the six towns. Historial geographers have long argued that the spatial organisation of a town tells us something about the economy and society of that settlement.[1] Moreover, as Conzen, Reed and more recently Borsay have argued, a town plan is a 'conservative morphological complex' and its enduring significance can effectively represent an aggregated record of the life history of a town's landscape development.[2] Even when towns expanded beyond their medieval limits they still followed the lines of ancient property boundaries. In this respect the Nottinghamshire market towns were little different to other urban centres. Their street plans until the 1770s were inherited from an earlier period, but from the late eighteenth century the pattern of expansion changed and for the first time since the Middle Ages new streets were added and new plan-units built on. This growth often had to be accommodated within old boundaries and administered for much of our period by ancient structures of local government. Inevitably this created problems of health and sanitation that were not taken seriously by central government until the 1840s. What all this change suggests is that the Nottinghamshire towns were experiencing new pressures, constraints and opportunities which, as in previous generations, left their mark on the urban landscape.

Evidence for expansion

Very little direct evidence for the physical expansion of the built-up area of any of the six towns exists for the years prior to the 1770s. It may be assumed that the increase of population between 1680 and 1801 must

[1] G. Sjoberg, *The Pre-industrial City. Past and Present* (Glencoe, Ill.,1960); J.E. Vance, 'Land assignment in pre-capitalist, capitalist and post-capitalist cities', *Economic Geography*, 47 (1971).

[2] M.R.G. Conzen, 'Alnwick, Northumberland. A study in town plan analysis', *Trans. Inst. British Geographers*, 27 (1969), p. 7; M. Reed, 'The urban landscape 1540–1700', in P. Clark (ed.), *The Cambridge Urban History of Britain. II. 1540–1840* (Cambridge, 2000), p. 313; P. Borsay, 'Early modern urban landscapes, 1540–1800', in P. Waller (ed.), *The English Urban Landscape* (Oxford, 2000), p. 99.

indicate some growth in housing, but residential development is only one demand on the use of space within a town. Before the late eighteenth century it is impossible to assess what other demands for space, for example commercial or institutional, might have existed. The overall picture that emerges is that relatively little extension of the built-up area occurred between 1680 and 1770, but that in the larger towns there was quite a rapid expansion between 1770 and 1840.

The argument that the towns saw some growth between 1680 and 1780 rests on three main sources: the hearth tax assessments (1664 and 1674), Archbishop Herring's visitation returns (1754) and the census returns from 1801 (Tables 3.1–3.3). Although these are not directly comparable, together they provide evidence of demographic and, by implication, physical growth from the late seventeenth century onwards, at least in relation to residential development.

In Newark, the largest of the six towns, 565 households were listed in 1664. This figure had dropped to 339 in 1674 but the latter returns did not include the households that were not charged. By 1745 the number of households had increased to 700 although this rounded figure suggests an estimate. On these figures Newark saw an increase of about one fifth in households between the late seventeenth century and 1743. In 1801 the census recorded 1,390 houses in the parish as a whole and in 1841 2,220, implying a fourfold increase in less than two centuries. A similar picture emerges for the three other larger towns (Mansfield, Worksop and East Retford), while even Bingham and Ollerton saw some growth.

Evidence for town expansion from 1780 to 1840 is abundant. The land tax assessments (1780–1832), the census (1801-41) and the tithe apportionments of the 1840s, together with maps, show that all but the smallest of the towns saw a considerable growth of the built-up area as a result of residential, economic and cultural demands. Between 1801 and 1841 all the towns saw at least a 26 per cent increase in the number of houses, with the figure in Worksop increasing by 52 per cent. Nationally the census shows that the housing stock roughly doubled between 1801 and 1851, although this figure needs to be treated with care as the census did not show separately houses that had been subdivided.[1] To this we can add the building of textile mills, malt kilns, corn mills, wharves, town halls, churches, schools and libraries.

[1] S. King and G. Timmins, *Making Sense of the Industrial Revolution. English Economy and Society 1700–1850* (Manchester, 2001), p. 239.

Table 3.1

Households in hearth tax assessments

Town	*1664 or 1674 total no. of households*	*Percentage of households not charged*
Newark*	565	43
Mansfield#	*c*.370	24
Worksop*+	358	50
East Retford*	210	29
Bingham#	*c*.145	35
Ollerton	50	30

* 1664 totals used because the 1674 totals do not include non-chargeable households.

\# Damaged assessments for 1664 for Bingham and Mansfield suggest that those for 1664 lack nearly 30 and over 50 non-chargeable households respectively, and so these figures have been added to the 1674 totals.

\+ The Worksop total uses the 1664 hearth tax assessment but this includes figures for Osberton, Scofton, Kilton, Welbeck, Radford, Gateford, Shireoaks and Ratcliffe. The figure for Worksop alone is 184 and this could represent the town's inhabitants.

The pattern of expansion, 1680–1770

Growth in this earlier period in the six towns, as elsewhere,[1] was accommodated either by in-filling and the intensification of land-use within the existing built-up area, or as a result of ribbon development, with new houses being built along the towns' principal roads. This is very similar to the organic pattern of town expansion that Keene highlights.[2] What was not common in this period was the development of new sites that significantly extended the built-up area. In many respects the expansion of these towns in this period was not accommodated by systematic planning. This was also the case in larger centres like Bath and Leeds and other smaller settlements such as Chorley and

[1] P.J. Corfield, *The Impact of Towns 1700–1800* (Oxford, 1982), pp. 170–1.

[2] D. Keene, 'The medieval urban landscape, AD 900–1540', in Waller, *English Landscape*, pp. 83–6.

Table 3.2

The number of families recorded in Archbishop Herring's visitation returns 1745

Town	*No. of Families*
Newark	700
Mansfield	600
Worksop	358
East Retford	215
Bingham	120
Ollerton	68

Note: The rounded figures for Newark and Mansfield suggest an approximation.

Alnwick.[1] Patterns of corporate and individual landownership were often inherited and could restrict 'large-scale modification of the urban form'.[2] As a result, until the 1770s the shape of the towns combined quite a dense nucleated centre with a sprawling, unplanned extension of building along main roads.

For example, Newark had once been enclosed by a town wall, although there is evidence to suggest that the built-up area had already extended beyond the walls by the mid sixteenth century. In 1553 a rental lists houses in Barnby Gate, Balderton Gate, Carter Gate, Mill Gate and North Gate, all of which continued beyond the walls (Fig. 2).[3] Between then and 1674 there seems to have been little change, other than the building of additional houses on the roads leading into the town and probably an intensification of land-use within the town centre. The hearth tax assessments of 1674 list 77 households in the Market Place, 32 in Castle Gate, 48 in Mill Gate, 35 in North Gate, 38 in Kirk Gate, 40 in Appleton Gate and Barnby Gate and 68 in Carter Gate and Balderton Gate.[4] Not until 1766 is there any evidence for new streets, when Wilson Street, just off the Market Place and thus right in the town

[1] Reed, 'Urban landscape', p. 297; A.M. Warnes, 'Early separation of homes from work-places and the urban structure of Chorley, 1780–1850', *Trans. Hist. Soc. Lancs. and Cheshire*, 122 (1970); Conzen, 'Alnwick'.

[2] Borsay, 'Early modern urban landscapes', p. 99.

[3] C. Brown, *A History of Newark* (Newark, 1904), ii. 4.

[4] National Archives, E 179/254/30.

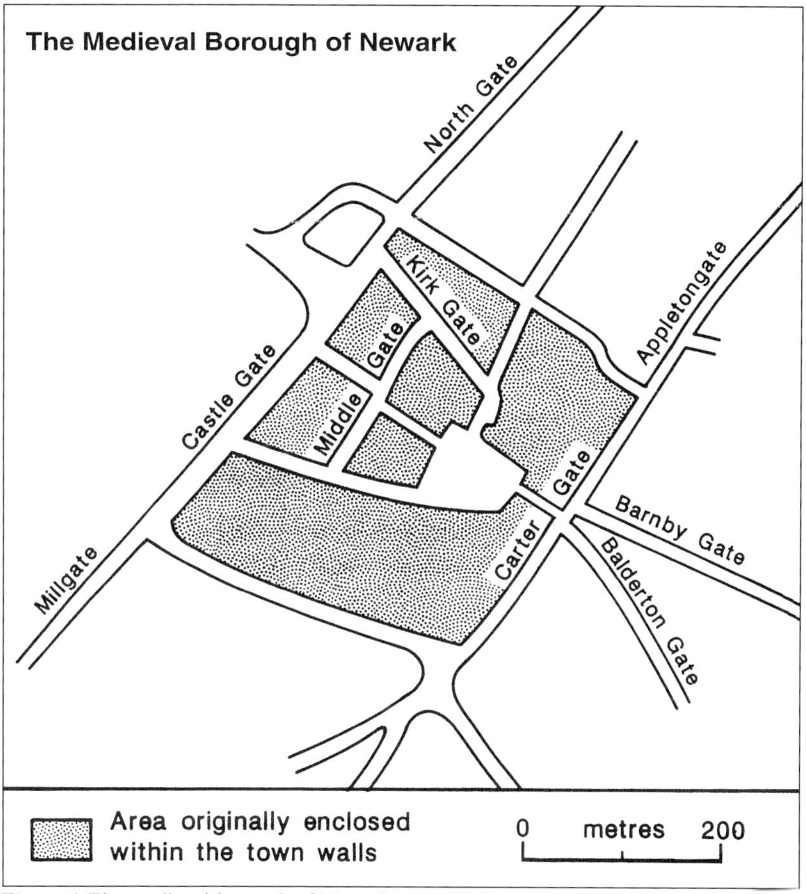

Figure 2 The medieval borough of Newark.

centre, was built, but there is no other evidence for new roads before 1770.

Worksop saw some expansion between the early sixteenth century, when Leland described it as a pretty market town with two streets,[1] and the mid seventeenth. In 1687 these two streets were mentioned again, together with a third, Newgate Street.[2] By 1754 a further nine streets were listed.[3] Between 1754 and 1770 there is very little evidence from which further conclusions can be drawn. Mansfield was described in

[1] L. Toulin-Smith (ed.), *The Itinerary of John Leland 1535–1543* (1904), p. 89.

[2] Sheffield Archives, ACM W8.

[3] Sheffield Archives, ACM W26.

Table 3.3

Census house data, 1801–41

	1801	*1811*	*1821*	*1831*	*1841*	*% increase*
Newark	1,390	1,504	1,691	2,093	2,220	37.4
Mansfield	1,245	1,458	1,717	2,017	2,200	43.5
Worksop	658	759	969	1,170	1,339	50.9
East Retford	428	471	510	546	581	26.4
Bingham	220	277	333	378	422	47.9
Ollerton	95	97	106	130	164	42.1

Note: The figures for Ollerton are for the chapelry rather than the parish.

1697 as a little market town. Thirty years later, it was considered large and well built, although there is no evidence to show how far the town had changed. In 1674 about 370 households were assessed to the hearth tax and in 1745 the town had 600 families, which suggests substantial growth in the intervening period. By contrast, Ollerton saw very little expansion for most of the eighteenth century and Bingham may have experienced a small decline in population (Tables 3.1 and 3.2).

In all the towns the rate of expansion was insufficient to force the development of new plots of land. The fact that what expansion did occur followed a pattern characteristic of urban development since the medieval period suggests little had changed in terms of where individuals felt they needed to—or could—live and work. As Borsay argues, 'growth was usually accommodated within or attached to a pre-existing urban form'.[1] The prime residential location remained either close to the town centre or along one of the principal roads leading to the town. One of the main considerations for most of the population was to be either in the trading heart of the town or in a position where people were likely to be regularly passing by. A town plan with a dense central core and ribbons of suburban development is typical of a place dominated by small scale, family businesses. For these tradesmen or craftsmen it was imperative that they lived and worked where they were going to attract custom. Moreover, as Corfield suggests, 'the prevailing transport technology' encouraged nucleation, with most people reliant on getting around by

[1] Borsay, 'Early modern urban landscapes', p. 100.

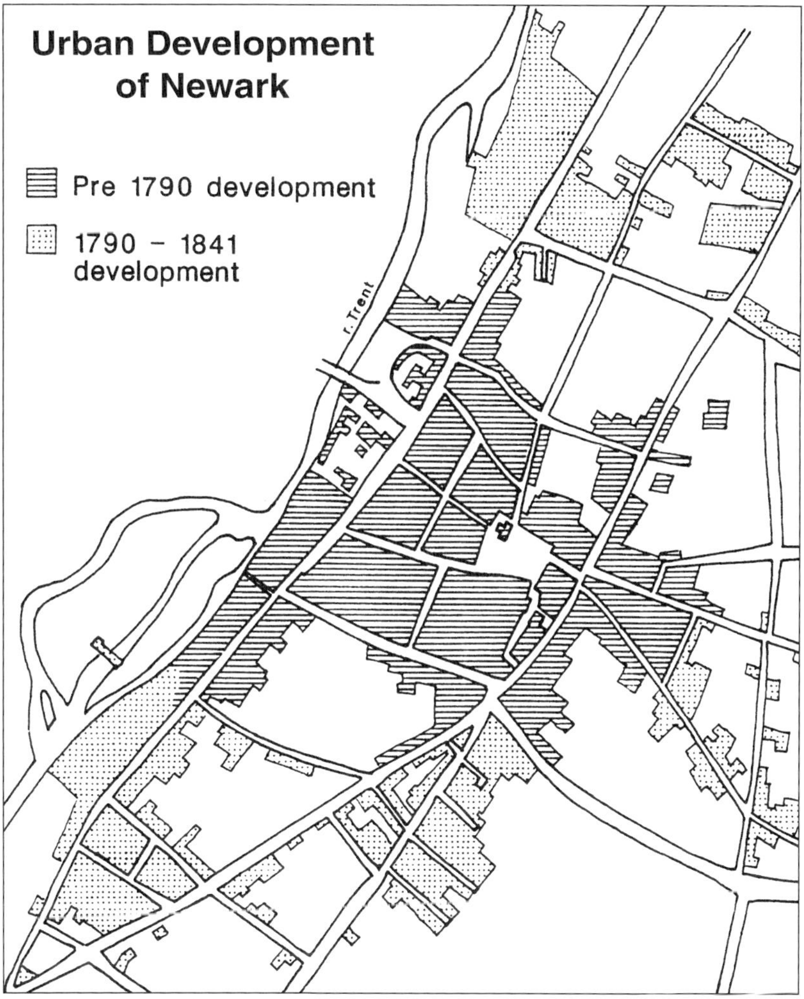

Figure 3 Urban development of Newark, 1790–1841.

foot.[1]

This organic pattern of town expansion was to change dramatically after 1770. New additions to the existing built-up area were created. The street system was expanded to accommodate these new sites, which for the first time were often not tied to existing main roads. This change suggests that the rate of population growth and economic development could not be accommodated in the traditional manner and also that some

[1] Corfield, *Towns*, p. 171.

individuals no longer needed to live facing a main road or close to the town centre. Most of these new sites of mainly residential development were for labourers or mill and foundry workers who were not reliant on selling goods.

The changing pattern of expansion, 1770–1841

Expansion from 1770 signalled the rapid economic, cultural and demographic growth the towns experienced at this time. New roads and streets were built at frequent intervals and land that had remained open for centuries began to be built on. Such developments occurred simultaneously with a continued intensification of land use within the town centre. These developments were most noticeable in Newark, Mansfield and Worksop, although East Retford and Bingham also saw substantial development for the first time in a considerable period. Ollerton saw very little expansion, and what there was could be accommodated by the addition of houses to the town's existing main street. Changes in physical appearance put greater distance than before between Ollerton and the other five towns.

The pattern of expansion changed as a consequence initially of economic growth. By 1840 all the towns except Ollerton and Bingham had acquired textile mills, large maltings, wharves, warehouses, iron foundries and a range of shops and leisure facilities. East Retford and Worksop had been provided with a canal. Improvements were undertaken to the river Trent at Newark and to most of the county's principal roads.

Fig. 3 illustrates the physical expansion of Newark between 1790 and 1841. New roads were set out, first to the north-east and south-east of the town and then to the south. In addition, the traditional pattern of town expansion, involving the building of one or two houses at a time, was superseded by the development of whole streets at once. In 1791 the *Lincoln and Stamford Mercury* reported that the call for new houses in Newark was so great that the 'bricklayers [had] scarcely time to build them so as to stand finishing'.

In 1780 the land tax assessment listed two new streets, St Mark's Lane and Hawton Lane, and also new rows of identically assessed houses in North Gate. By 1785 seven tenements had been added to Cross Keep, 15 to North Gate and four to Bow Lane.[1] In 1790 Newark had

[1] NAO, QDE 1/4.

two further streets: Pelham Street and Portland Street.[1] Between 1790 and 1829 14 new streets were added with further housing development on those already in existence.

In 1829 the town centre had 36 terraces, rows, squares and places, with a further 12 lanes between the principal streets.[2] Continued infilling increased the density of building in the town centre between then and 1841, when the census enumerators recorded a further three streets, 15 yards and 12 rows.[3] One of the most common areas to be developed in this way were the yards of inns and taverns. In 1829 two houses were recorded in the yard of the Black Bull inn; by 1841 this had increased to seven. The number of houses in White Hart Inn Yard increased from four to seven over the same period. Similar developments were found in Alnwick and Ashbourne.[4] Between 1750 and 1841 the population increase of Wolverhampton was largely accommodated by 'infilling, cramming courts at maximum density into any available gaps'.[5]

This new pattern and increased rate of expansion of Newark's built-up area was matched by developments in Mansfield and, to a lesser degree, Worksop and East Retford. In fact, the population of both Mansfield and Worksop was increasing in the early nineteenth century at a faster rate than that of Newark (Table 4.2). In 1674 71 houses were listed in one of Mansfield's principal streets, Stockwell Gate; by 1824 the number had increased to 123.[6] In 1832 the town was described as consisting of four main streets which 'communicate with several shorter streets, and with many courts, lanes and alleys'. It was also noted that the town had seen 400 houses built in the last ten years, most of stone and many forming 'large and handsome villas',[7] although the census records only 300 houses built between 1821 and 1831. Over the period 1801 to 1841 as a whole the number of houses in Mansfield had almost doubled (from 1,245 to 2,200 (Table 3.3).

From 1780 most of Worksop's growth was restricted to the north of the town, close to the Chesterfield Canal, whose completion in 1777 encouraged the building not only of wharves and warehouses, but also

[1] These are first shown on a map of Newark of 1790.

[2] NUMD, Newark Election Poll Listing (Newark, 1829).

[3] NUMD, Newark Census Enumerators Books 1841.

[4] Conzen, 'Alnwick', p. 65; Henstock, *Ashbourne*, p. 17.

[5] John Smith, 'Industrialisation and social change: Wolverhampton transformed', in Stobert, *Towns, Regions, Industries*, p. 139.

[6] NAO, DDH 1354/60.

[7] *White's Directory*, p. 519.

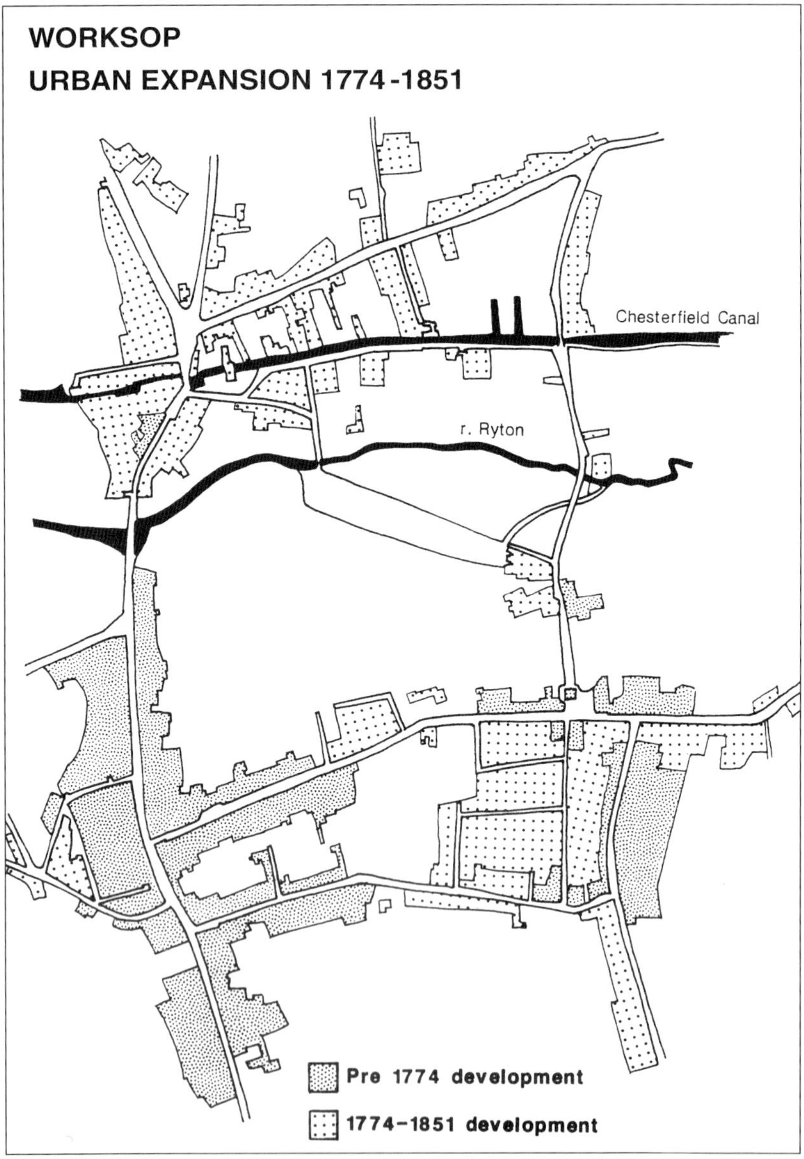

Figure 4 Worksop: urban expansion, 1774–1851.

a mill, numerous malt kilns and a large number of houses (Fig. 4). Between the river Ryton and the canal three residential streets had developed, and between the canal and East Gate more industrial development took place in the form of malt kilns, a corn mill, two public houses, three wharves and a number of private houses. This area had

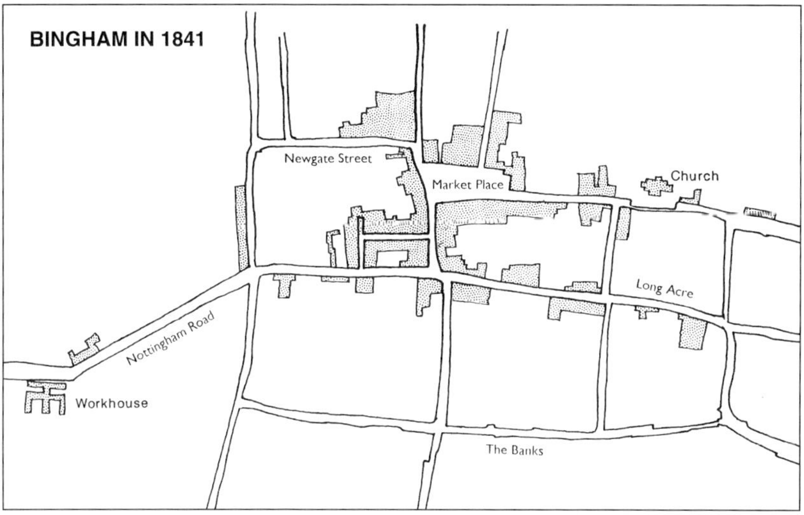

Figure 5 Bingham in 1841.

been common land until 1803, when under the enclosure Act it was allotted to the duke of Norfolk who agreed to its development.

East Retford, Bingham and Ollerton saw much less expansion of their built-up area. The evidence of directories suggests that East Retford had seen some infilling and two new streets are also mentioned. Between 1832 and 1842 the town acquired Union Street (leading west off the market place) and new houses were built in Leverton Road. In Bingham two new streets, Union Street and Needham Street, were developed in the late eighteenth century but the town remained relatively undeveloped even in the early nineteenth (Fig. 5). Ollerton still had only one main street in 1841.

The intensification of land-use, initially through infilling in the town centre, followed by the expansion of the built environment, particularly from the 1770s, is the first evidence to suggest that the economy and society of all but the smallest Nottinghamshire towns was changing. The layout of the towns remained relatively unchanged, particularly in the town centres, except in Mansfield, as will be discussed in the next section. Nevertheless, the extension of the built-up area from the 1770s and the changing pattern of that expansion to include new building for residential, economic and cultural purposes added a new chapter to the landscape of these towns. The two phases of development highlighted are consistent with evidence for other small towns like Alnwick and Ashbourne. In Alnwick Conzen argued that the key period of building fell between 1775 and 1851, while Henstock argued that there was a building boom in late eighteenth-century Ashbourne.[1] Both suggest that the late eighteenth century was a prosperous time for these towns. While the scale of expansion may not have matched that of larger centres like Birmingham or Manchester, they still shared an experience reflecting the new demands on urban living.

The changing urban fabric, 1680–1840

The continued infilling in the town centres and the extension of the built-up area was to accommodate one or more of three types of development: an increase in the number of public, industrial or residential buildings. Each of these made different demands on the townscape. Together, they contributed to the first major reorganisation, and in some cases restructuring, of the town plan since the Middle Ages.

Public buildings are discussed more fully in Chapter 6. Chronologically this development can be traced to the mid eighteenth century, with the building of Mansfield's town hall in 1752. New town halls, libraries, theatres, indoor markets, schools, churches and workhouses were in varying degrees to become common to all the towns. Even Bingham and Ollerton had, respectively, a theatre and new school by 1841.

Buildings with a civic and social role were conspicuously present in the town centre. Their construction often involved the demolition of existing buildings and sometimes the amalgamation of older plots. In Newark the town hall, completed in 1772, occupied in part the site of the old moot hall but its grandeur and size meant that an inn and a number of houses had to be demolished.[2] Fig. 6 shows the town hall next to the Green Dragon inn, which by 1774 had been demolished to make space for a wing of the still incomplete building.

Mansfield's market place was completely redeveloped from 1823, both to accommodate a new town hall and also to create a much more obvious and noteworthy town centre. In August that year a programme of purchasing and demolishing buildings was instituted by the improvement commissioners, and in October £3,135 was paid to seven individuals for their properties.[3] In Newark and Mansfield the changes to these market places are the first clear signs that inherited property boundaries were changing. The centres of Worksop, East Retford, Bingham and

[1] Conzen, 'Alnwick', p. 49; Henstock, *Ashbourne*, pp. 18–20.

[2] R.P. Shilton, *History of Newark. Part II* (Newark, 1820), pp. 366–7.

[3] NAO, DCM 2/1, 1 Aug., 6 Oct. 1823.

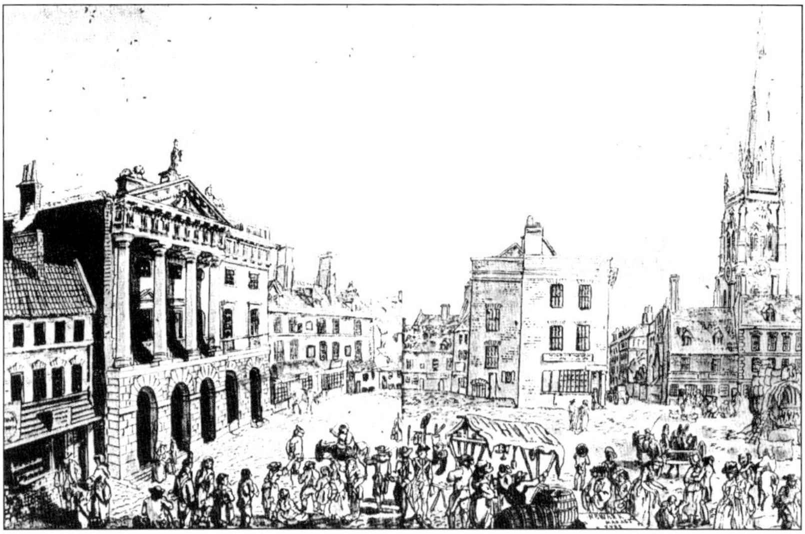

Figure 6 Newark market place, *c.*1790.

Ollerton were not affected in the same way. Although East Retford acquired a new town hall, the building was confined to the site of the previous moot hall. As Borsay notes, property demolition was fairly rare, primarily because of cost.[1]

Schools, churches and workhouses tended to be built on new, undeveloped plots and so did little to change town plans. Similarly, the development of large industrial premises usually took place on the outskirts of the towns. Many had to be located close to a water supply both for power and also because water was often essential for processing.

Mills and iron foundries were a new and symbolic addition to the townscapes of Newark, Mansfield, East Retford and Worksop. In Newark, in particular, the riverside area along Mill Gate to North Gate saw extensive development. In 1790 there was one mill straddling the Trent; by 1829 there were two more. North of the town, two maltings and a foundry were built between 1790 and 1840. At the centre of this area was Castle Hill (Fig. 7) with the main public wharf for the town. To the south of this was Castle Wharf, a coal wharf with three shipping places, a house and counting house, and beyond this Cuckstool Wharf. By 1804 the open spaces around the castle ruins had been filled with tenements and workshops, a candle manufactory and a number of

[1] Borsay, 'Early modern urban landscapes', p. 99.

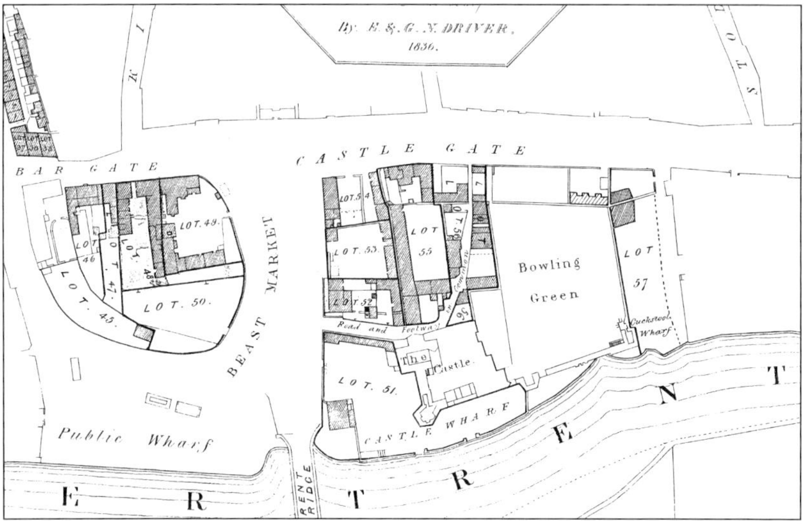

Figure 7 Castle Gate Wharves, Newark, in 1836.

outhouses.[1] To the north of the public wharf were the premises of W.F. & J. Handley, maltsters and brewers, and beyond this by 1830 lay another malthouse, owned by J.H. Massey, and the Wellington iron foundry.

In Mansfield new industrial buildings were to be found both on the outskirts of town and close to the centre. Harrod's *History of Mansfield* (1801) lists five cotton mills, including Stanton's Mill, in Bath Lane, south of the town centre (Fig. 8), and a further 50 were believed to lie within 20 miles of the town. The number close to the town had increased to seven by 1832, by which date there were also several corn mills, three foundries near Portland Wharf, malthouses and a gasworks in Limetree Place.[2] In Worksop and East Retford large industrial and commercial buildings were located close to water, although they formed only a small part of the townscape by 1841. The location of industrial and commercial buildings, and later housing, on the outskirts of the towns and close to water was a common feature of urban growth.[3] Such developments do not in themselves denote a wholesale shift from domestic to industrial production but they are tangible evidence of a new chapter in the

[1] National Archives, MR 1/1132; NAO, Catalogue for the Sale of Crown Lands (1836).

[2] *White's Directory*, p. 521.

[3] King and Timmins, *Industrial Revolution*, pp. 342–6.

Figure 8 Stanton's Mill, Mansfield.

economic history of the towns (see Chapter 4).

By far the biggest addition to the towns in terms of both chronology and space was residential building. In one sense it is misleading to describe the building of houses in this period as purely residential development. Many of these houses, right up until the end of the period considered here, combined the role of home and workplace.[1] Even the wealthier members of the community ran their businesses from home. This in Newark in 1798 Mrs Handley (a member of a very successful brewing family) had a house with offices sharing the ground floor with the hall, drawing room, dining room and kitchen.[2] Similarly, the homes of John Baker (a currier), along with that of George Stevenson (a chemist), William Barnard (a clockmaker) and Joseph Heppenstall (a cordwainer), all included a shop.[3] Those lower down the social scale were even more likely to have similar arrangements. In the early nineteenth century George Scales built a row of cottages (Scales' Row) for his employees with specially constructed cellars to accommodate their

[1] Warnes, 'Chorley'.

[2] NAO, DC/NK 2/1.

[3] NUMD, Ne S 145.

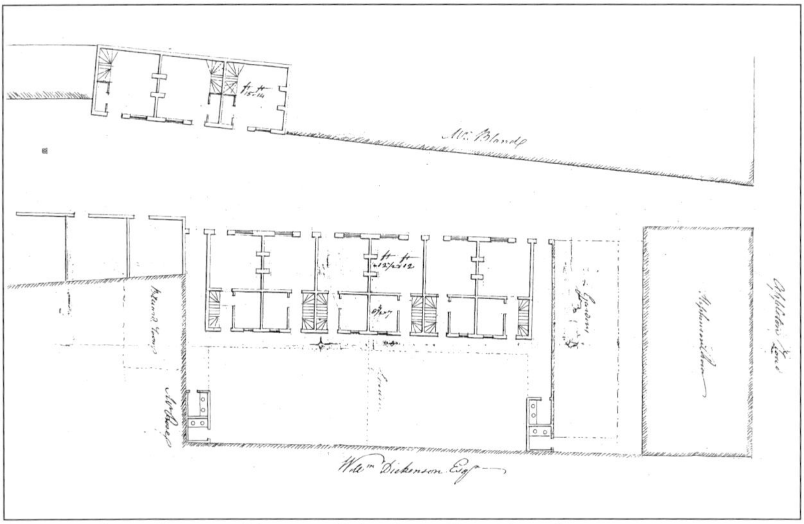

Figure 9 Plans of proposed houses off Appleton Gate, Newark.

looms. The eighteenth century did see a number of fine purely residential Georgian houses built (Chapter 6), but they were far outnumbered by more modest terraces.

From the late eighteenth century rows of houses were built over very short periods of time. Many lined the new streets laid out in the four larger towns, but a number were also built in the numerous yards, alleys and rows off the main streets. Most of these houses were small, often consisting of two rooms on the ground level and two above (Fig. 9). Plans for those in West Gate, Worksop, show that the main front room measured 11 ft by 11 ft, with the back kitchen just 6 ft 4 in. by 7ft 8 in. A narrow passage led to a common yard shared by the two houses (Fig. 10). By 1798 Newark had houses of only two rooms.[1] Typically, these were situated within a yard and were characteristic of the types of buildings developed off the main streets and filling spaces between existing buildings. The houses were small and cramped; those in Cross Guns Yard in Newark were remembered as hovels, 'built upon the flat principle … the central block containing 56, and the sides about 10 cottages each … They were occupied by over 100 families, the total number of human beings … herded together [reaching] 300 people'.[2] In 1835 most of the new houses in Newark were felt to be 'of an inferior

[1] NAO, DC/NK 2/1.

[2] *Nottingham Journal*, 3 Jan. 1834, p. 3.

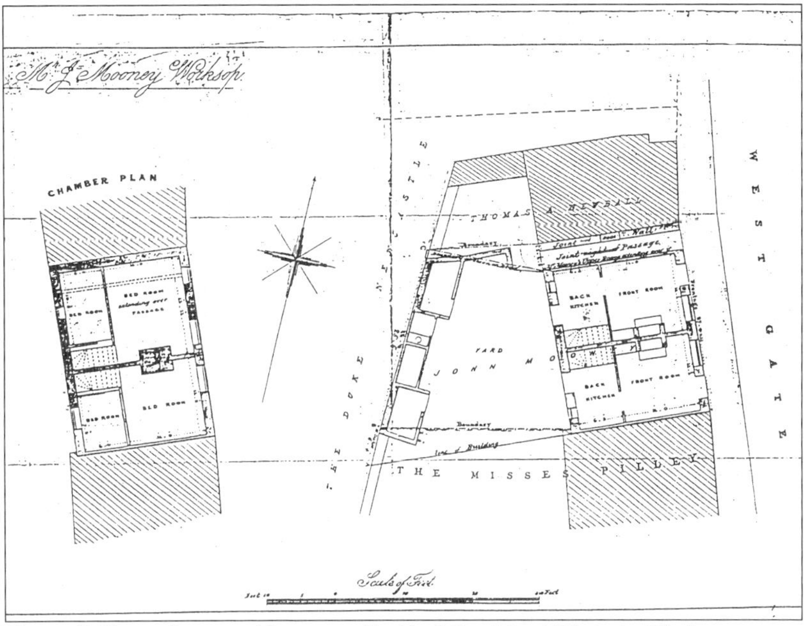

Figure 10 Plans of proposed houses on the Norfolk estate at Westgate, Worksop.

class'.[1]

Similarly, in Mansfield in 1824 some houses in the numerous courts and alleys covered as little as 18 or 16 square yards.[2] Such cramped conditions were accompanied by a lack of fresh water and poor ventilation. Again, such places were to be found in the courts and alley ways behind the buildings that faced the main streets. Table 3.4 lists just some of the courts and alleys that were tucked away behind Stockwell Gate in Mansfield.

East Retford, with 2,680 inhabitants in 1841, had houses packed into most pub yards. These housed, as the census shows, the town's labourers, pedlars, hawkers, washerwomen and chimney sweeps. In 1849 a Board of Health inquiry noted the existence of dark, ill-ventilated courtyards containing small and inconvenient dwellings.[3] Even in Bingham, tenements and small houses were being built in 1841. Fourteen

[1] *Report of the Royal Commission on Municipal Corporations* (Parl. Papers, 1835 (116), XXV), p. 1948.

[2] NAO, DD1354/60, pp. 41–2.

[3] *Report to the General Board of Health on a Preliminary Inquiry into the Sewerage, Draining and the Sanitary Condition of the Inhabitants of the Borough and Parish of East Retford and the Parishes of West Retford, Clarborough and Ordsall* (1849), pp. 11–17.

Table 3.4

Courts and alleys off Stockwell Gate in Mansfield in 1824

Street name	*Buildings*	*Average square yards per house*
King's Head Court	4 houses, 1 yard	21.5
Chandler's Court	21 houses, 1 yard	26.3
Greyhound Court	13 houses, 1 shop, 1 yard	22.2
Plumber's Court	12 houses, 1 yard	24.2
Malt Court	4 houses, 1 yard, 1 malt kiln, 1 house and garden	27.5
Carpenter's Court	3 houses, 1 yard	28
Bakers Court	3 houses, 1 house and garden, 1 house, shop and garden, 1 court	19.3
Rosemary Alley	7 houses, 1 shop	29.7
Peacock Court	5 houses, 1 brewhouse, 1 public house	38.6
Wheatsheaf Court	9 houses, 2 yards, 1 shop	29.8

tenements were built on a plot of land measuring 24.5 perches (53.4 yards). Ollerton by comparison saw no such development. Many of these houses were built by the owners of large commercial and industrial enterprises and most of the yards took their names from their owners. Some, the better quality ones, were built by subscription, for example Wilson Street in Newark (1766) and Norfolk Street in Worksop (*c.*1790), which consisted of '60 houses, built uniformly, with small gardens attached'.[1]

Clearly, even towns with a population of less than 3,000 in 1841 could suffer from the cramped conditions that are more generally associated with the larger industrial centres.[2] These areas became prone to cholera, typhus and small pox in the 1820s and 1830s (see Chapter 6). This constant infilling suggests that space in the town centres was at a premium, with the worst examples of cramped terraced houses found directly behind the prestigious Georgian buildings that lined the main streets. Even in a small town, families of different wealth and status could have a very different experience of the urban environment, yet live in close proximity. It remains to be seen whether the expansion of the market town economy and the introduction of large-scale industry and

[1] J. Holland, *History of Worksop* (Sheffield, 1828), p. 145.

[2] J. Ellis, *The Georgian Town, 1680–1840* (Basingstoke, 2001), ch. 5, pp. 87–105.

large-scale agricultural processing, together with the growth of slum areas in the town centres, encouraged the development of residential segregation that is believed to be more characteristic of larger towns in the nineteenth century (Chapter 5).

The morphology of the market town can only be understood within a wider economic and social framework. In the towns studied here there appear to be two phases of growth between 1680 and 1840. Up to *c.*1770 they followed a pattern common to pre-industrial towns, including London.[1] A second period, starting in the late eighteenth century, reflects their demographic and economic development (see Chapter 4). There is a distinct change in the pace and pattern of expansion from 1770 in Newark, Mansfield and Worksop, accompanied by new types of building, especially public, civic and industrial buildings, signposting the cultural and economic development of these towns. The conspicuous absence of such developments in Bingham and Ollerton, whose physical appearance remained virtually unchanged between 1680 and 1840, highlights their relative decline in the late eighteenth century.

In Newark and Mansfield it was not just the town plan that changed. New streets were, for the first time, given names with a national frame of reference, such as Parliament Street, King Street, Queen Street, George Street, Albion Street and Chatham Street in Newark and Queen Street in Mansfield. At the same time some old street names were altered: in Newark Potters Dyke became Lombard Street in the late eighteenth century, explained by one local historian as the 'accidental circumstance of a banking house being established' on it.[2] Indeed, street names can throw light on the history of communities, since they are as much part of the town plan as its morphology. Their meaning highlights the context of their initial selection and subsequent change and it is no coincidence that such names began to appear as the economic and social horizons of these towns were broadening.

[1] P. Waller, 'Introduction. The English urban landscape yesterday, today and tomorrow', in idem (ed.), *English Urban Landscape*, p. 11.

[2] W. Dickinson, *The Town of Newark* (1816), p. 7.

FOUR

Population Growth and Economic Change

This chapter looks first at the growth of population in the six towns in relation to both the national and regional context. Demographic trends can be used as a crude indicator of levels of economic activity and thus, once the demographic pattern for the Nottinghamshire towns is established, their economic development is explored. In this context, particular attention is paid to the growth of retailing and craft specialisation, often for the local or home market. Alongside this we also see the introduction of textile manufacture and an increase in the scale of agricultural processing industries like malting, which catered more for national and international markets, and sometimes relied on imported raw materials, such as cotton. The scope for new directions in the market town economies did not come at the cost of older, more established roles. The eighteenth and early nineteenth centuries continued to see these towns function as market and service centres, and there was even some expansion and specialisation in these areas. For the larger towns of Newark, Mansfield and Worksop, economic growth and diversification were reflected in their demographic fortunes, and together this suggests that the eighteenth and early nineteenth centuries, particularly from *c.*1770, were a time of prosperity. To some extent this was also true of East Retford, but less so for the smaller and more isolated towns of Bingham and Ollerton. The fortunes of the six towns adds further weight to those historians who look to the home market as well as international trade in assessing eighteenth-century economic developments. However, it is worth remembering that market towns were also producing for export and that this was not confined to places like Manchester, Leeds and Nottingham. Thus any link between industrialisation and urbanisation needs to include the experience of these smaller towns.

Population growth

Between 1681 and 1841 England's population appears to have grown by about 200 per cent.[1] The population may have fallen between 1675 and 1680 but by 1685 had begun to expand again. Growth was maintained until the late 1720s, when the estimated death rate once again exceeded the birth rate, but this proved to be a short lived setback which had resolved itself by the late 1730s. From then total population continued to increase to the 1840s and beyond.[2] These national figures obviously mask regional variations and also fail to measure the increasing proportion of the population living in towns. It has been estimated that the percentage of town dwellers rose from 2.6 in 1700 to 7.9 by 1801, although these figures only include settlements of 2,500 or more.[3]

In the case of regional variations, it has been suggested that between 1642 and 1676 Sussex and Nottinghamshire saw a decline in population of up to 20 per cent.[4] In Nottinghamshire, this appears to have been a short-term crisis with growth once again evident from the last decade of the seventeenth century or early in the eighteenth century, so that by 1725 the population may have been 30 to 40 per cent higher than in 1670.[5] Like the country as a whole, Nottinghamshire experienced a short-term decline in in the late 1720s.[6] Burials reached a peak in the county between 1727 and 1729,[7] years of bad weather and poor harvests.[8] After 1730 there appears to have been an upward trend until the end of this study in 1841, although throughout the eighteenth century population growth was more rapid in the north-west and Yorkshire than elsewhere and the proportion of the population living in the East Midlands may actually have been falling (Table 4.1).[9] If this was the case it did not lead to population decline in the towns studied here (Table 4.2). Langton argues that the county and cathedral towns of the

[1] E.A. Wrigley and R.S. Schofield, *The Population History of England 1541–1871. A Reconstruction* (Cambridge, 1989 edn), p. 208.

[2] Ibid, p. 498.

[3] P.J. Corfield, *The Impact of English Towns 1700–1800* (Oxford, 1982), p. 9.

[4] D. Turner, 'A lost seventeenth-century demographic crisis? The evidence of two counties', *Local Population Studies*, 21 (1978), pp. 14–17.

[5] J.D. Chambers, *Nottinghamshire in the Eighteenth Century* (1966 edn), p.ix; J.V. Beckett, *A History of Laxton, England's Last Open-Field Village* (Oxford, 1989), p. 325.

[6] J.D. Chambers, 'The Vale of Trent, 1670–1800. A Regional Study of Economic Change', *Economic History Review Supplement* (1957); Beckett, *Laxton*, pp. 80–2, 325.

[7] Chambers, *Nottinghamshire*, p. 29.

[8] Beckett, *Laxton*, p. 81.

[9] R. Lawton, 'Population and society 1730–1900' in R.A. Dodgshon and R.A. Butlin, *An Historical Geography of England and Wales* (Harlow, 1978), p. 320; R. Sweet, *The English Town 1680–1840. Government, Society and Culture* (Harlow, 1999), p. 12 is more optimistic.

Table 4.1

Regional distribution of the English population, 1701–1851

Region	*1701*	*1751*	*1801*	*1851*
South East	29.7	29.7	30.1	30.5
West Midlands	9.5	9.8	10.3	10.2
East Midlands	9.0	8.3	7.7	6.9
East Anglia	9.5	8.5	7.6	6.3
South West	19.6	19.5	16.2	13.4
Yorks./Humberside	7.5	8.1	9.8	10.8
North West	6.3	7.5	10.6	15.1
North	8.9	8.7	7.6	6.9

Source: R. Lawton, 'Population and society 1730–1900', in R.A. Dodgshon and R.A. Butlin, *An Historical Geography of England and Wales* (1978), Table 12.2, p. 320.

East Midlands had a higher than average growth rate from the late seventeenth century. This, as he points out, is 'intriguing because urban growth was generally relatively muted in the region before 1841'.[1]

A comparison of the increase in the population of the six towns with England as a whole shows that the former experienced far higher growth rates between about 1670 and 1790. From 1790 their rate of growth falls more in line with the national trend and in some towns fell below the national average. The overall pattern for the sample towns is very similar to that found for small towns in general by Clark from the late seventeenth century to 1811. Such figures support 'a more optimistic interpretation of the performance of small towns in this period'.[2] This runs counter to other suggestions that most country towns saw only modest population growth, especially in comparison with industrial, port and spa towns, and large towns generally.[3] Some have argued that many small towns failed even to double their population in the course of the century. While few towns achieved this rather arbitrary benchmark, Table 4.2 shows that all but one of the Nottinghamshire towns more than doubled in size between 1743 and 1801. It is important to note that the

[1] J. Langton, 'Urban growth and economic change: from the late seventeenth century to 1841', in P. Clark (ed.), *The Cambridge Urban History of Britain. Volume II. 1540–1840* (Cambridge, 2000), pp. 477–8.

[2] P. Clark, *Small Towns in Early Modern Europe* (Cambridge, 1995), p. 99.

[3] Lawton, 'Population and society', p. 326; Corfield, *Towns*, p. 21.

Table 4.2

Population estimates and census enumerations for the Nottinghamshire market towns, 1664–1841

Estimated Population

Town	*1664/74*	*1676*	*1743*	*1801*	*1811*	*1821*	*1831*	*1841*
Bingham	580	490	510	1082	1326	1574	1738	1989
Retford	840	600	914	1948	2030	2461	2491	2680
Mansfield	1480	1490	2550	5988	6816	7861	9426	9388
Newark	2260	1850	2975	6730	7236	8084	9557	10,195
Ollerton	200	–	289	439	462	576	658	777
Worksop	1432	1800	1521	3263	3702	4567	5566	6197

Intercensal change (%)

Town	*1664/7–1676*	*1676–1743*	*1743–1801*	*1801–1811*	*1811–1821*	*1821–1831*	*1831–1841*
Bingham	-15	4	112	22	19	10	14
Retford	-29	52	113	4	21	1	8
Mansfield	1	71	135	14	15	20	0
Newark	-18	61	126	7	12	18	7
Ollerton	–	–	52	5	25	14	18
Worksop	26	-15	114	13	23	22	11

Notes: Hearth tax: a multiplier of 4.25 has been used (for Retford the 1664 figures have been used because those for 1674 did not include non-chargeable households). Compton Census: a multiplier of 1.5 has been used. Herring's visitation: a multiplier of 4.25 has been used. 1801–41: The census figures are for the parish except for Ollerton, which are for the chapelry.

figures from the census (which except for Ollerton are for the parish) are not directly comparable with earlier estimates. In Worksop, for example, many of the inhabitants of the parish lived outside the town.

Between 1801 and 1841 all six towns continued to grow, with an average population increase of 43 per cent, although the census of 1841 records a slight drop in population for Mansfield from 1831. Clark argues that by 1811 England was on the eve of large-scale industrial transformation and that this had a detrimental effect on smaller towns, which 'became increasingly marginalised from the accelerating juggernaut of urbanisation'.[1] The sample towns did see a slight decline in growth rates from the early nineteenth century, which seems to fit the national picture, suggesting that it is from this time that the larger provincial towns, specially in the textile areas of Lancashire and Yorkshire and the metal-working areas of the West Midlands, begin to grow much faster than other centres. This did not, however, lead to an absolute decline of smaller towns which, in Nottinghamshire, was feared if not realised in the 1840s. Nevertheless, between 1801 and 1841 each of the towns, except East Retford, managed to increase its population by over 50 per cent. Interestingly, the highest growth rates were to be found in the more rural parishes of Worksop and Bingham and the chapelry of Ollerton (Table 4.2).

Five of the six Nottinghamshire market towns doubled their total population during the eighteenth century. This is despite the fact that population growth for the Midlands as a whole is usually attributed to the industrial districts and those towns which had an excess of 15,000 people at the beginning of the eighteenth century.[2] As Wanklyn argues, this population increase in the Midlands was linked with 'a massive increase in productive employment, and thus in the quantity of goods being bought and sold'.[3] This is clearly demonstrated in the Nottinghamshire market towns: trades and crafts, services and manufactures all expanded from 1680 and especially between 1770 and 1840.

Economic development

Economic development was common to, though not evenly distributed between, all six towns. Newark, Mansfield, Worksop and, to a lesser extent, East Retford saw significant economic development from 1680 to 1840. Bingham and Ollerton were not so fortunate.

Behind the success of exploiting local, national or even international markets lay access to good communications. Prosperity, as Dyer argues, came to many small towns located on busy roads especially in a period where the 'scale of road use escalated' and so too did the amount of

[1] Clark, *Small Towns*, p. 100.

[2] M. Wanklyn, 'National and international trade and the Midlands economy', in J. Stobart and N. Raven, *Towns, Regions and Industries. Urban and industrial change in the Midlands, c.1700–1840* (Manchester, 2005), p. 206.

[3] Ibid.

business from travellers.[1] The eighteenth century brought improved road, river and canal links to the midlands.[2] This not only ensured that regional produce could be exported but also that essential raw materials, such as cotton, could be brought into the region.

As a county, Nottinghamshire benefitted from its central location between the expanding industrial centres of the north and markets to the south, including London. It had a natural advantage in the river Trent, the navigation of which was improved in 1772, and good road communications. The Great North Road was vital to the fortunes of Newark and, after it was redirected in 1776, to East Retford, of which one local writer commented that 'commerce [had begun] to shed [its] invigorating influence over the town', bringing a 'gaiety and bustle', in view of the number of coaches and travellers that now passed through.[3] Similarly, the Fosse Way, which crossed the southern part of the county on a east-west axis, also passed through Newark. The Fosse Way ensured good links with the rest of the East Midlands and Lincolnshire.

Recognition of the need to build on Nottinghamshire's potential resulted in continued communication improvements in the eighteenth and early nineteenth centuries. Between 1725 and 1840 24 Acts were passed creating new turnpike trusts in Nottinghamshire, together with 21 extending the powers of earlier Acts, ten to repeal others, and one amending Act.[4] As Raven and Stobart note, most road improvements in the East Midlands came after 1760, later than in the West Midlands, with earlier efforts focused only on routes to London. The later improvement of routes to the north and west reflected the changing direction of some of the local market town economies. For instance, the growth of Mansfield's textile industry was dependent on the import of cotton from America via Liverpool. Canal building was less marked in the East Midlands, reflecting at this stage the more mineral-based economy in the West Midlands.[5] Nonetheless, the Chesterfield Canal, authorised in 1771 and completed six years later, provided Worksop and Retford with better

[1] A. Dyer, 'Small towns in England, 1600–1800' in P. Borsay and L. Proudfoot, *Provincial Towns in Early Modern England and Ireland. Change, Convergence and Divergence* (Proceedings of the British Academy, 108, 2002), p. 60.

[2] Ibid., p. 193.

[3] J.S. Piercy, *The History of East Retford* (Sheffield, 1828), p. 154; W. White, *History, Gazetteer and Directory of Nottinghamshire* (Sheffield, 1832), p. 303.

[4] A. Cossons, *The Turnpike Roads of Nottinghamshire* (Historical Association, 1934) p. 42.

[5] N. Raven and J. Stobart, 'Networks and hinterlands: transport in the Midlands', in *Towns, Regions and Industries*, p. 87.

access to the Trent. Both towns contributed to the capital needed to build one of the most ambitious projects of its day.[1]

Four types of economic development can be distinguished in the six towns. The first, dating from the late seventeenth century, relates to the occupational structure of the towns and their increasing diversification and sophistication as a consequence of the growth of retailing and small craft-based or artisan production. As the eighteenth century progressed, a number of specialised trades were to be found in the towns, many of which can be linked to the production and retailing of fashionable consumer items, especially clothes and furniture. These new trades and crafts catered mainly for a local market. Second, no doubt closely linked to the rise of these specialised luxury trades and crafts, was the growth of a professional middle class, such as attorneys, land agents, surveyors, insurance agents, doctors, veterinary surgeons and school teachers. Third, traditional and established economic enterprises also experienced change. The scale of flour and malt production dramatically increased in the eighteenth century as national demands for such goods developed. Flour mills often stood alongside the new textile mills that were built in four of the towns between 1770 and 1828. Finally, an element entirely new to the towns was large-scale textile production. Its presence alone signifies that the eighteenth-century market town was no longer catering purely for a local market but also for a national and overseas demand. These new features of the towns' economies by no means totally superseded older functions such as catering for travellers and the marketing of local produce, but they did transform them from that of a predominantly exchange and service economy to one in which manufacture was more important.

Diversification of occupations

There is no doubt that in each of the six towns, irrespective of their size, the eighteenth century saw an increase in the range of trades and professions. Most of these, like their older counterparts, were small in scale, often based on the household, and catered for the growing demands of a local market. Until recently the growth of the home market in this period has been undervalued, perhaps because it is difficult to measure. Yet the evidence for growing home consumption, particularly

[1] C. Richardson, *The Waterways Revolution. From the Peak to the Trent, 1768–1778* (Stourport on Severn, 1992).

of relatively luxurious food items, clothes and furniture among a greater proportion of the population suggests domestic demand was flourishing.[1] The small scale of such enterprises should not obscure the cumulative boost they must have given the local economy.

This new demand can be seen indirectly in the increasing range of occupations found in small towns. In this respect, the Nottinghamshire towns shared in a much broader experience. Whereas only a few hundred job titles are used in the earliest directories of the late seventeenth century, by the 1780s, nearly two thousand were being used.[2] This multiplication of occupations became more marked from the late eighteenth century onwards, and these tradesmen, craftsmen and professionals, were not only producers but also consumers of fashionable and luxury goods (see Chapter 5). This expansion in the range of crafts and trades was closely linked with the rise of a 'middling sort' in towns.[3]

Wills and inventories name 69 different occupations (excluding 'gentleman' and 'esquire') in the six towns studied here between 1680 and 1720, 76 in 1721–60, 89 in 1761–1800, and 108 in 1801–41. The largest range was to be found in Newark, with 72 between 1801 and 1841 (Table 4.3). By comparison, 38 occupations were recorded in 1695 in Kendal, whose population was then about 2,500,[4] larger than any of the Nottinghamshire towns. An analysis of occupations in East Anglia between 1650 and 1699 (not compiled solely from probate records) lists 74 occupations in Norwich, but most of the smaller towns had no more than 30 and often far fewer. There was a clear hierarchy of East Anglian towns in terms of the occupations they supported, with the presence of certain occupations clearly denoting a higher degree of sophistication.[5] This is equally true of the Nottinghamshire market towns. Newark and Mansfield thus had a relatively wide range of occupations in the late seventeenth century. The same could be said of Worksop and East

[1] N. McKendrick, N. Brewer and J.H. Plumb, *Birth of a Consumer Society: The Commercialisation of Eighteenth-century England* (1983); L. Weatherill, *Consumer Behaviour and Material Culture in Britain 1660–1760* (1988); M. Douglas and B. Isherwood, *The World of Goods: Towards an Anthropology of Consumption* (1980); J. Brewer and R. Porter (ed.), *Consumption and the World of Goods* (1993).

[2] P.J. Corfield in *The Times Higher Education Supplement*, 13 Sept. 1985.

[3] J. Rule, *The Vital Century. England's Developing Economy 1714–1815* (Harlow, 1992), p. 257.

[4] J.D. Marshall, 'The rise and transformation of the Cumbrian market town 1660–1900', *Northern History*, 19 (1983), pp. 138-9, 162.

[5] J. Patten, *English Towns 1500–1700* (Folkestone, 1978), p. 283.

Table 4.3

Occupations recorded in probate documents

Town	*1680–1720*	*1721–1760*	*1761–1800*	*1801–1840*
Newark	42	53	66	72
Mansfield	41	39	29	34
Worksop	27	23	41	37
East Retford	26	33	34	51
Bingham	18	16	26	26
Ollerton	7	5	11	12

Source: NAO, PRNW and PRMW, Nottinghamshire Probate Inventories.

Retford, considering that their populations were probably below 1,000 in 1700 (Table 4.2).

The most frequently recorded occupation in all six towns was farmer, highlighting the continued importance of agriculture to these towns. Other common occupations were maltsters, innkeepers, shoemakers, butchers, bakers, mercers, tanners, apothecaries, blacksmiths, barbers, labourers, chandlers, carpenters, tailors, ironmongers, joiners, fellmongers, dyers, wheelwrights and masons. Thus, between 1680 and 1720 a Nottinghamshire market town could offer a range of services, including provisioning (maltsters, innkeepers, butchers, and bakers), building and construction (joiners, carpenters, masons), metalware (blacksmiths, ironmongers), leather goods (tanners, fellmongers and shoemakers), textiles (mercers and dyers), as well as barbers and apothecaries. In addition, the larger towns supported more specialised trades, such as haberdashery, saddle-making, bodice-making and the manufacture of cutlery. Occupations found only in the two largest towns, Newark and Mansfield, include a brewer, whitesmith, hatter, framework knitter, gardener, clerk, doctor, drawer, merchant, collar-maker and clockmaker.

Certain tradesmen, such as joiners, gardeners and seedsmen, bricklayers, grocers and merchants, became common to most of the towns as the eighteenth century progressed. Even so, Newark and Mansfield still supported a wider range of specialist activities (Table 4.4). By contrast, only 13 different occupations were found in probate records for Ollerton, the smallest of the towns, between 1801 and 1841, and none of these was particularly specialised.

From the early nineteenth century directories show that the occupational structures of all the towns had become more complex than the probate records suggest. By 1832 even Bingham and Ollerton had watch- and clockmakers, tea dealers, an attorney, a confectioner, a hatter, china and glass dealers, druggists, tobacconists, wine and spirit merchants, cabinet makers and paper makers.[1] In contrast, Newark had printers, bankers, stencillers, musical instrument makers, upholsterers, eating-house owners, insurance agents, perfumers, dealers in London hats, iron and brass founders, professors of dancing and music, portrait painters, jewellers, silversmiths, toy dealers and tobacco manufacturers. Judging by the destinations of carriers operating from the town, the demand for such services came from a wide area. Ashbourne in Derbyshire had over 300 tradesmen and professional people listed in Pigot's *Directory* of 1835, yet the town's population did not exceed 2,000 at the time.[2] A significant proportion of the residents of both the towns themselves and nearby villages must have had both the income and the desire necessary to keep these traders in business.

Even in Bingham, with a population of only 1,574 in 1821, it was possible for a few specialist traders and retailers to make a living. This should not be surprising in one respect, given that Mui and Mui suggest that the ratio of population to shops declined to very low levels in the eighteenth century and part of this fall, according to Shammas, was as a result of the growth in number of 'country' shops.[3] Between 1801 and 1840 inventory declarations of £450 each were left by a grocer-iron-monger and a watchmaker.[4] Jon Stobart's analysis of the north-west of England shows that while trades and services such as mercers, drapers and apothecaries were common to large and small towns alike, higher-status service functions and 'luxury trades' were restricted to the larger urban centres.[5] In 1841 the census recorded 242 occupations in Newark, 245 in Mansfield, 153 in Worksop, 134 in East Retford, and 88 in Bingham. Ollerton, with only 777 inhabitants in 1841, boasted 62

[1] White, *Directory*, pp. 423–4, 482–4.

[2] Dyer, 'Small towns', p. 58.

[3] H.C. Mui and L. Mui, *Shops and Shop-keeping in Eighteenth-Century England* (London, 1989), pp. 45, 297; and C. Shammas, *The Pre-Industrial Consumer* (Oxford, 1990), pp. 225–65.

[4] NAO, PRNW, John Doncaster (1821), William Stubbs (1822).

[5] J. Stobart, 'Leisure and shopping in the small towns of Georgian England. A regional approach', *Journal of Urban History*, 31 (4) (May 2005), 486–9.

Table 4.4

New tradesmen and professionals appearing in probate documents, 1721–1841

Period	*Occupations*
1721–1760	soap boiler, shopkeeper, pewterer, confectioner, basket maker, wool comber, cabinet maker, stationer, bookseller, musician, chair maker
1761–1800	excise officer, chemist, corn factor, paper maker, hardware dealer, clog maker, steward, plasterer, painter, tool maker, instrument maker, hosier, gunsmith, surveyor, china and glass dealer
1801–1841	brush maker, book keeper, map maker, broker, linen manufacturer, patten maker, coal dealer, lace worker, spoon maker, flaxmonger, bleacher, mealman, attorney, machine maker, horse dealer, engraver, pipe maker, auctioneer, architect, frock maker

Source: NAO, PRNW and PRMW, Nottinghamshire wills and probate inventories, 1721–1840.

occupations. Two-thirds of Ollerton's population at this time were labourers and servants, but the town also had grocers, druggists, surgeons, merchants, watch- and clockmakers, together with a surveyor, a carver and gilder, a vet, a straw bonnet maker, a chair-maker and a bookseller,[1] all of whom, except the bookseller, not only lived within the town, but had shops there.[2] In terms of size Ollerton was little different to Weobley in Herefordshire, which had 45 tradespeople listed in a directory of 1835.[3] This range of occupations may be compared to that of one of the largest villages in Nottinghamshire at this time, Laxton, which in 1841 had a population of 641, including 22 trades and professions, all concerned with farming.[4] Ollerton would rarely be classified as a town, even in the nineteenth century, on the basis of its population, but it clearly functioned as a service centre of sorts. What we are seeing at the county level in Nottinghamshire is a spatial hierarchical

1 National Archives, HO 107/850–851.

2 Pigot & Co., *Directory of Nottinghamshire* (1841), pp. 53–4.

3 Dyer, 'Small towns', p. 59.

4 Beckett, *Laxton,* pp. 149, 202.

interaction between neighbouring towns in relation to the provision of goods and services, much like that found by Patten in East Anglia and Stobart in the north-west of England.[1]

The areas in which the range of occupations grew first seem to have been the retailing of clothes and textiles, the production and retailing of fashionable furniture, and general grocery stores, which often sold a range of goods from the colonies, thus lending support to the idea of a consumer revolution. Even such highly specialised traders as parfumiers, spoon makers and instrument makers could be found locally. From the late eighteenth century, this development is accompanied by a rise in the number of professionals and also dealers and manufacturers, who were presumably catering for external markets. It is, of course, unwise to place too much confidence in occupations recorded in the 1841 census,[2] since both probate inventories and directories reveal individuals pursuing multiple occupations in a way in which the census does not. Nominally specialist traders could be found selling a range of unexpected goods (often groceries), which suggests that most retailers were opportunists and sought to make profits however they could.[3] Thus in 1700 a Newark mercer, Thomas Newham, left not only hose and gloves, drapery ware, silk ware and haberdasher's ware in his shop, but also groceries. Similarly, John Reynolds of East Retford, whose occupation was tallow chandler, left not only 30 lb of currants, 68 lb of starch, 65 lb of sugar, and some claret, but also tobacco, ginger, indigo, rice, soap and thread in his shop in 1704.

Besides the general grocery shops, there were more specialised retailers, usually dealing in clothes or textiles. In 1701 Mary Manning's haberdashery shop contained nine 'old fashioned caster hats', 12 bury hats, 18 straw hats, 11 chip hats, hatbands, a further 216 hats of various types, and some 'oyle cloths and cases'.[4] Charles Wilson's shop, also in Newark, was stocked with a wide range of materials in 1730, including calico, crêpe, cotton, camblin, Spanish poplin, flannel, serge, tammy, mohair, half printed linen, black mantua silk, white lambs gloves. Similar inventories can be found for mercers and haberdashers in Mansfield and

[1] Patten, *English Towns*; Stobart, 'Leisure and shopping'.

[2] P.H. Lindert, 'English occupations, 1670-1820', *Journal of Economic History*, 40 (1980).

[3] J.D. Marshall, *Autobiography of William Stout of Lancaster, 1665–1752* (Manchester, 1967); T.S. Willan, *An Eighteenth-century Shopkeeper: Abraham Dent of Kirby Stephen* (Manchester, 1970); D. Flemming, 'A Local Market System 1549–1720' (Unpublished M.A. thesis, University of Leicester, 1980), p. 15.

[4] NAO, PRNW.

East Retford. It has been argued that shops became increasingly specialised during the eighteenth century,[1] but there are so few inventories for shops in our area, particularly after 1740, that it is difficult to test this proposition. On the other hand, the growing range of shopkeepers listed in directories from the early nineteenth century indirectly points to increasing specialisation and suggests, as Stobart has argued, that leisure and luxury retailing offered a route to prosperity, even in small towns.[2]

Not all these businesses were necessarily small enterprises with only a local market. Although the demand for goods was mainly local, lists of debts suggest the supply of goods came from much further afield. Many of the shops stocked goods acquired from outside the county or even imported. Dutch thread and cloth, Irish and Russian cloth, German steel, Persian rugs, Manchester ware, ginger, tobacco, sugar and other groceries also found their way into local shops.[3] Some shopkeepers had outlets in more than one town. John Calvert's inventory (1689) detailed stock in his shop at Newark but also referred to stock in another shop in Grantham.[4] In 1726 Amos Torr, a Worksop brazier, had goods in his shop at Worksop as well as in shops in Tuxford and Retford, the two nearest towns.

The range of goods sold and the distance over which some of these items had to be transported underlines the need for efficient communications. Not surprisingly, the range of even the most specialised shops in Bingham and Ollerton was limited, since neither was on or near a major traffic artery. Although we can see how far the range of shops and trades had increased since the late seventeenth century, we cannot tell from directories how successful these businesses were. In 1832, Bingham's market place was described as being 'disgraced by some mean looking shops, which are seldom occupied ... '.[5] A decade later Bingham remained 'rather unfortunately situated and circumstanced' between Nottingham and Newark 'with a population too small to command any material consumption, and too remote from the Trent or any great road,

[1] N. Cox, 'The distribution of retail tradesmen in north Shropshire, 1660–1750', *Journal of Regional and Local Studies*, 13 (1) (1993).

[2] Stobart, 'Leisure and shopping', p. 495.

[3] E.g. the inventories for John Calvert, bodicemaker (Newark 1689); Matthew Derry, ironmonger (Newark, 1727); William Townsend, mercer (Mansfield, 1729); Alex Guthrie, draper (Newark, 1759).

[4] NAO, PRNW.

[5] White, *Directory*, p. 480.

to form a depot ... '.[1] By contrast, East Retford, which had no industrial interests by 1835, was entirely dependent 'upon the retail trade carried on with the inhabitants of the surrounding agricultural districts'.[2] Its ability to survive almost solely as a retailing centre was undoubtedly due to the rerouting of the Great North Road through the town in 1766, which made it the principal post and staging town in north Nottinghamshire.

The level of demand within each town determined whether tradesmen and craftsmen had to supplement their income through farming or some other occupation. Hey found that metal workers in rural parts of Sheffield frequently combined their trade with farming,[3] and Hudson came to the same conclusion for textile workers in West Yorkshire.[4] Inventories reveal that for many Nottinghamshire tradesmen in the late seventeenth and early eighteenth centuries, some involvement in farming was commonplace. For some this amounted to no more than keeping a few pigs, probably for their own consumption. Others were clearly producing for market. In 1689 Robert Moore, described as a cordwainer, left not only leather and hide in his shop but also 201 sheep, five horses, a bull, 42 stone of wool, 12 quarters of oats and four quarters of wheat.[5] The incidence of dual occupations appears to decline between 1680 and 1760 in the larger towns. Up to 1720 23 out of 73 Newark inventories recorded agricultural stock for individuals not specialising in farming, including five innkeepers, chandlers, bakers, one waterman and one glazier, whereas forty years later the proportion was only 26 out of 135.[6] Nine of these were for innkeepers and another four were for butchers, the rest including three bricklayers, a barber, millwright, miller, carpenter, plumber and brazier.

Newark may have generated sufficient local demand to allow most tradesmen to concentrate on their craft rather than dividing their time between that and farming. This was not the case in Worksop, where 45 per cent of inventories for people with non-agricultural occupations

[1] J. Curtis, *A Topographical History of Nottingham* (1843–4), p. 25.

[2] NAO, DDHO 4/11.

[3] D.G. Hey, *The rural metalworkers of the Sheffield region: a study of rural industry before the Industrial Revolution* (Leicester University, Dept of English Local History, Occasional Papers, 2nd ser., 5, 1972), pp. 16-41.

[4] P. Hudson, 'Land, the social structure and industry in two Yorkshire townships, *c.*1660–1800' in P. Swan and D. Foster (ed.), *Essays in regional and local history: essays in honour of Eric M. Sigsworth* (Beverley, 1992), pp. 27–31.

[5] NAO, PRMW 40/60a.

[6] Cf. Flemming, 'Market System', p. 15.

recorded some agricultural goods, including a number of gentlemen who may in fact have been farmers. Between 1721 and 1760 the figure dropped to 34 per cent. In Bingham, the proportion fell from 77 per cent to 20 per cent in the later period, while in Ollerton the figure for the earlier period was even higher. In Bingham it seems that chandlers, mercers, wheelwrights, cordwainers, barbers, glaziers, grocers, framework knitters, nailers, coopers and carriers all needed to supplement their livelihoods with some farming.

Three conclusions can be drawn from the occupational evidence. First, whereas most of the towns appear to have had no more than a basic range of facilities in the late seventeenth century, by 1841 all of them, irrespective of size, supported a considerably increased range of trades and services, albeit with a clear hierarchy as to the range each supported. Newark and Mansfield had nearly double the number found in Worksop and East Retford, which in turn had more than Bingham or Ollerton. Even in Ollerton there was a sufficient range to suggest that it functioned as a town, serving local villages. The late eighteenth century seems to have seen the most rapid extension of services and trades in the Nottinghamshire towns and this chronology is reflected elsewhere. Burslem saw limited service expansion for most of the eighteenth century, with local inhabitants having to travel to Newcastle-under-Lyme. By the early nineteenth century, however, Burslem had increased its range of services dramatically, despite the proximity of Newcastle.[1]

Second, communications were essential to the success of these towns, perhaps more than ever before. The turnpiking of roads, the building of the Chesterfield Canal and the improvements undertaken to the Trent meant the market radius and sphere of influence of the larger towns had increased. By 1841 it was easier for people living close to Bingham or Ollerton to get to other towns and therefore these both were more directly in competition with their neighbours than before. This is probably why the incidence of dual occupations remained higher, although as a general feature of market town life this phenomenon seems to have been on the decline.

Finally, economic development between about 1680 and 1770 predominantly catered for a local market, even if the businesses themselves operated on a wider scale. This does not, however, diminish the importance of such development to the local community, or, when set alongside similar growth elsewhere, to the national economy.

[1] J. Stobart and B. Trinder, 'New towns of the industrial coalfields: Burslem and West Bromwich', in *Towns, Regions and Industries*, p. 125.

In a sense, the diversification of occupations and the growing sophistication of trades and craft was no more than the rejuvenation of the traditional role of these towns as trading and service centres catering mainly for local demand. The scale of this role had changed but its nature had not. None of these towns, however, remained merely producers and retailers of goods to meet local demand. From the late eighteenth century they were also involved in new, large-scale production for national and overseas markets, as well as receiving raw materials and finished goods from them. This change in function has been described as 'one of the most neglected aspects of industrial history'.[1] The three industries that were particularly successful in Nottinghamshire were malting, milling and textile manufacture. The first two were long established, but both were transformed in the eighteenth century. Textile manufacturing, particularly of cotton, was new to the towns.

Agricultural processing, 1760–1841

The fortunes of the six towns, like that of most other market towns, had always been closely bound up with agriculture.[2] Petitions for or against river improvements in the late seventeenth century show that all the larger towns were actively involved in exporting wheat and malt from the county.[3] By the early nineteenth century, much of this produce was being processed locally before being exported. Newark was producing flour for a national market by 1800, when 'placards announcing the sale of Newark flour could be seen all over the country'.[4] The town was supplied with grain from both within the county and nearby Lincolnshire, with boats collecting wheat from farmers along the Trent and delivering it to millers in Newark.[5] By the early nineteenth century one large watermill and one steam mill were in operation. It was estimated that the steam mill 'could and did grind 2,500 quarters of wheat per week, and worked day and night in the busy season'.[6] With the establishment of mills capable of producing flour on this scale we begin to see the impact

[1] A. Everitt, 'The Banburys of England', *Urban History Yearbook* (1974), p. 36.

[2] Dyer, 'Small towns in England', pp. 56–7.

[3] *Journals of the House of Commons*, xi. 398, 414, 434.

[4] 'Reminiscences of a septuagenarian', *Newark Advertiser*, July 1894.

[5] The Royal Commission on Canals and Waterways (1908) refers to the former great trade in agricultural traffic along the Trent to Newark.

[6] *Newark Advertiser*, July 1894.

of technological innovation in the late eighteenth century. Furthermore, the actual building of these mills required relatively large sums of capital of which the origin is uncertain. By 1832 Newark had 11 corn merchants, six corn millers and 19 flour dealers. There were 20 corn mills close by.[1] The 1841 census listed 77 millers and four flour dealers and in the same year two Newark businesses sold 80,000 sacks of flour, generating a revenue of £92,000.[2]

Worksop, the other main flour producing centre, had two mills on the river Ryton in 1774.[3] By 1828 the town had three mills, one each powered by wind, water and steam. The steam mill was said to be capable of handling 100 loads of corn per day.[4] Milling was still Worksop's major industry in the 1850s, supplying local markets like Mansfield and Sheffield as well as London.[5] East Retford had four mills by 1774, but these were less successful and by 1832 two had been converted to paper manufacture.[6]

The second major agricultural processing industry found in all the larger towns was malting, which has been described as one of the quintessential urban occupations of the first half of the nineteenth century.[7] But as Trinder points out there was a distinction to be made between production simply for local markets and that which catered for further afield.[8] Inventories show that malting was a long established Nottinghamshire trade (Table 4.5), for which the county was well served with raw materials. Hops were grown locally, especially around Ollerton and in the north of the county, and at Newark, Mansfield, Worksop and East Retford water was readily available. As in the case of milling, the scale of the industry changed in the late eighteenth century.

In 1698 Mansfield was described as a 'principal trading Town ... especially in malt' which was sent to 'Cheshire, Lancashire and other parts', by which hundreds of families were maintained.[9] In 1727 the

[1] White, *Directory*, p. 619.

[2] S. Lewis, *Topographical Dictionary of England* (1841), iii. 335.

[3] J. Chapman, *Map of Nottinghamshire* (1774).

[4] J. Holland, *History of Worksop* (Sheffield, 1828), p. 5.

[5] E. Eddison, *The History of Worksop* (Sheffield, 1854), p. 5.

[6] Chapman, *Map of Nottinghamshire* (1774); White, *Directory* (1832), pp. 323–4.

[7] 'Towns and industries: the changing character of manufacturing towns', in Stobart and Raven (ed.), *Towns, Regions, Industries*, p. 108.

[8] Ibid., p. 104.

[9] *Journals of the House of Commons*, xii. 500.

Table 4.5

Inventories and inventory declarations for maltsters

Town	*1680-1720*		*1721-1760*		*1761-1840*	
	No.	*Value*	*No.*	*Value*	*No.*	*Value*
			(£)		*(£)*	*(£)*
Newark	5	456	5	373	8	911
Mansfield	8	626	8	210	4	263
Worksop	6	394	5	373	7	1413
East Retford	0	0	1	185	0	0

Source: NAO, PRNW and PRMW, Probate inventories for Newark, Mansfield, Worksop and East Retford, 1680–1840. The figures in the second column in each period are the average value of the number of inventories given in the first column.

town was similarly said to be 'deriving a great Trade in malt'.[1] Between 1680 and 1760 a greater number of inventories survive for maltsters than for any other occupation in Mansfield, or for maltsters in any of the other five towns. Malt production was still flourishing in the town in the early nineteenth century, when William Brodhurst was said to have had the largest malting business in England.[2] By 1843 Mansfield's malt trade had been affected by the success of the Worksop maltsters and the advantage Worksop had in the Chesterfield Canal which 'afforded a superior facility of cheap conveyance'.[3]

Prior to the eighteenth century the other main malt producing town was East Retford, although by 1727 it was said to have lost most of the trade to Worksop.[4] By the late eighteenth centur Newark and Worksop had probably become the county's principal producers of malt. In the 1790s Newark's chief trade was 'in the malting line', which was described as 'considerable and greatly increasing'.[5] In 1798 Robert Lowe argued that the Newark breweries were comparable with those of

[1] T. Cox, *A New Survey of Great Britain* (1727), p. 74.

[2] S. Lewis, *Topographical Dictionary* (1831), p. 247; White, *Directory*, pp. 521, 540–1.

[3] J. Curtis, *A Topographical History of Nottinghamshire* (1843–4), p. 138.

[4] Cox, *New Survey*, p. 138.

[5] *Universal British Directory of Trade and Commerce* (*c*.1790–8), i. 57.

Burton-upon-Trent, especially as regards their trade to the Baltic.[1] A large malting and brewing establishment in the town had a long history of trade with Russia until a duty was imposed on the import of British beer, after which the market became wholly domestic. In 1816 Newark was supplying Nottinghamshire, Lincolnsire, Staffordshire, Cheshire, Warwickshire and Yorkshire.[2] By 1830 the town's malt kilns were producing upwards of 480,000 bushels of malt and the duty paid on this was almost £67,000.[3] Ten years later 50,000 quarters of malt were sent annually to Manchester, Liverpool and London.[4]

The situation was similar in Worksop where, by the early nineteenth century, it was impossible to miss 'the great number of malt kilns standing almost in every direction'.[5] Duty paid by the town's maltsters was over £50,000 in 1821, but this fell to around £36,600 after 1825.[6] In 1832 Worksop had 40 maltsters but by 1841 only 13,[7] a decline explained at the time as a result of the growing importance of Newark's malting trade.[8]

It seems that competition between the towns eventually led to the concentration of malting first in Worksop and Newark, and then in Newark alone. In the early eighteenth century Newark, Mansfield, Worksop and, to a lesser extent, East Retford all had successful maltsters. By the end of the century Newark and Worksop emerged as the two main producers, since both had the benefit of cheap transport by river or canal to the growing markets north of Nottinghamshire. By the 1840s only Newark retained a large industry. This centralisation did not automatically lead to the decline of the other towns, although the loss of East Retford's malting industry early in the eighteenth century is one explanation as to why the town failed to share the growth experienced by Newark, Mansfield and Worksop. The decline of malt production in Mansfield was to some extent masked by the growth of the textile industry and stone quarrying. By the late eighteenth century the manufacture of cotton and linens had been introduced to Worksop, East

[1] R. Lowe, *A General View of the Agriculture of the County of Nottingham* (1798), p. 138.

[2] W. Dickinson, *The Town of Newark* (1826), pp. 137–8.

[3] White, *Directory*, p. 605.

[4] Lewis, *Topographical Dictionary*, p. 335.

[5] Holland, *History of Worksop*, p. 4.

[6] White, *Directory*, p. 455.

[7] White, *Directory*, p. 455; National Archives, HO 107/852.

[8] Eddison, *Worksop*, p. 5.

Retford and Newark with varying success, and in the early 1830s one of the largest quarries, owned by Charles Lindley, was selected to provide the stone for the Houses of Parliament.[1]

Textile production, 1760–1841

In 1790 Mansfield, Newark, East Retford and Worksop all had textile mills. One of the earliest to be built in the county was at Papplewick on the river Leen in 1785. This mill was 100 ft long, 30 ft wide and six storeys high.[2] It was a purpose-built mill, of which there were some fifteen or twenty in Britain by 1780.[3] It functioned on a 24-hour basis, without stop. Between 300 lb and 500 lb of thread was turned each twenty four hours, with an average of 2,000 lb a week.[4] The Papplewick mill was an early sign that cotton production could be introduced to areas with adequate water supply, such as Mansfield or Newark. Cotton production became a new and an important part of Mansfield's economy from the late eighteenth century. By 1801 there were five mills on the Maun, which flows through what were then the outskirts of the town. In 1829 the number had increased to eight.[5] A calculation in 1816 estimated that the average mill in Mansfield was employing 211 workers.[6] A ledger of 1818–19 shows that raw cotton was imported from America and Brazil at Liverpool, from where it was taken by canal and road to Mansfield, and that hosiery and sewing cotton were exported to Philadelphia.[7] In 1841 40 per cent of Mansfield's population was employed in the textile industry, including 167 cotton spinners, seamers, cleaners, winders, corders reelers or doublers, as well as 109 factory hands, 106 lace makers, runners, dressers and corders, 95 seamers, 85 twist mill hands, 29 mill hands, 17 needle makers, 16 bleachers, nine silk spinners, four lace manufacturers and merchants, two needle women, two hosiery warehouse men, a factory manager, a lace pattern maker and a

[1] Pigot, *Directory* (1841), p. 7.

[2] NAO, DD4P 79/63.

[3] M. Berg, *The Age of Manufactures 1700–1820. Industry, Innovation and Work in Britain* (1994 edn), p. 40.

[4] NAO, DD4P, 79/63.

[5] W. Harrod, *A History of Mansfield* (Mansfield, 1801), p. 5; Pigot & Co., *National Commercial Directory* (1828–9), p. 629.

[6] J.H. Clapham, 'Some factory statistics of 1815–1816', *Economic Journal*, 25 (1915), pp. 475–7.

[7] NAO, DD 1175/3.

cotton merchant.[1]

At Newark a mill was built across the Trent in 1790 and four years later Eden wrote of cotton as being the principal manufacturing concern within the town.[2] He referred to a mill that employed 'upwards of 300 people, chiefly women and children' in the production of cotton thread for the town's hosiers, but much of this would have also been for external markets. By the early nineteenth century George Scales, a local linen manufacturer, had built a mill on the southern outskirts of the town and also a row of houses (Scales' Row) with specially converted cellars so that many of his weavers could work from home.[3] It has been argued that the production of linen has not been given sufficient consideration in indices of economic growth for the eighteenth century[4] and certainly in Newark the linen industry thrived until the late 1830s.[5] However, textile production in Newark never came to dominate the community to the same extent as in Mansfield and in 1841 only 13 per cent of the town's working population was employed in the industry.[6]

Nationally, the quantity of raw cotton imported into Great Britain rose from 2.5 million pounds in 1760 to 22 million by 1787.[7] In 1788 Major John Cartwright set up the Revolution Mill in East Retford. The mill had 6,000 spindles, powered by steam and operated by 600 employees. Within three years, however, the business was struggling and eventually collapsed, because of lack of cheap transport, the owner's inexperience, and the absence of any local tradition of large-scale enterprises in such a specialised field, which meant that there was no pool of skilled labour locally.[8] One other mill was set up in East Retford and two in Worksop, none of which survived for more than a few years.[9] This was not

[1] National Archives, HO 107/859.

[2] F.M. Eden, *The State of the Poor* (1928 edn), p. 273.

[3] 'Reminiscences of a Septuagenarian. Newark 60 Years Ago', *Newark Advertiser*, 4 July 1894.

[4] Berg, *Age of Manufactures*, p. 43.

[5] One local inhabitant remembered, as a child, watching 'the operatives weaving beautiful table cloths and other articles' with these items being laid out to dry or bleach in a nearby field. *Newark Advertiser*, 4 July 1894.

[6] National Archives, HO 107/850.

[7] D.S. Landes, *The Unbound Prometheus. Technological change and Industrial Development in Western Europe from 1750 to the Present* (Cambridge, 1969), p. 42.

[8] W.H. Chaloner and J.D. Marshall, 'Major Cartwright and the Revolution Mill, East Retford, Nottinghamshire', in N.B. Harte and K.G. Ponting (ed.), *Textile History and Economic History* (Manchester, 1973), esp. pp. 285–8.

[9] White, *Directory*, p. 310; Holland, *History of Worksop*, p. 145.

untypical of smaller centres elsewhere.[1]

The introduction of mills powered by water or steam in the late eighteenth century did not totally displace domestic production in Nottinghamshire. In all the towns studied here inventories list spinning wheels or looms. In 1689 Samuel Clark, a tanner, had three wheels and in 1721 William Simpson, a webster, had three looms in his shop and three wheels in his chamber. A number of widows and spinsters left spinning wheels and one wife left wheels and spools in her parlour. In Ollerton, one yeoman (John Turner, 1723) left a spinning wheel. In Bingham 14 inventories recorded spinning wheels or knitting frames. The majority of inventories that listed frames and wheels were for farmers or husbandmen, but a butcher, a labourer and a widow also had wheels. Spinning was predominantly a female occupation and the number of households with spinning wheels is a reminder of the role of women in the domestic economy. The situation did not change much with the introduction of mills. As late as 1841, many families in Mansfield, Newark and Bingham were relying on the income generated by both wives and children. For example, Robert Simpson, a Mansfield framework knitter, had three daughters, aged 15, 13 and 11, working as factory hands. In the same town Thomas Stevenson worked as an engineer, while his wife Sarah and daughter Sophia were factory hands.[2]

Framework knitting, by contrast, was a male occupation. In 1801 there were said to be 700 stocking frames in Mansfield.[3] The 1841 census listed 562 framework knitters, 81 stockingers and 25 framesmiths in the town, whereas Bingham had 63 stocking makers, 50 lace runners or carriers, 13 seamers and needleworkers and nine framework knitters. East Retford had 16 staymakers, seven weavers, three stockingers, three spinners, and two lace makers. Worksop had only seven framework knitters and two stocking makers and in Ollerton there were no domestic textile workers at all.[4]

The evidence for large-scale production emphasises the opportunities that industry could offer market towns well situated in terms of both communications and natural resources. As Dyer illustrates, a range of

[1] J. Ellis, 'Regional and county centres 1700–1840', in P. Clarke (ed.), *The Cambridge Urban History of Britain. Vol. II* (Cambridge, 2000), p. 682; J.D. Marshall and C.A. Dyhouse, 'Social transition in Kendal and Westmorland, *c.* 1760–1860', *Northern History*, 12 (1976), pp. 127–57; D.J.W. Dawson, 'Brampton in the 1790s', *Trans. Cumb. & Westmorland Antiq. & Archaeol. Soc.*, 72 (1973), pp. 299–316.

[2] National Archives, HO 107/859.

[3] Harrod, *Mansfield,* p. 6.

[4] National Archives, HO 107/850–853, 859, 868.

industrial activities were to be found in small towns from the seventeenth century and into the eighteenth century, the attraction possibly lying in low labour costs. At the same time it is also clear that large-scale manufacturing in cotton could exist alongside spinning and framework knitting on the domestic scale. While Bingham clearly suffered from its close proximity to Nottingham as a market centre, it still gained some benefit from Nottingham's framework knitting and hosiery industry and thus, as Dyer argues, 'the growing industrial strength of the major towns could be a help as well as a hindrance to the continuing prosperity of the small town'.[1]

Distribution and marketing in the early nineteenth century

In 1816 the historian of Newark believed that improvements to the river Trent had increased the trade, population and importance of the town, within the last few years, 'in a proportion that almost exceeds credibility'.[2] Coal and corn were the main items that passed along the river. In 1810 43,000 tons of goods were said to be delivered and loaded at Newark, and in 1818 over 50,000 tons, a year in which 6,650 boats passed Newark Lock.[3] The presence of such a convenient and cheap means to supply traders and manufacturer gave a tremendous boost to Newark's economy. In 1841 there were 85 watermen, 39 boatmen and boatwrights, five sail-cloth makers and menders, a lock keeper and a wharfinger in Newark.[4] As a result of their position on the Chesterfield Canal, Retford supported 13 boatmen, six watermen, two boat builders, two wharfingers and one lock keeper, while Worksop had 15 boat builders and boatmen.[5]

Road transport was another important local employer. Table 4.6 shows the weekly coaches running from each of the six towns. The pattern of services emphasises the strong links between these towns and the textile towns and ports of the north and north-west. Thus Mansfield, with its strong textile interests, had services to Leeds, Manchester, Halifax, and Huddersfield. Newark had a weekly service to most of the main northern towns and a number of ports and county towns in East Anglia, possibly

[1] Dyer, 'Small Towns in England', pp. 60, 63–4.

[2] Dickinson, *Newark*, p. 137.

[3] R.P. Shilton, *History of Newark. Part II* (Newark, 1820), p. 542.

[4] National Archives, HO 107/868.

[5] National Archives, HO 107/851–852.

Table 4.6

Weekly coach destinations from the Nottinghamshire towns in 1832

	Newark	*Mansfield*	*Retford*	*Worksop*	*Bingham*
Nottingham	✓	✓	✓	✓	✓
Doncaster	✓	✓	✓	✓	
London	✓	✓	✓		
York	✓	✓	✓		
Leeds	✓	✓	✓		
Manchester	✓	✓		✓	
Lincoln	✓	✓			✓
Gainsborough	✓	✓			
Sheffield		✓	✓	✓	
Newcastle	✓		✓		
Edinburgh	✓		✓		
Derby	✓	✓			
Chesterfield		✓		✓	
Stamford		✓	✓		✓
Norwich	✓				
Cambridge	✓				
Glasgow	✓				
Halifax		✓			
Huddersfield		✓			
Liverpool		✓			
Sleaford	✓				
Boston	✓				
King's Lynn	✓				

Source: W. White, *History, Gazetteer and Directory of Nottinghamshire* (Sheffield, 1832).

✓ denotes at least one weekly service.

because of the town's large agricultural processing industries. Most of the towns with which East Retford had contacts with lay on the Great North Road, while Worksop and Bingham had more local services. Ollerton had no coach services, but was served by weekly market carriers to most neighbouring towns. It is clear from the coach destinations that Nottinghamshire's market area, at any rate by the early nineteenth century, lay to the north and east of the county.

The coaches and carriers operated from the principal inns in each town (Table 4.7). Such was the importance of this type of activity that both Newark and East Retford were in the top twenty of Midland towns

Table 4.7

Inns, taverns and beerhouses in Nottinghamshire market towns

Town	*1832*	*1841*
Newark	76	74
Mansfield	56	61
East Retford	38	38
Worksop	34	30
Bingham	10	10
Ollerton	6	3

Source: W. White, *Nottinghamshire* (1832); Pigot & Co., *Nottinghamshire* (1841–2).

deriving a significant living from passing coach trade.[1] In the 1830s Newark was 'alive with the bustle of trade, of coaches and carriages and heavy draught wagons',[2] while East Retford owed much of its 'gaiety and bustle' to the Great North Road, which brought 'to it daily great numbers of coaches and travellers of every grade'.[3] Newark alone had 76 carriers in 1832.[4] By 1841 both towns had coach builders, coach painters, coachmen, carters, carriers and carriers' agents, gig hirers, coach offices and livery stables.[5]

The movement of heavy goods like coal, lead and stone was increasingly common, although the Newark area was already estimated to be consuming 16,000 tons of coal a year in 1655.[6] The advent of steam powered mills, iron foundries and other new industry substantially increased the demand for coal. The Nottinghamshire market towns were reasonably well placed in relation to coal resources, with the output in the East Midlands (meaning principally Derbyshire in this period) rising

[1] Raven and Stobart, 'Networks and hinterlands: transport in the Midlands', in *Towns, Regions and Industries*, Table 5.5, p. 93.

[2] 'Newark Sixty Years Ago. Reminiscences of a Septuagenarian', *Newark Advertiser*, 6 June 1894, p. 8.

[3] White, *Directory*, p. 303.

[4] Ibid., pp. 624–5.

[5] *Pigot & Company's National & Commercial Directory* (1841), pp. 11, 18.

[6] J.U. Nef, *The Rise of the British Coal Industry* (1932), i. 60.

from 75,000 tons in 1700 to 1,700,000 in 1830.[1] As in most areas, the opening of the Chesterfield Canal in 1777 led to a fall in the price of coal along its route.[2] The trading interests of Mansfield were further enhanced by the construction of eight miles of railway linking the town with the Cromford Canal at Pinxton, completed in 1819 at a cost of £33,000.[3]

There is no doubt that for Newark, Mansfield, Worksop and East Retford the eighteenth century and early nineteenth was a period of considerable economic growth and prosperity. Even Bingham and Ollerton saw some increase in the number of trades each supported. All shared in the depression after 1815. For example, in 1827 Retford's savings bank was in difficulties because of 'the low ebb of agricultural affairs, and consequently the general depression of trade'.[4] Despite such setbacks, of greater consequence to these towns was the expansion of agricultural processing and the introduction of textile mills, which demonstrates that the towns benefitted from technological innovation and the growing exploitation of inorganic fuel resources. They were able to do this because the requirements of coal had not yet become so crucial as to warrant the relocation of industry in and around the coal fields themselves. By contrast, later in the nineteenth century East Retford failed to share in the industrialisation taking place elsewhere in the East Midlands and South Yorkshire because it lay some distance from a coalfield.[5] Nor had large-scale production completely superseded domestic industry. The structure of the economy still relied in part on established practices and patterns, and it is this that allowed towns like Newark, Mansfield, Worksop and even East Retford to prosper. From the 1840s, with the growth of the railway system and more rapid industrialisation elsewhere, the towns faced an uncertain future. Domestic industry was in decline, cotton manufacturing became largely the preserve of Lancashire, and the railways took away the long-distance carriage of both goods and people from the roads.

[1] M.W. Flinn, *The History of the British Coal Industry. Vol. 2. 1700–1830: The Industrial Revolution* (Oxford, 1984), p. 26.

[2] A. Cossons, *Inland Waterways of Great Britain and Ireland* (1960), p. 147.

[3] Lewis, *Topographical Dictionary* (1831), p. 247.

[4] Piercy, *Retford*, p. 169.

[5] A.J. Barber, 'Change in the Town of Retford, 1801–1901' (Unpublished M.A. thesis, University of Nottingham, 1993), pp. 113–17.

Conclusion

The evidence presented in this chapter illustrates how a growing domestic market from the early seventeenth century ensured that for Newark Mansfield, Worksop and to some extent East Retford the eighteenth century brought a rejuvenation and expansion of their marketing, retailing and servicing functions. Behind the growth of each town lay factors such as access to external markets, the means to transport heavy goods and raw materials, the investment of local entrepreneurs, and the ability of local inhabitants to spend. Change was evident in even the most traditional aspects of the market town economy in this period. The busiest day of the week in all six towns was still market day. Local officials of manor or borough continued to appoint leather searchers and sealers, to monitor weights and measures and to ensure fair trading as they had since the Middle Ages. But throughout the eighteenth century no prosecutions for engrossing, forestalling or regrating cereal and grain products came before the local courts, while the collection of tolls declined. In 1766 East Retford corporation abandoned the collection of tolls on corn and fruit, together with a charge for entering the town across the bridge.[1] In 1785 William Wood, who had leased the market rights, complained that there were no tolls for corn and fruit at Mansfield market,[2] and in 1793 the tolls at Newark were described as so trifling that exemption from them was unnecessary.[3] The presence of hawkers, higglers, corn merchants, factors and other middlemen in early directories is an indication that goods were being distributed beyond the immediate locality.

It may have been the increasing scale of transactions that encouraged the establishment of more specialised markets from the late eighteenth century. In 1793 the *Newark Herald* announced that a new fatstock market was to be opened in the town.[4] Mansfield also acquired a new cattle and sheep market in the early nineteenth century, together with an annual market for the hiring of servants, while in Worksop and East Retford the existing markets were said to be well supplied and flourishing.[5]

The long eighteenth century saw a transformation of the market town

[1] White, *Directory*, p. 520.

[2] NAO, DD3P 14/16.

[3] *Newark Herald*, 14 Aug. 1793.

[4] Ibid.

[5] White, *Directory*, p. 520.

economy. Change was most marked in the period 1770 to 1840, the classic period of the Industrial Revolution, but this did not take the form of radical change in the way the local economy worked or in how goods were produced. Essentially, these towns continued to balance a mixed economy of trades, crafts and manufacturing. Their range increased to accommodate the growing demand for luxury and consumer goods in the home market, and from the late eighteenth century the scale of production in malting and grain milling increased to exploit growing domestic and international markets. None of these industries, however, came to overwhelm the older market town economies sufficiently to make them highly specialised sites of production. Most of these developments in local urban economies remain hidden in national aggregate figures which concentrate on exports. Yet as Rule suggests, 'it remains the case that in Britain there was an unprecedented structural shift in employment away from agriculture ... a unique increase in urbanisation and, above all, an ability to increase total output ahead of what was by some margin Europe's most rapidly increasing population'.[1] The evidence presented in this chapter is ample testimony to this view.

[1] Rule, *Vital Century*, p. 38.

FIVE

Wealth, Status and Association

What of the people themselves? This chapter examines the experience of different social groups in the light of the economic development of the six market towns. First, the different socio-economic groups are identified. Second, the balance between these groups is examined to see if any broad changes in the social structure developed in this period. Levels and types of wealth are examined in the third section: the focus will be on property ownership and material wealth as displayed at home. The fourth section discusses changes in the cultural relationships between different social groups at this time and whether a growing concept of social space encouraged residential segregation.

To many eighteenth-century commentators, economic development inevitably brought social change. While some acknowledged the material benefits from the rise in trade and commerce, others were less sure about the social, religious and moral change that seemed to accompany it. Goldsmith warned that where wealth accumulated men decayed and Mandeville satirised a society based on the acquisition and accumulation of material wealth.[1] Historians are no more certain of either the material benefits or the social change that accompanied and encouraged economic development.

Interest has centred on the fact that, in general, the accelerating pace of urbanisation and economic change from the late seventeenth century, with high levels of migration from countryside to town, did not apparently lead to 'any great upsurge of social instability in towns' or any 'traumatic breakdown of the urban social order', despite a rise in urban poverty.[2] This stability has been explained by three developments: the containment of poverty, the 'advent of a more sectored, multi-linear and diffuse social hierarchy', and the growth of voluntary clubs and societies in towns.[3] Why a more diffuse social hierarchy should act as

[1] O. Goldsmith, *The Deserted Village* (1769); B. Mandeville, *The Fable of the Bees* (ed. P. Harth) (1970).

[2] P. Clark (ed.), *The Transformation of English Provincial Towns* (1984), p. 30.

[3] Ibid.; P. Clark, *Urbanity and Sociability: Clubs and Societies in the Eighteenth-century City* (Leicester, 1986).

a solvent for social instability is not clear but presumably the existence of more subtle gradations between levels of wealth encouraged a sense of mobility and therefore a vested interest in personal achievement and in maintaining social order. Borsay suggests that the concept of space was the central characteristic of the developing urban culture of this period. In particular, he refers to the 'implanting of the idea of social space in people's minds', and the towns, by servicing this demand, encouraged the pursuit of status, social emulation and possibly even the Industrial Revolution.[1] This argument has been taken a step further to suggest that not only did the concept of emulation and social climbing help to maintain order, but that it was also a mechanism that encouraged consumer demand and economic growth.[2] Porter, for example, argues that 'newly accepted acquisitiveness and opportunism had certain socially accommodating and integrative effects, helping to create a consensus amongst the affluent and aspirant'.[3] According to both Borsay and Wahrman, this consensus extended beyond the locality and was central to the development of a 'national society'.[4]

Social emulation and the pursuit of status are closely linked to the rise of middle income groups in towns. It has been suggested that one of the most fundamental long-term changes in the English urban social structure was a growth in the number, affluence and influence of the 'middling sort'.[5] It might be expected that the development of a large and more diverse middle class would fill the space between rich and poor and create a less polarised society. Arguably, it produced exactly the opposite. While Laslett has proposed the notion of a one-class society in this period, others have preferred to see eighteenth-century society as either one governed and controlled through property ownership and patronage or one in which a profound distance opened up between the

[1] P. Borsay, 'The English Urban Renaissance: the development of provincial urban culture *c.*1680–*c.*1760', in P. Borsay, *The Eighteenth-century Town, 1688–1820* (1990).

[2] E.A. Wrigley, 'A simple model of London's importance in changing English society and economy 1650–1750', *Past and Present*, 37 (1967); M.J. Daunton, 'Towns and economic growth in eighteenth-century England', in P. Abrams and E.A. Wrigley (ed.), *Towns in Societies: Essays in Economic History and Historical Sociology* (Cambridge, 1978); N. McKendrick, 'Home demand and economic growth', in N. McKendrick (ed.), *Historical Perspectives* (1974).

[3] R. Porter, *English Society in the Eighteenth Century* (Harmondsworth, 1982), p. 17.

[4] P. Borsay, 'The London connection: cultural diffusion and the eighteenth-century provincial town', *The London Journal* 19, 1 (1994), pp. 21–34; D. Wahrman, 'National society, communal culture: an argument about the recent historiography of eighteenth-century England', *Social History* 17, 1 (1992), pp. 43–72).

[5] Borsay (ed.), *Eighteenth-century Town*, p. 15.

culture of the patricians and the plebeians.[1] Clark has even argued that England remained, in the eighteenth century, firmly rooted in the *ancien régime* with 'Gentlemen, the Church of England and the Crown' ensuring, between them, social hegemony. The upper ranks of the middling sort, by participating in a cultural world dominated by the landed elite with their hold over the church and state, were accepting and strengthening the leadership of that elite.[2]

There are several problems with these general models. Those who, like Thompson and Clark, adopt a bipolar model of society and culture have been criticised for the neglect or marginalisation of the middling sort and for constructing a model more relevant to rural than urban society.[3] Is it safe to assume that as the middling sort grew in wealth and affluence they unreservedly joined the ranks of the gentry elite? In any case, there may have been a lack of homogeneity even among the urban middling ranks themselves.[4] On the one hand, there were those who were nationally orientated, looking to London as their centre; on the other hand, there were those who identified more with a local or provincial urban culture. There are problems even with this simple division. While the middling orders were actively creating their own leisure pursuits and a 'polite', urbane culture in many provincial towns (including, as we shall see, market towns), such developments so closely mirrored those of London that it is difficult to see how the middle ranks can be separated on national and provincial lines.[5] It is, of course, possible that provincial and national identities could co-exist and serve to reinforce one another. For example, in a period in which we are told that we can see the growth of a more nationally oriented culture, overwhelmingly focused on London, there were over two dozen active

[1] P. Laslett, *The World We Have Lost* (2nd edn, 1971), H. Perkins, *Origins of Modern English Society* (1969); E.P. Thompson, *Customs in Common* (New York, 1991), ch. 2.

[2] J.C.D. Clark, *English Society, 1688–1832* (Cambridge, 1985); L. and J.C.F. Stone, *An Open Elite? England 1540–1880* (Oxford, 1984).

[3] P.J. King, 'Edward Thompson's contribution to eighteenth-century studies. The patrician–plebeian model re-examined', *Social History*, 21 (2) (1996); J. Barry, 'Bourgeois collectivism? Urban association and the middling sort', in J. Barry and C. Brooks (ed.), *The Middling Sort of People. Culture, Society and Politics in England, 1550–1800* (1984), p. 88.

[4] Wahrman, 'National Society'.

[5] P. Borsay, *The English Urban Renaissance, Culture and Society in the Provincial Town, 1660–1770* (Oxford, 1989), P. Earle, *The Making of the English Middle Classes. Business, Society and Family Life in London, 1660–1730* (Berkeley, Calif., 1989); P. Langford, *A Polite and Commercial People. England 1727–1783* (Oxford, 1989).

regional societies in the capital from the late Stuart period onwards.[1] As Helen Berry has argued, provincial centres did not simply emulate London, and the practice of London coffee houses taking provincial newspapers fostered an interest in provincial affairs.[2]

As far as the development of local urban culture in Nottinghamshire is concerned, there is some evidence for the polarisation of elite (or polite) and popular culture, particularly from the mid to late eighteenth century. It was the urban gentry and middle ranks who combined to form the elite in this context, not least as a result of the growth of clubs and associations. Clark has suggested that this development was crucial to the stability of urban society, absorbing newcomers, providing different groups with a meaningful, collective life and, in some instances, bridging the gap between different social strata.[3] Langford talks of 'politeness' being a solvent between a broadening group of urban elites.[4] Through such 'middle class devices' as subscription and balloted membership the exclusiveness and thus sanctity of this group was maintained. However, we can question the extent to which the growth of a distinctive polite culture necessarily means that we have to look for the withdrawal of the elite from popular activities or even their mounting attack on traditional customs. In Bristol traditional popular customs and values continued to appeal to the elite until the late eighteenth century.[5] There are certainly instances in Nottinghamshire which we might consider to be an attack on, or an attempt to reform, popular culture, but none appears to amount to a persistent campaign.

Social groups in Nottinghamshire towns

For the purpose of this study, six social groups were distinguished: (1) the urban poor; (2) servants and waged labourers; (3) artisans, tradesmen, craftsmen and husbandmen; (4) retailers, merchants and manufacturers, farmers, graziers and yeomen; (5) professionals; (6) urban gentry. This division was primarily developed from records that give an indication of wealth, whether in terms of property ownership or material possessions.

[1] P. Clark, *Sociability and Urbanity*, p. 10.

[2] H. Berry, 'Promoting taste in the provincial press: national and local culture in eighteenth-century Newcastle upon Tyne', *British Journal for Eighteenth-Century Studies*, 25 (1) (Spring 2002), pp. 1–17.

[3] Clark, *Sociability*.

[4] Langford, *Polite and Commercial People*, p. 116.

[5] Borsay, *Eighteenth–century Town*, p. 35.

The six groups can be distinguished both in terms of the way they derived their income and the levels of wealth they achieved. There are of course cases where a tradesman appeared to have had more wealth of a certain kind than a gentleman, and the evidence from this study shows that individuals in groups 3, 4, 5, and 6 were all capable of amassing relatively high levels of wealth in this local context. In general, however, these groups can be distinguished on the basis outlined here.

In terms of absolute numbers, the majority of the employed population in the sample towns were waged labourers or servants. What distinguished members of Groups 1 and 2 from the other categories was their reliance on the market economy for the sale of their labour. The urban poor (Group 1) can be further distinguished by their unemployment and the need to supplement their income with, or become wholly dependent upon, charitable relief. In contrast, the servants and labourers in Group 2 were usually employed. Together these two groups comprised the lower stratum of urban society.

Groups 3, 4 and 5 represent the middle ranks in society with group 6, the urban gentry, at the top of the social ladder. The artisans, traders and craftsmen in Group 3 earned their living by producing goods or services in relation to their acquired skill or trade. Most of these individuals had small-scale businesses in which they combined both the production and retailing of their goods. Borsay has classified such people as the 'petty bourgeoisie' and considers them in general to be of lower middle rank status.[1] Included in this group are husbandmen, who do not appear to have had the same levels of wealth as yeomen or graziers. The latter two occupational descriptions appear in Group 4, together with individuals who basically retailed or dealt in goods but who were not usually involved in the production of their merchandise. Also included in Group 4 are the maltsters and manufacturers who were often employing quite large workforces by the end of the eighteenth century. The final group (Group 5) falling into the broad category of the urban middle ranks is composed of those that followed a profession. Langford suggests that these individuals—the doctors, attorneys, clerks, land agents and apothecaries—had a superiority by reason of their education and a more formal recognised training which entitled them to adopt the title of esquire or gentleman,[2] a view expressed by the Municipal Corporations Commission when considering Newark in 1832.[3]

[1] Borsay, *Eighteenth-century Town*, p. 15.

[2] Langford, *Polite and Commercial People*, p. 72.

[3] *Report of the Royal Commission on Municipal Corporations*, iv. 1938.

As will become apparent, individuals within Groups 3, 4 or 5 could aspire to the status of a gentleman. Indeed, it has been suggested that the title, like that of esquire, depreciated in value as the eighteenth century progressed and that this in itself is a mark of a fundamental transformation in society.[1] Langford has also argued that such titles were particularly worthless in an urban context. Everitt too prefers to use the term 'pseudo-gentry' to distinguish those in urban communities from their rural namesakes.[2] In short, it is generally accepted that urban gentlemen did not command the same wealth and lifestyle of those who possessed a country seat. However, I would argue that all of these terms were locally specific and that the term 'gentleman', as used in the Nottinghamshire towns, did imply recognition of a certain level and type of wealth. The fact that a variety of individuals from trade, agriculture or more professional occupations could (and did) aspire to the title of gentleman does not mean that, in their eyes at least, the term had depreciated in value or meaning during our period.

It is often difficult to discover how the urban gentry made a living. Inventories demonstrate that many were farmers and directories show that others were mercers or dealers. We have 52 detailed probate inventories for gentlemen or esquires for the period 1680 to 1832, with valuations ranging from £14 to £1,712. Seventeen list agricultural stock (either crops or animals) and it is clear that a number of the town gentry made their living from farming. For example, William Martin of Newark (1702) had 202 sheep, as well as malt floors and stall gear, and in 1714 Thomas Rippon, also of Newark, was described as both a gentleman and a yeoman.[3] A further 22 inventories mention money owed in the form of either rent or debts, with substantial sums tied up in mortgages, bills and bonds. One inventory gave a solicitor the title of esquire and another referred to the deceased as both a gentleman and a doctor. Thus the term did not necessarily refer to certain occupations but to levels and types of wealth. Individuals from a variety of backgrounds might be recognised as 'gentlemen', although most practised a profession rather than a trade. More important than social background was the fact that the individual was (at least in part) of 'independent means', as contemporaries put it.

[1] Langford, *Polite and Commercial People*, p. 66.

[2] A.M. Everitt, 'Social mobility in early modern England', *Past and Present*, 33 (1966), pp. 70–2.

[3] NAO, PRNW.

Changes in the social structure of the towns

Two broad structural changes in eighteenth-century urban society have been identified in recent writing. Clark and Corfield have suggested that the increase in population, together with higher levels of migration and rapid economic growth, created a 'rising tide of urban poverty';[1] at the same time there was a growth in the middle ranks of society, both in London and provincial towns. In all towns an apex of wealth rested on a broad base of relative poverty.[2] Table 5.1 illustrates the distribution of hearths in 1674 in the sample towns, on the assumption that the number of hearths indicates the approximate size of the house, and therefore at least roughly the wealth of its occupants. A large number of households had one or two hearths and very few had five or more. In fact it is likely that the number of houses with one or two hearths is underestimated because in three of the six towns 'not chargeable' households were excluded.

In three of the towns the number of households exempt from the tax are recorded. In Mansfield 12 per cent of households were too poor to pay, in Bingham 19 per cent, and in Ollerton 30 per cent. Alone, these figures tell us little except that the smaller towns had a higher proportion of houses discharged. These percentages are high compared with market towns in Yorkshire[3] but lower that those for Newcastle, Norwich and Exeter.[4] Only with Eden's *State of the Poor* (1790) do we have any comparable information, and then only for Newark, where he calculated that 605 households paid tax and 500 were exempt,[5] 45 per cent of the total. Eden certainly thought the poor had increased in number in Newark, as in other towns in the late eighteenth century.[6] In 1801 the local historian William Harrod believed that 916 houses paid assessments in Mansfield.[7] The census that year recorded 1,245 houses, suggesting that 26 per cent of households did not pay. Harrod also believed the

[1] P.J. Corfield, *The Impact of Towns, 1700–1800* (Oxford, 1982), p. 135; P. Clark (ed.), *The Transformation of English Provincial Towns* (1984), pp. 31–2.

[2] Corfield, *Impact of Towns*, p. 130.

[3] D.E. Smith, 'Otley: a study of a market town in the late seventeenth and eighteenth centuries', *Yorkshire Archaeological Journal*, 52 (1980), p. 145.

[4] J. Ellis, 'A dynamic society: social relations in Newcastle-upon-Tyne 1660–1760' in Clark (ed.), *Transformation of Towns*, p. 197.

[5] F.M. Eden, *The State of the Poor* (ed. A.G.L. Rodgers, 1928), p. 273.

[6] Clark, *Transformation of Towns*, p. 32.

[7] W. Harrod, *History of Mansfield* (Mansfield, 1801), p. 5.

Table 5.1

Distribution of hearths in Nottinghamshire market towns in 1674

No. of hearths	*Percentage of households*
1	29.2
2	24.6
3	20.5
4	11.1
5	5.4
6	3.1
7	1.3
8	1.5
9	1.1
10+	2.1

Source: National Archives, E 179/254/30.

town had 1,000 paupers, or 17 per cent of a population of 5,988.

Poverty is a relative term: there were degrees of poverty which could range from relative solvency to destitution.[1] It was in the periods in which the distinction between bare solvency and destitution decreased that there was a more general and vivid appreciation of hardship. Then local newspapers would tend to stimulate public concern over the plight and action of the poorer members of society. In 1795 a group of 'riotous' people assembled in Newark, as they did in many other places, to seize and sell corn, which was to go to the local millers, at the price they determined. The wheat was taken by women and placed in the market place, where it was seized by soldiers.[2] The town authorities were clearly disturbed by such occurrences, especially in the 1790s when 'the minds of men were maddened by the absurd idea of equality'.[3] Many years later, in 1822 Newark Corporation resolved that £25 of William Leevers's yearly rent should be returned to him because of the depression in prices for agricultural produce,[4] and in 1830 the *Notting-*

[1] Corfield, *Towns*, pp. 134–6.

[2] *Lincoln & Stamford Mercury*, 24 July 1795, p. 3.

[3] R.P. Shilton, *The History of the Town of Newark upon Trent* (1820), ii. 504.

[4] Newark Town Hall, Corporation Minutes, 18 Feb. 1822.

ham & Newark Mercury noted the price of butter at Newark's market had fallen, one of 'the many proofs of the want of employment and the scarcity of money'.[1] However, to judge from the press, the instances of riot in Nottinghamshire towns were few and far between. Because the occasional riot was usually effectively contained, we might suggest that, at least in relation to public order, poverty and its more disruptive effects were controlled. In any case, the growth in voluntary associations and self-help groups may have helped to alleviate the problems of those who found themselves impoverished.

Of vital significance to the general argument that this period saw rising levels of urban poverty was the decline of the pre-modern dual economy, whereby most households combined their services as labourers with some agricultural production, often on a very small scale.[2] With the onset of industrial and agricultural specialisation, these people became increasingly dependent on waged labour which enhanced their vulnerability to the market economy, particularly when there was a shortage in demand for labour and high unemployment. Towns in particular saw a large increase in industrial labourers from the late eighteenth century. In Nottinghamshire towns, as elsewhere, opportunities for such employment existed but it is difficult to assess whether this contributed to greater poverty. It has also been argued that increasing employment opportunities for women and children, particularly in textile mills, increased the number of wage earners in poorer households. In 1790 Eden alluded to the importance of the cotton thread mill in Newark, which employed mostly women and children who earned between 1s. and 5s. a week. He also noted that ten of the fifteen children currently in the workhouse were employed at the mill.[3]

Without data on wages and the price of basic provisions it is impossible to measure absolute levels of poverty. In any case, there is no general agreement as to what criteria we should employ to assess the standard of living, what periods we should compare, or how local and regional variations should be accommodated.[4] Some have argued that from the second half of the eighteenth century population growth depressed the national average wage, while others have emphasised that wages varied between regions and did not fall in the midlands and

[1] *Nottingham & Newark Mercury*, 2 Jan. 1830.

[2] Clark (ed.), *Transformation of Towns*, p. 32.

[3] Eden, *State of the Poor*, p. 273.

[4] Borsay, *Eighteenth-century Town*, p. 16.

north.[1] It has been suggested that not until 1781 was there a considerable improvement in workers' living standards, with most gains coming after 1820, or that such an improvement may not have begun until the 1840s.[2]

Less controversy surrounds the expansion in the number and affluence of the middle ranks in society. One of the signs of this was the growing demand for domestic servants, since the middle classes were keen to employ servants as a sign of gentility and status.[3] In 1777 the government imposed a tax of 1 guinea per manservant on their employers.[4] The number of employers of manservants ranged from one, John Swan, in Ollerton to 34 in Newark.[5] In fact Newark was one of the 53 towns highlighted by Schwarz to have a sufficient number of employers (30 or more) to be considered a 'leisure town'.[6] Mansfield had 21 employers, East Retford 18, Workshop 12 and Bingham three.[7] A lack of reliable population figures prevents a calculation of what percentage of the towns' population these employers comprise but the number for East Retford is relatively high. This picture is further confirmed when we analyse the wills and inventories for Retford. Where we have further information on the employers of these manservants it is clear that the majority were urban gentlemen, professionals and successful manufacturers and merchants. If it is accepted that the employment of a manservant was a sign of gentility then the aspiration was clearly evident among those who could afford such a luxury, and according to Schwarz this was a small proportion of the population in the Nottinghamshire market towns.

The single most common occupation in 1841 in all six Nottingham-

[1] R.D. Lee and R.S. Schofield, 'British Population in the eighteenth century' in R. Floud and D. McCloskey, *The Economic History of Britain since 1700. 1. 1700–1860* (Cambridge, 1981); E.A. Wrigley and R. S. Schofield, *The Population History of England 1541-1871. A reconstruction* (Cambridge, 1981), pp. 432–5; E.H. Hunt and R.W. Botham, 'Industrialisation and regional inequality: wages in Britain, 1760–1914', *Journal of Economic History*, 46 (1986) and 'Wages in Britain during the Industrial Revolution', *Economic History Review*, 40 (1987).

[2] P.H. Lindert and J.G. Williamson, 'English workers' living standards during the Industrial Revolution: a new look', *Economic History Review*, 2nd series, 36 (1983); J. Moykr, 'Is there still life in the pessimist case? Consumption during the Industrial Revolution 1790-1850', *Journal of Economic History*, 48 (1988).

[3] Corfield, *Towns*, p. 128.

[4] L. Schwarz, 'Residential leisure towns in England towards the end of the eighteenth century', *Urban History*, 27 (1), (2000), p. 53.

[5] National Archives, T 47/8.

[6] Schwartz, 'Residential leisure towns', Table 1, pp. 56–7.

[7] National Archives, T 47/8.

shire towns was female servant. As there are few references to servants in any source until the 1841 census, it is impossible to assess whether, and to what extent, there was a growth in domestic service during the previous century. A small number of inventories refer to a servant's room or a servant's bed but tell us nothing quantifiable. By 1841, however, 22 per cent of houses in Newark had at least one servant. Most of these were headed by people described as of independent means, although, butchers, plumbers, joiners, even journeymen and one labourer could afford a servant.

Borsay has suggested that four developments contributed to the growth of the urban middle class: the rising numbers and affluence of the professions; the emergence of a leisured, residential and quintessentially urban group of what he calls pseudo-gentry; the increasing body of merchants, manufacturers, financiers and wealthy tradesmen; and the development of a distinct petty bourgeoisie of prosperous shopkeepers, craftsmen and victuallers.[1] The growth of trades and crafts in each of the Nottinghamshire towns (see Chapter 4) reflects an increase in the numbers of those constituting the lower middle ranks. With them came, by the late eighteenth century, a growing range of professionals, such as teachers, doctors, attorneys, surveyors, architects, ministers, bankers and clerks, together with merchants, manufacturers, corn factors, cattle dealers and grocers involved in either large-scale production or distribution. Everitt found that, in towns like Northampton, while the number of professionals may have been small, their proportionate wealth, as assessed from probate inventories, rose between 1611 and 1640.[2] This was not the case in Nottinghamshire, where very few inventories exist for professionals from 1680 to 1840. On the other hand, property transactions in the towns and their farming hinterland provided a stimulus for the legal profession and this in turn increased the need for bankers, land agents, appraisers, auctioneers and insurance agents. All are found in Newark, Mansfield, Worksop and East Retford. Occupations culled from wills and inventories, freeman's lists and directories demonstrated the development of a more diverse middle class in the larger towns and, to a lesser extent, in Bingham and Ollerton.

The fact that the records more often than not relate to wealth or status says something in itself. For example, the freeman's list for Mansfield in 1739 includes 15 gentlemen, nine retailers or dealers and ten tradesmen.

[1] Borsay, *Eighteenth-century Town*, p. 15.

[2] A. Everitt, *Change in the Provinces: the Seventeenth Century* (Leicester, 1969), p. 44.

The next surviving list (1780) shows the number of gentlemen had fallen to 13 and that six freemen were professionals, 27 were retailers or dealers and 23 were tradesmen.[1]

Levels of material wealth based on inventory values, 1680-1840

The growing prominence of the middling sort, particularly in terms of wealth, is more clearly evident from an analysis of probate documents between 1680 and 1840. In his study of London Earle suggested that the middling ranks could be distinguished by earning £50 or more on an annual basis and possessing several hundred pounds in wealth.[2] An income of £40 is considered to have been twice as much as was necessary for subsistence and therefore such an income offered the possibility of consumer spending.[3] We have no information to shed light on the annual incomes of different social and occupational groups in the Nottinghamshire market towns, but the inventories do give us one indication of the relative levels of material wealth individuals could amass prior to their death.

Based on Earle's suggestion that a few hundred pounds in wealth was a fair sum to have acquired, at least in London, the Nottinghamshire inventory totals were broken down into six categories: those valued at £1,000 or more, £500–£999, £200–£499, £100–£199, £50–£99 and £1–£49 (Table 5.2). Using Earle's figures and taking £200 as a minimum, 38.1 per cent of the sample town inventories were of sufficient value to be classed as representing the middle ranks if living in London. In a provincial town, should the figure be £100 (i.e. 55.7 per cent)? A social analysis of inventory totals based on the divisions given above revealed two developments in our period: first, that the percentage number of inventories valued at £200 or more increased from 1760 (Table 5.3) and second, that it does appear that as the eighteenth century progressed it was not only the middling ranks in society, particularly retailers, dealers and professionals, who had amassed these higher levels of wealth but also a number of specialist trades and crafts.

The fact that the number of inventory valuations increased significantly between 1801 and 1840 cannot be taken as indicating that, in general, there was more wealth in the market towns at this time than earlier.

[1] NAO, QDJ 1/1–2, 2–5.

[2] Earle, *English Middle Class*, p. 14.

[3] Langford, *Polite and Commercial People*, pp. 62–3.

Table 5.2

Distribution of inventories by value

Value	*Number*	*Percentage of total*
£1,000+	135	7.2
£500–£999	177	9.4
£200–£499	404	21.5
£100–£199	331	17.6
£50–£99	334	17.8
£1–£49	499	26.5

Source: NAO, PRNW and PRMW, Nottinghamshire Probate Inventories and Inventory Declarations, 1680–1840.

From the 1770s, rather than full inventories of goods being taken, the increasing practice was to give only one inventory declaration and an approximate valuation of wealth at that time. The inventory declarations were rounded figures giving the ceiling value of the deceased's property. Such declarations survive in greater numbers than inventories themselves. This change does not, however, mean a social analysis of wealth is any less informative, since it applies to all the six towns and thus the information remains comparable.

To try to establish who, in the sample towns, were able to amass high levels of wealth, an analysis of probate inventories valued at £1,000 or more and between £500 and £999 was undertaken. Bearing in mind the fact that Earle felt that a few hundred pounds was a fair sum to have acquired in London, having £500 or more in a provincial town should reflect a good standard of living. The results for those having inventories valued at £1,000 or more are given in Table 5.4, which shows that the most likely social group to leave inventories of this value was retailers/manufacturers (Group 4), then artisans/traders (Group 3) and gentlemen (Group 6). This corroborates the evidence in Chapter 4 for the growth in business and trade and shows, as Jon Stobart has illustrated, the importance of consumption and culture in shaping economic as well as social and cultural life in 'virtually all towns in eighteenth-century

Table 5.3

Distribution of higher value inventories

Period	*No. of inventories valued at >£200*	*Percentage of total*
1680–1720	91	23
1721–1760	88	23
1761–1800	119	31
1801–1841	416	58

Source: as for Table 5.2.

England'.[1] More specifically, from 1761 we see the appearance of professionals in this group and even in 1824 one Newark individual described as a labourer whose inventory was valued at £3,000.[2] It is also clear that from 1761 we see the growing presence of retailers and merchants (for instance a stationer, merchant, hardwareman and six grocers) together with, from 1801, the first hosier and a number of more specialised tradesmen like the watchmaker and cabinetmaker.

If this analysis is taken one step further to examine who among the market town populations were most likely to have inventories valued at between £500 and £999, a similar picture emerges (Table 5.5). This time, inventories for a merchant and stationer appear between 1721 and 1760 and then more specialist and professional occupations increase from 1761.

An occupational analysis of inventories valued at between £200 and £499 shows that the number for specialist craftsmen, professionals and merchants declined from 1680 to 1840 but that, at the same time, there was a broader range of what we could consider to be more basic trades and crafts (petty bourgeoisie), like plumbing, brickmaking, weaving and tailoring. The number of individuals falling into the petty bourgeoisie increased as a whole and in general across the period and the trend was replicated for the category of those with wealth of between £100 and £199 and for those valued at less than £100.

1 J. Stobart, 'Leisure and shopping in the small towns of Georgian England. A Regional Approach', *Journal of Urban History,* 31 (4) (2005), p. 498.

2 N.A.O., PRNW, Robert Peet, Labourer, Newark, 1824.

Table 5.4

Inventories valued at over £1,000

Period	*No. of inventories valued at >£1,000*	*Social group and occupation or status*
1680–1720	11	Group 6: Gentleman [9%] Group 4: Maltster (2), Mercers (2), Innkeeper [45%] Group 3: Ironmonger, Stapler, Cordwainer, Butcher, Tanner [45%]
1721–1760	12	Group 6: Esquire [8%] Group 4: Mercer/Draper (6), Innkeeper, Yeoman [67%] Group 3: Ironmonger, Bricklayer, Grazier [25%]
1761–1800	16	Group 6: Gentleman (3) [19%] Group 5: Surgeon (2) [12.5%] Group 4: Maltster (2), Merchant, Stationer, Mercer, Steward, Publican [44%] Group 3: Ironmonger, Cordwainer [12.5%] Other: Spinster (2) [12.5%]
1801–1840	96	Group 6: Gentleman (15) [16%] Group 5: Surgeon (2), Clerk, Minister, Surveyor [5%] Group 4: Farmer (9), Grocer (6), Merchant (4), Innkeeper (4), Victualler (3), Maltster (3), Corn Factor, Mercer, Hosier, Hardwareman [34%] Group 3: Baker (3), Tailor (2), Miller (2), Painter (2), Barber (2), Whitesmith, Seedsman, Cabinetmaker, Frock maker, Sergeant at Mace, Watchmaker, Butcher, Wheelwright, Gardener, Ironmonger, Saddler, Plumber [24%] Group 2: Labourer [1%] Other: Widow/Spinster (19) [20%]

Notes: Where more than one inventory is left by individuals in the same trade, the number is given in round brackets. The percentage figures in square brackets refer to the number of inventories and inventory declarations in each social group as a percentage of the total number of inventories and inventory declarations for each period.

Table 5.5

Inventories valued at between £500 and £999

Period	*No. of inventories valued at £500–£999*	*Social group and occupation or status*
1680–1720	23	Group 6: Gentleman (3) [13%] Group 4: Yeoman (5), Maltster (4), Innkeeper (3) [52%] Group 3: Butcher (3), Chandler, Tanner, Baker [26%] Other: No Trade Given (2) [9%]
1721–1760	26	Group 6: Gentleman (6) [23%] Group 4: Maltster (4), Yeoman (3), Merchant (2), Stockmaster, Stationer, Mercer [46%] Group 3: Plumber, Baker, Husbandman [11%] Other: Widow/Spinster (4), Minor [19%]
1761–1800	36	Group 6: Gentleman (5) [14%] Group 5: Surgeon [3%] Group 4: Maltster (3), Mercer/Draper (2), Grocer Supervisor, Book seller, Publican [25%] Group 3: Builder, Tanner, Cordwainer, Butcher, Saddler, Fellmonger, Gardener, Currier [22%] Other: Widow/Spinster (10), No Trade (3) [36%]
1801–1840	92	Group 6: Gentleman (10) [11%] Group 5: Doctor, Reverend [2%] Group 4: Farmer (15), Grocer (4), Innkeeper (3), Merchant (2),Maltster (2), Victualler (2), Auctioneer, Shopkeeper, Boat Owner [34%] Group 3: Plumber (2), Miller (2), Currier (2), Builder (2) Butcher, Patten Maker, Painter, Coach Maker, Confectioner, Hairdresser, Brazier, Fellmonger, Machine Maker, Brickmaker, Baker, Map Maker, Boat Owner, Seedsman, Fishmonger, Whitesmith, Boat Builder [26%] Group 2: Labourer (3) [3%] Other: Widow/Spinster (21), No Trade [24%]

Note: Where more than one inventory is left by individuals in the same trade, the number is given in round brackets. The percentage figures [] refer to the number of inventories and inventory declarations in each social group as a percentage of the total number of inventories and inventory declarations for each period.

The evidence of inventories suggests a hierarchy that can be related to status and occupation. It also suggests that the hierarchy was headed by a broad middling group of merchants, dealers and manufacturers, including traders and artisans, and then gentlemen and professionals. This trend is particularly noticeable from 1760 onwards. It would be wrong to assume, however, that total inventory values are a good index of relative standards of living. For example, the inventories of a Mansfield blacksmith, William Mirfin, and John Clay, a Mansfield hatter and haberdasher, demonstrate how misleading the assumption that total inventory values indicate the degree of domestic comfort or daily existence. The total inventory value for William Mirfin was £129 2s. 11d. in 1741.[1] However, of this £106 5s. 7d. represented goods in his shop. The only possessions of note in his house were one clock and case, a writing desk and 12 prints of the Apostles. By contrast, John Clay's inventory of 1783, valued at £72 16s. 6d, shows an elaborately furnished house with four-poster beds, mahogany card- and tea-tables, crimson damask curtains, carved mirror frames and several pieces of silverware.[2] In short, there is no direct correlation between total inventory values and levels of material or domestic comfort, which raises the question of who, in these towns, were the urban consumers of luxury and fashionable goods.

Domestic possessions

In 1838 William Howitt described how 'every man lives now-a-days for public observance. He builds his house and organises his establishment so as to strike public opinion as much as possible'.[3] Massie's original tables, purporting to show economic and social ranks, divided each group according to what was drunk, coffee or chocolate, on the grounds that this could be taken as an indication of how frequently sugar was consumed.[4] In the eighteenth century consumer goods were seen as a sign of wealth and status and, as will be demonstrated, increases in material wealth appear to have been limited to the middle and upper groups in society. In this respect they perhaps served to unite these

[1] NAO, PRMW 74/10d, William Mirfin, Mansfield, 1741.

[2] NAO, PRMW 81/11b, John Clay, Mansfield, 1783.

[3] W. Howitt, *The Rural Life of England* (1838), i. 108.

[4] P. Mathias, 'The social structure in the eighteenth century: a calculation by Joseph Massie', *Economic History Review*, 2nd ser. 10 (1957), p. 36.

groups with each other. At the same time they also distanced both groups from the rest of the urban community.

De Vries has argued that the role played by urbanisation was crucial to the rise in consumption.[1] Similarly, Overton has demonstrated how the adoption rate of new material goods was generally higher in urban than rural parishes between 1600 and 1750, although they argue that the rural–urban dichotomy can be overplayed and factors such as status and occupation often produced different levels of material possessions between rural parishes.[2] Eversley suggests that, taking an income of around £50 a year as a threshold, three million households in England were above this level in 1800 and can therefore be counted as potential consumers.[3] His group included the better paid artisans and even rural manufacturing groups like hand-loom weavers and framework knitters. McKendrick has argued that where opportunities for the employment of women and children existed (as in our market towns), total family earnings could combine to bring a significant number of their households into the group of consumers.[4] The evidence for the advertising and supply of consumer goods together with the wage-earning potential has led McKendrick to assert that eighteenth-century England saw a 'consumer revolution' with 'more men and women than ever before in history' able to enjoy the experience of acquiring possessions.[5]

Shammas and Weatherill produced evidence from probate inventories and Customs records to show there was indeed an unprecedented increase in the consumption of such goods as exotic groceries and household durables in late seventeenth- and eighteenth-century England and America, but the recent work of Styles throws serious doubt on

[1] J. De Vries, 'Between purchasing power and the world of goods: understanding the household economy in early modern Europe', in J. Brewer and R. Porter (ed.), *Consumption and the World of Goods* (1993).

[2] M. Overton, J. Whittle, D. Dean and A. Hann, *Production and Consumption in English Households, 1600-1750* (2004), pp. 167–8.

[3] D.E.C. Eversley, 'The home market and economic growth in England 1750-80' in E. Jones and G.J. Mingay (ed.), *Land, Labour and Population in the Industrial Revolution,* (1967), pp. 211–14.

[4] N. McKendrick,'Home demand and economic growth: a new view of the role of women and children in the industrial revolution', in N. McKendrick (ed.), *Historical Perspectives*, pp. 184–90.

[5] N. McKendrick, J. Brewer and J.H. Plumb (ed.), *The Birth of a Consumer Society* (1982), pp. 9, 53.

whether this increase constituted a revolution.[1] Styles denounces the loose use of such terms as 'mass consumption' and 'mass production' to describe the experience of eighteenth-century England. So who were the consumers? Earle suggests that the group to benefit the most was the poorer members of the middle ranks (the petty bourgeoisie); Weatherill's work suggests that it was the middling ranks as a whole who experienced most change and in Kent and Devon it appears to have been those involved in service, retail or maritime activities.[2] My own study would seem to confirm these findings and to suggest that household possessions served to reinforce social divisions in the urban community.

The vast majority of late seventeenth-century homes in Nottinghamshire market towns were rather sparsely furnished. Tables, chairs, fire irons, feather beds, couch chairs, pewter dishes and brass pots and pans were the commonest items. Several houses had curtains and cushions. The most elaborately furnished rooms appear to have been the main chamber or bedroom. Very little descriptive detail on furniture and furnishings is given in inventories from between 1680 and 1720 and this in itself would suggest there was little new to attract the attention of appraisers. When something of value or something unusual was found the appraisers would give more detail. Items of note between 1680 and 1720 included cane furniture, leather upholstery, holland sheets, carpets, pictures, silver and glass ware.

In the late seventeenth century luxury items were most likely to be found only in the houses of gentlemen. For example, Richard Mason of Newark had four tables, eight leather chairs and five bass chairs in his hall in 1688.[3] The parlour contained a further two tables, twelve cane chairs, five turkey-work chairs, six cushions and some pictures. Upstairs the chambers and garrets had 'mat and cord' bedsteads, feather beds, counterpanes, valences, bolsters, pillows, stuffed chairs, couch chairs and curtains. Mason also had a large collection of silver ware which was individually itemised and included a sugar bowl, 14 salt cellars and two

[1] C. Shammas, 'Changes in English and Anglo-American consumption from 1550–1800'; L. Weatherill, 'The meaning of consumer behaviour in late seventeenth- and early eighteenth-century England'; J. Styles, 'Manufacturing, consumption and design in eighteenth-century England', in J. Brewer and R. Porter (ed.), *Consumption*, pp. 527–54.

[2] Earle documents a major up-grading of domestic interiors, especially among poorer members of the middle income groups in London (*The Making of the English Middle Class* (1989), pp. 281, 300), but Weatherill examines a much broader range of English society in *Consumer Behaviour and Material Culture in Britain, 1660-1760*, and demonstrates the growth of consumer goods is evident in a wider range of households. For Kent and Devon see Overton, *Production and Consumption*, pp. 150–1.

[3] NAO, PRNW, Richard Mason gent., Newark, 1688.

sweetmeat spoons. Compared with most inventories compiled between 1680 and 1720, his described a well furnished and comfortable house. Individual items found in Mason's house were also present in the homes of those lower down the social hierarchy but the full range and quantity of his possessions were rarely found in anything other than a gentleman's house.

Successful late seventeenth-century tradesmen, merchants and professionals invested some of their wealth in household goods. John Swift, a Newark tanner, left leather, cane and turkey-work chairs and a clock, in addition to more usual items, in 1694 and in the same year Thomas Watnaugh, a maltster from Worksop, left leather chairs, carpets and rugs, a clock and curtains.[1] In 1699 the inventory for Mathias Cumberland, a Newark yeoman, details a parlour furnished with one oval table and six leather and four turkey-work chairs.[2] Upholstered furniture, like turkey-work chairs, also appeared more often in Kent inventories from the late seventeenth century.[3] The more unusual items to appear at this time included an hour-glass (Mansfield, 1689), a striking clock (East Retford, 1698) and a weather glass (Worksop, 1700). This suggests that, for those who had the means, there was the desire to furnish houses more comfortably and to purchase items that were either unusual or signified a degree of wealth. These items were clearly available in the seventeenth century and affordable not only to the local gentry but also to the wealthier traders. The fact that many of these items are found earliest in the houses of the town gentry, and then later appear in the houses of traders, might suggest that the latter group were emulating their social superiors. However, recent work has challenged such an explanation. Campbell claims that there is no evidence that people bought new goods in order to emulate their betters and Vickery has suggested that social differentiation, rather than emulation, may have been important.[4]

Irrespective of the motives for possessing consumer goods, the inventories show that such goods were becoming increasingly common in urban homes in the eighteenth century. Nonetheless, it is undoubtedly the case that inventories underestimate the spread of consumer items

[1] NAO, PRNW John Swift, tanner, Newark, 1694; T. Watnaugh, maltster, Worksop, 1694.

[2] NAO, PRNW, Mathias Cumberland, yeoman, Newark, 1699.

[3] Overton, *Production and Consumption*, p. 95.

[4] C. Campbell, 'Understanding traditional and modern patterns of consumption in eighteenth-century England: a character-action approach'; and A. Vickery, 'Women and the World of goods: a Lancashire consumer and her possessions, 1751–81', in Brewer and Porter (ed.), *Consumption*, pp. 40–57 and 274–301.

Table 5.6

Frequency of items recorded in inventories, 1680–1832

Item	*1680–1720*		*1721–1760*		*1761–1832*	
	No.	*%*	*No.*	*%*	*No.*	*%*
Pictures	35	11.1	69	23.3	19	36.5
Clocks	36	11.4	86	29.1	28	53.8
Leather chairs	21	6.6	8	2.7	1	1.9
Goldware	7	2.2	9	3.0	3	5.8
Silverware	52	16.5	70	23.6	16	30.8
Delftware	3	0.9	13	4.4	7	13.5
Maps	3	0.9	18	6.1	3	5.8
Cane furniture	8	2.5	12	4.1	1	1.9
Books	29	9.2	23	7.8	7	13.5
Musical instruments	4	1.3	1	0.3	0	0
Watches	4	1.3	7	2.4	4	9.6
Oak furniture	2	0.6	11	3.7	8	15.4
Mahogany furniture	0	0	5	1.7	10	19.2

The first figure under each date is the total number of references to each item; the second figure is the percentage of all inventories containing those items as a percentage of the total number of inventories for that period which list household goods. The latest inventories to have sufficient detail to be used in this analysis for each town were 1767 (Ollerton), 1787 (Worksop), 1822 (Bingham and Mansfield), 1826 (Newark) and 1832 (East Retford).

because the number that were sufficiently detailed to list these goods declined as the eighteenth century progressed. Many late inventories simply list the total value of goods for individual rooms without itemising their contents. In this respect, it is important to remember the point made by Overton that inventories cannot be used to claim particular items were not present.[1] Moreover, the range of individuals possessing these items also increased. The frequency with which thirteen key items were recorded in inventories between 1680 and 1832 is listed in Table 5.6.

An analysis of who possessed these items over the same periods shows that the ownership of material possessions was largely restricted to the middle ranks and above (Table 5.7). In particular, the recording of material or consumer items in the inventories of those classified as

[1] Overton, *Production and Consumption*, p.18.

Table 5.7

Occupation or status of those possessing consumer goods

1680–1720	Group 6: Gentlemen (19) [19%] Group 5: Apothecary (2), Doctor, Schoolmaster, Surgeon [5%] Group 4: Innkeeper (6), Mercer/Draper (6) Maltster (4) Framework Knitter, Haberdasher [18%] Group 3: Chandler (6), Yeoman (6), Barber (5),Tanner (5), Cordwainer (3), Fellmonger (3), Wheelwright (2), Baker, Bricklayer, Butcher, Carpenter, Cutler, Husbandman, Ironmonger, Joiner, Laceworker, Saddler, Stapler, Tailor, Webster, Whitesmith, Woolmaker [45%] Group 2: Waterman [1%] Other: Widow (13) [13%]
1721–1760	Group 6: Gentlemen (9) [6%] Group 5: Doctor (2), Reverend [2%] Group 4: Innkeeper (21), Yeoman (11), Maltster (7), Mercer/Draper (6), Framework Knitter (2), Stationer, Stockmaster, Wood Merchant [34%] Group 3: Cordwainer (8), Blacksmith (6), Bricklayer (6) Baker (5), Butcher (5), Husbandman (5), Fellmonger (3), Glover (2), Joiner (3), Mason (3), Brazier (2), Cooper (2), Miller (2), Plumber (2), Tanner (2), Currier, Dyer, Furrier, Gardener, Glover, Grazier, Ironmonger, Saddler, Soap Boiler, Tailor, Victualler, Wheelmaker, Woolcomber, Weaver [47%] Group 2: Labourer [0.5%] Other: Widow (13), Spinster (3) [11%]
1761–1832	Group 6: Gentlemen [2.5%] Group 5: Reverend [2.5%] Group 4: Innkeeper (9), Framework Knitter (3), Maltster (2), Grocer, Haberdasher, Postmaster, Shopkeeper, Yeoman [47.5%] Group 3: Blacksmith (3), Cordwainer (2), Tailor (2), Carpenter, Cooper, Fellmonger, Flaxdresser, Mason [30%] Group 2: Labourer, Servant [5%] Other: Widow, Spinster (4) [12.5%]

Note: Where more than one inventory is left by individuals in the same trade, the number is given in brackets ( ). The percentage figures [ ] refer to the number of inventories in each social group as a percentage of the total number of inventories for each period.

retailers or manufacturers (Group 4) rose dramatically in the period 1680–1832. This seems to confirm both Weatherill's and Earle's findings that it is in the households of middle income groups that can be found a growing number of consumer items. Between 1721 and 1832 only two labourers had any of the items listed in Tables 5.6 and 5.7. One Bingham labourer left a clock in 1751 and one Newark labourer possessed some pictures in 1763. There is no evidence here to suggest the growth of mass consumption, at least in relation to household possessions. Even among the middle and upper ranks in the market town communities the possession of material items was much more marked in the larger towns of Newark, Mansfield, Worksop and East Retford. These were the places that had the shops and it would appear that as a result local inhabitants were either more likely to buy goods or attached more significance to domestic comfort. Moreover, the houses of farmers, yeoman and husbandmen, especially those who lived in Bingham and Ollerton, but also many in the larger towns, had very little in the way of consumer goods. Few people involved in agricultural occupations are listed in Tables 5.7 and in 5.8. The average value of household goods in the inventories of yeomen, farmers and husbandmen is also relatively low. Yet the total value of inventories for these individuals was often high (Tables 5.4 and 5.5), suggesting that they were simply not interested in the acquisition of fashionable consumer goods. This seems to be true of farming households elsewhere. Weatherill, Shammas and Overton have all stressed the conservatism of English and American farmers in relation to the ownership of consumer goods.[1]

More recently Scammell has argued that urban life was not such an important focus for the ownership of domestic goods. By selecting certain items (such as china, curtains, clocks, books and earthenware) and comparing their presence in rural and urban homes she concludes that location was not important for many of these items.[2] Ownership might have been easier in towns but, where ownership related to certain domestic activities, the difference between urban and rural homes was not pronounced. From the range of goods selected by Scammell, her findings are not surprising, but if a broader and less commonplace range of goods was selected the findings might be quite different. Certainly the inventories analysed for this study show that individuals with more rural occupations did not own the same range of consumer items as those practising urban trades and crafts.

Although Amanda Vickery and T.H. Breen have argued that 'social

[1] Weatherill, *Consumer Behaviour*, ch. 8; C. Shammas, 'Consumer behaviour in colonial America', *Social Science History*, vi (1982), pp. 77–8; Overton, *Production and Consumption*, p. 151.

[2] L. Scammell (formerly Weatherill), 'Town versus country: the property of everyday consumption in the late seventeenth and early eighteenth centuries', in J. Stobart and A. Owens (ed.), *Urban Fortunes: Property and Inheritance in the Town, 1700–1900* (Aldershot, 2000), pp. 26–49.

Table 5.8

Average value of household goods in inventories by occupation and status

Occupation/status	*No. of Inventories*	*Average Value £*
Gentlemen	43	77
Innholders/Victuallers	62	71
Chandlers	10	52
Mercers/Drapers/Haberdashers	28	45
Framework Knitters	9	37
Maltsters	34	36
Barbers/Peruke makers	11	32
Butchers	24	28
Cordwainers/Shoemakers	31	27
Glover/Fellmonger	13	27
Blacksmith/Ironmonger	25	26
Tanner	8	26
Yeoman/Husbandmen	85	25
Joiner	10	24
Bricklayer/mason	16	24

meaning cannot be read off the bare fact of ownership',[1] it does seem that owning material possessions of the type listed in Table 5.6 was both open and important to the middling and upper ranks in urban society, and within these groups it was tradesmen, craftsmen and retailers rather than farmers, who seemed to attach most significance to the possession of these items. Langford's description of the middling sort as a 'class defined by material possessions' is an accurate one.[2] In a community where status divisions were clearly important but perhaps increasingly blurred, at least among the middling groups, the type of possessions and level of comfort in the domestic environment may have seemed to them important. Nonetheless, Table 5.7 shows the clear distinction between the urban gentry and the value of their domestic goods and the tradesmen and retailers below them. The title 'gentleman' still denoted a certain level of conspicuous consumption in the market town community that

[1] Vickery, 'Women and the world of goods', p. 276; T.H. Breen, 'The meaning of things: interpreting the consumer economy in the eighteenth century', in Brewer, *Consumption and the World of Goods*, p. 251.

[2] Langford, *Polite and Commercial People*, p. 121.

few individuals could aspire to. The next section will examine wealth in relation to property ownership where the dominance of the urban gentry became even more apparent.

Ownership of property, 1780–1841

This examination of property ownership is confined to the period 1780 to 1841 because there are no adequate sources before the surviving land tax assessments become available. These are the first comprehensive, though by no means complete, record of landownership that exist for the towns until the tithe apportionments were compiled between 1840 and 1853.[1] Both sets of records were used to construct a social register of wealth in the form of property. The major limitation of this analysis is that it excludes consideration of property owned outside the towns by the market town populations, although the evidence of wills suggests few individuals were in such a position.

The proportion of the urban population of Nottinghamshire owning land or property within the towns was very small, even by 1841. Yet the occasional references suggest that by this time the ownership of property had actually become more widespread than in earlier times, at least in the minds of nineteenth-century commentators. One Newark inhabitant believed 'real property [was] much more diffused in the town' in his day (1816) and in Worksop the sale of some of the duke of Norfolk's property as building plots had enabled 'numerous individuals [to] become occupants and proprietors, where it was not probable at one period, they would have become either'.[2] However, a comparison of the Newark tithe apportionment (1841) with the census for the same year shows only 8.7 per cent of householders owned property at that date, 3.1 per cent of the total population. Nor was Newark an exception. In East Retford only 3.3 per cent of the total population were landowners as late as 1848. The pattern was similar for Mansfield and Worksop, while in Bingham and Ollerton landownership was even more exclusive. In 1840 the earl of Scarbrough owned 86.5 per cent of the land recorded in the tithe apportionment for Ollerton. The Church owned a further 9.5 per cent and the remaining 4 per cent was owned by 19 individuals, or 2.4 per cent of the population. This pattern was not untypical. In 1842 ten

[1] Record linkage between the land tax assessments from 1780 and directories was used to compile a socio-economic profile of Otley (Smith, 'Otley', p. 152).

[2] Dickinson, *Newark*, p. 141; W. Holland, *History of Worksop* (Sheffield, 1828), p. 145.

owners held more than 66 per cent of tithable land in Wolverhampton, with much of the remainder owned by the Church.[1] The ownership of property was more diffuse in the borough towns of Newark and East Retford than in the other four manorial towns. This was probably due to political considerations but even here few individuals appear to have been able to invest in property. As Howitt noted in 1838 the ownership of land still remained the privilege of the aristocracy:

> imagine the possessor of a noble estate coming down to receive his friends at home. To a high and generous mind this must be something very delightful. When he enters his own neighbourhood, he enters his own kingdom. The very market-town through which he last passes, is probably, totally or three-fourths of his property.[2]

In the Nottinghamshire towns the ownership of land or property served to identify or distinguish those who were right at the top of the social ladder. More subtle distinctions in material possessions, the conspicuous deployment of labour and the type and style of town houses helped to accentuate differences in status and wealth among the rest of the urban elite. It might be that, as Vickery suggests, differentiation rather than emulation is the key to understanding the meaning of possessions to eighteenth-century urban dwellers. If so, we might also expect a more individualistic society to develop from this, but Barry has argued that the increasingly fragmented and fluid nature of urban society actually encouraged a more collective response to urban, mass living.[3] A similar point was made as early as 1828 by a Worksop historian:

> In towns where the relative distinctions of personal or family importance, are not broken down, or abraded by the effects of trade, and the feeling of mutual independence, the reciprocal duties of friendship and good neighbourhood, are most likely to be confined or neglected: as, in such cases, there wants the circulation medium of free and universal intercourse; for which, insulated independence, however multiplied, is no equivalent. In no situations do men more certainly rise and sink in their relative

[1] J. Smith, 'Industrialisation and social change: Wolverhampton transformed, 1700–1840', in Stobart, *Town, Regions and Industries*, p. 139.

[2] Howitt, *Rural Life*, i. 28.

[3] A. Vickery, 'Women and the world of goods' and J. Barry, 'Bourgeois Collectivism? Urban Association and the Middling Sort', in Barry and Brooks (ed.), *Middling Sort*, pp. 84–112.

> importance or non-importance in the scale of society, than when they are constantly brought into contact with their equals, or their superiors; and no where is this less the case, than in those places where the privileges of social intercourse are defined or limited.[1]

From a different perspective Borsay has also argued that from 1660 we see the development of an elite polite culture which served to unite the middling and upper groups in urban society. His analysis is restricted to the larger provincial towns, but it is clear from this study and others that have focused on smaller urban communities, that the growth of an elite polite culture was equally common in the more substantial market towns.[2]

Social and cultural development

It has been argued that one of the problems in attempting to understand the mechanisms and success of the assimilation of migrants in towns is that of integrating a heterogeneous body of people into a viable community. Some forms of association were more formal than others. For example, East Retford and Newark had both acquired borough status (in 1246 and 1559 respectively) and with this a formal administrative framework had long been established. In East Retford a charter granted in 1608 ruled that the town should have a 'common council' which was to be governed by a senior and junior bailiff and twelve burgesses chosen as aldermen. The bailiffs and aldermen chose a recorder, who had limited civil and criminal jurisdiction, and the recorder had the power to appoint a town clerk. Qualification as a burgess could come automatically through birth (by being the oldest son of a burgess) or by serving a seven-year apprenticeship with a burgess. Only burgesses had the right to vote for borough representatives in Parliament. In 1831 East Retford's burgesses numbered 200 out of a population of 2,491 (8 per cent). Furthermore, half of these burgesses did not reside within East Retford. However, as a result of a parliamentary from 1827 it was decided that, to avoid corruption, the franchise should be extended to the whole of the Bassetlaw hundred, which may have increased the number qualified to

[1] Holland, *Worksop*, p. 156.

[2] P.J. Corfield, 'Small towns, large implications: social and cultural roles of small towns in eighteenth-century England and Wales', *British Journal of Eighteenth-Century Studies*, 10 (1987); M. Reed, 'The cultural role of small towns in England 1600–1800', in P. Clark (ed.), *Small Towns in Early Modern Europe* (Cambridge, 1995).

vote.

Other older institutions that had survived from the Middle Ages included the manorial courts in Worksop, Mansfield, Bingham and Ollerton, together with the church vestries which, right up until the end of our period, were still responsible for aspects of town up-keep and improvement and could control considerable charitable funds (especially in the case of Newark). The role of the manorial courts had survived to varying degrees in the different towns. In Ollerton only a court leet was held once a year whereas in Bingham and Mansfield a court baron was held every three weeks and a leet twice a year. Jurymen for both courts were selected from the towns' freeholders. Like the burgesses in Newark and East Retford, many of the freeholders in Bingham, Mansfield and Worksop were not resident. For example, the freemen's lists for Bingham in 1805 listed nine out of the 17 (53 per cent) as non-resident, with others living in Nottingham, Cambridgeshire and Leicestershire.[1] Involvement in town affairs could therefore come automatically as a result of economic status within the community.

Apart from these established and necessarily formal types of association, it has been claimed that the social and cultural roles of towns had become a more difficult problem in post-Reformation Europe where 'the collapse of traditional collective forces in town life was a central feature'.[2] Borsay argues the collapse had become a particular problem in the seventeenth century with the decline of other traditional forms of association, such as the parish and the gild.[3] Clark describes this process as 'the fragmentation of the communal coherence, the diminution of the organised sociability, and the sundering of the powerful cultural identity of the older medieval city'.[4] By the late seventeenth century the need to assimilate townspeople may have led to the development of some predominantly, if not uniquely, urban forms of social organisation which provided specific groups with a meaningful collective life. Clark argues that it was the 'resurrection of urban sociability' that helped to 'create a new, dynamic, secular vision of the urban community'.[5] The institutions and organisations involved, which were often based around inns, coffee houses, churches and chapels,

[1] NAO, QDE 5/1.

[2] J. Barry, 'Bourgeois Collectivism', in *Middling Sort*, p. 87.

[3] P. Borsay, '"All the town's a stage": urban ritual and ceremony 1660–1800', in Clark (ed.), *Transformation of Towns*, pp. 228–58.

[4] Clark, 'Sociability', p. 4.

[5] Ibid., p. 6.

served a vital function in developing an informal web of association that gave urban society a measure of coherence and community.[1] Some of these associations, like the friendly, charitable and cooperative societies, operated as self-help groups, while others, like the coffee and news clubs, were orientated more towards conviviality.

The Nottinghamshire towns, like the larger provincial centres, shared in this expansion of social, cultural and self-help groups, which have been more broadly described as part of an urban renaissance and an English Enlightenment. Clubs and societies appeared in all the towns from the late eighteenth century. Most would have met informally in public houses leaving little, if any, record of their existence. Newspapers are often the only source to mention the existence of such groups and they themselves were undoubtedly selective in their coverage.

Together with the associations listed in Table 5.9 Mansfield had, by 1832, 44 friendly and two cooperative societies, Newark had seven friendly societies and two charitable institutions, East Retford had six charitable and seven friendly societies, and Worksop had 12 friendly and four charitable societies.[2] The smaller towns of Bingham and Ollerton clearly could not sustain such groups at this time.

The late eighteenth century also saw the establishment of theatres in all the towns except Ollerton and a carefully co-ordinated county circuit of assemblies between Nottingham and the principal market towns (Newark, Mansfield, East Retford, Worksop). On 17 November 1781 the *Nottingham Journal* announced that the manager of the Mansfield assemblies had decided to change the days on which they were held 'as those in several local towns are scheduled close together'. On average assemblies were held monthly in Newark and Mansfield and every two or three months in Worksop and East Retford. These were newsworthy affairs with the regular announcements of forthcoming assemblies and a detailed assessment of those just past. Often with the announcement of assemblies came advertisements for dancing schools for classes in 'plain minuet, Pargrave minuet, De La Cour minuet, Devonshire minuet, English rigadoon, allemande, quadrille, cotillions and country dances'.[3]

Both the clubs and societies and the assemblies shared the use of subscription or balloted membership to control who could participate. Langford describes both methods as 'middle class devices' for excluding

[1] P. Clark, *British Clubs and Societies 1500–1800. The Origins of an Associational World* (Oxford, 2000), ch. 4.

[2] White, *Directory*, pp. 315, 456, 529, 614.

[3] *Nottingham Journal*, 22 Feb. 1783.

Table 5.9

Clubs and societies in Nottinghamshire market towns, 1782–1840

Date	*Town*	*Society*
1782	Mansfield	Harmonic Society
1787	Mansfield	Friendly Society of Gentlemen Florists
1790s	Mansfield	Coffee Club
1820	East Retford	Book Club and Newsroom
1825	Newark	Subscription Library and Newsroom
1825	Mansfield	Newsroom
1828	Mansfield	Circulating Library; second Coffee Club
1831	Worksop	Subscription Library and Newsroom
1836	Mansfield	Floral and Horticultural Society
1840	East Retford	Agricultural Society
1840	Ollerton	Agricultural Society

unworthy members.[1] The subscribers to East Retford's newsroom were elected by ballot and in 1828 included 40 gentlemen. The rules stated that no strangers were to be admitted unless accompanied by a member, with the one exception being Navy or Army officers.[2] In 1801 Mansfield's coffee club had the support of 'noblemen and gentlemen of the country, and principal tradesmen in the town', all of whom were chosen by ballot.[3] The second coffee club to be set up in Mansfield (1828) had, at the top of its list of members, the duke of Portland, Lord William Bentinck and Lieutenant-General Need. Among the non-town resident members were three magistrates, one barrister and several esquires. Town members included most of the gentry and main tradesmen and professionals, including a linen and woollen draper, a tea dealer and grocer, maltster, bleacher, surgeon, attorney, cotton manufacturer, banker's clerk, merchant, farmer, coach proprietor, surveyor, a registrar of wills and the clerk to the Mansfield improvement commissioners.[4] All these people would be classified in Groups 4, 5 and 6 of the social groups adopted here and therefore represent the upper middle ranks and urban gentry. Even the friendly societies which might be expected to include those of

[1] Langford, *Polite and Commercial People*, pp. 101–2.

[2] J.S. Piercy, *The History of East Retford* (Retford, 1828), p. 147.

[3] Harrod, *Mansfield*, p. 7.

[4] NAO, DD 1354/54.

a lower social status had their criteria for excluding undesirable members. In Newark members had to be over 18 and below 30 years of age and to be 'free from the King's evil, falling sickness, lameness, venereal disease and any other distemper'.[1]

Exclusion by controlling membership was reinforced by spatial segregation. In the larger provincial towns many of these new forms of urban association were conducted in private premises, such as new assembly rooms, coffee clubs and libraries.[2] In the towns studied here, most of the societies met in a principal inn and the assemblies would be held in a specially designed room in the new town halls, as Borsay has argued for elsewhere.[3] In two cases new, purpose-built buildings were erected, a newsroom by East Retford corporation in the early nineteenth century and Lord Middleton's new building, in the market place, for Newark's coffee club.[4] Presumably the more limited resources in the market towns, both in terms of people and money, inhibited the development of new more private buildings for the social elite.

It has been argued that critical to this whole process of social and cultural development in the towns were changes in the intellectual and cultural milieu of better-off townsmen. The end result was the growing polarisation of polite and popular culture in the eighteenth century. On the one hand, new forms of association served to unite the middling and upper social groups, while also signalling a widening gap between these groups and those below them.[5] Thus, as Earle argues, 'politeness' became a solvent between a broadening group of urban elites, while for Barry the growth of clubs and societies was a necessary form of 'reconciliation' for urban society because of the growing economic and occupational specialisation and fragmentation which, he argues, lay at the 'root of urban life'.[6] This is a difficult theory to test and it could be argued that Earle's notion of 'politeness' acting as a solvent and Barry's notion of reconciliation over-simplify the nature of socialising within urban society. For example, Shani D'Cruze's work illustrates how individual town inhabitants developed informal and formal forms of association that operated on different levels and amongst different types

[1] Rodgers (ed.), *State of the Poor*, p. 273.

[2] Borsay, *Urban Renaissance*, passim.

[3] Ibid., p. 111.

[4] Piercy, *East Retford*, p. 147; White, *Directory*, p. 609.

[5] Porter makes this point arguing that the eighteenth century saw a 'simultaneous process of cultural concensus [among the elite] and cultural polarisation': *English Society in the Eighteenth Century*, p. 17.

[6] Earle, *English Middle Classes*; Barry, 'Bourgeois Collectivism', p. 89.

of people simultaneously.[1] Where wealth and status did play a role was in either opening or closing the number of associations accessible to an individual. The more wealth an individual had, the greater the number of options available to him. Thus, while the concept of 'politeness' is a useful descriptive tool, it can obscure the diversity of urban associations and the subtle distinctions that may have existed between them and their clientele.

Even more problematic is the argument that as an elite urban culture developed, those who could participate not only increasingly dissociated themselves from popular culture and tradition but also became extremely contemptuous of it, attempting both to reform and abolish certain customary pastimes. For example, activities such as bull-baiting and cock-fighting were increasingly condemned nationwide.[2] And, perhaps not surprisingly, one Worksop historian demonstrated in 1828 his familiarity with such concerns by arguing 'the time is past when the abusing of cocks and the baiting of bulls can be admitted as a necessity', describing the latter as 'a relic of a barbarous taste'.[3] Bull-baiting had been stopped in Worksop by the beginning of the nineteenth century. Similarly, the sale of a wife in Newark's market place in 1835 caused some consternation for at least one local inhabitant.[4] At the same time, cock fights were still frequently held and 'widely and fashionably attended', and there is little evidence from the press that there was a sustained effort to reform many popular customs between the late eighteenth century and 1840. Moreover, it seems that those in authority were quick to accept the more ritualistic and rowdier modes of popular culture when they had a message to get across to the general public. For example, after a meeting at Mansfield town hall in 1793, where inhabitants of all classes openly declared their 'firm and unshaken attachment to his Majesty King George III', the 'polite attenders' celebrated with an 'excellent dinner', while a hogshead of ale was given to the general populace who 'amused themselves by exhibiting Tom PAINE (with his bosom friend the Devil, peeping over his shoulder) through the town, and then hanging the noble pair … '.[5]

Although the threat of riot and general disturbance concerned those

[1] S. D'Cruze, 'The middling sort in eighteenth-century Colchester: independence, social relations and the community broker', in Barry and Brooks, *Middling Sort*, pp. 181–207.

[2] Borsay, *Urban Renaissance,* ch. 10.

[3] Holland, *Worksop*, p. 5.

[4] *Nottingham & Newark Mercury*, 8 Feb. 1835.

[5] *Nottingham Journal*, 5 Jan. 1793, p. 2.

in authority, popular customs seem to have been tolerated, if we can judge by the few complaints voiced in newspapers. It is difficult to assess whether the upper ranks withdrew their support for popular customs. The fact that other forms of association were developed and that these were on the whole exclusive in nature does not mean popular customs and rituals came under attack. Peter Burke has shown that popular culture served to reaffirm economic, social and political inequalities by inverting them, turning the world upside down, but not challenging the structure of society.[1] Even Thompson's work, which demonstrates how vibrant popular culture was, shows many customs and practices, even in riots, conformed to established traditional notions of a moral but none the less unequal society and economy.[2]

The question of distinction between urban social groups raises the issue of whether there was any shared experience between urban dwellers irrespective of their wealth or status: was there something unique to urban society and culture in this period? Borsay suggests that the central defining characteristic of urban culture at this time was the concept of space. Not physical space, because in many ways we associate urban living with exactly the opposite, but above all 'social space', the separation of individuals by status.[3] Social space, it would seem, can be demonstrated in terms of domestic possessions and by the development of exclusive cultural clubs and societies for the urban elite, but how far did a concept of social space manifest itself into physical space in terms of residential segregation in our period?

Social geography and social class

In the 1960s and 1970s, Sjoberg and Vance postulated a model of spatial organisation common to pre-industrial towns and cities.[4] According to them the geographical hallmark of a pre-industrial urban settlement was the way the wealthy lived in the urban centres while the poorer citizens inhabited areas on the periphery. After industrialisation class-based

[1] P. Burke, *Popular Culture in Early Modern Europe* (1978).

[2] E.P. Thompson, 'Patrician society, plebian culture', *Journal of Social History*. 7 (1974), 382–405.

[3] P. Borsay, 'The development of provincial urban culture *c*. 1680–*c*. 1760', in Borsay (ed.), *Eighteenth-century Town*, pp. 180–1.

[4] G. Sjoberg, *The Pre-industrial City: Past and Present* (Glencoe, Ill., 1960); J.E. Vance, 'Land assignment in pre-capitalist and post-capitalist cities', *Economic Geography* 47 (1971).

segregation becomes manifest.[1] The Vance-Sjoberg model has been criticised for being over-simplified and too static, with two major concerns emerging. The first, exemplified in the work of Langton, demonstrates that the core–periphery model of segregation is not demonstrable in most pre-industrial towns. The second suggests that some class-based segregation emerged before the Victorian period with which it is traditionally associated.

From his studies of Dublin, Exeter and Newcastle, Langton has argued that while there was a tendency for the more affluent citizens to live in the town centres, wealth and status were not the sole residential determinants. In Newcastle some occupational segregation was evident with the existence of a mercantile quarter and a degree of class-based zoning.[2] Prior's study of Oxford, and Priestley's of Norwich, have also shown that occupational zoning was not unusual in these towns in the seventeenth and eighteenth centuries.[3] Nor do influences on residential zoning appear to have differed much according to size. In his study of London, by relating social status to differing tax-paying categories Schwarz concludes that while there was a clear tendency for the wealthier and less well-off to concentrate in different areas, this was just a tendency, and there was no simple division between a richer town centre and a poorer periphery.[4] Malmgreen showed that in mid eighteenth-century Macclesfield 'all ranks of residences, from wealthy merchants to the poorest labourers lived in close proximity', even in the town centre where 'one could find buildings suitable to each grade on the social scale'.[5] Similarly, for the even smaller town of Grantham, it was found that Sjoberg's and Vance's model is not applicable.[6]

Carter has argued that it is a mistake to see the eighteenth-century

[1] J. Langton, 'Residential patterns in pre-industrial cities: some case studies from seventeenth-century Britain', *Transactions of the Institute of British Geographers*, 65 (1975), p. 1.

[2] Ibid., pp. 16–18, 21.

[3] M. Prior, *Fisher Row: Fishermen, Bargemen, and Canal Boatmen in Oxford 1500–1900* (Oxford, 1982), pp. 10–12; U. Priestley, '"The fabric of stuffs": the Norwich textile industry *c.*1650–1750', *Textile History*, 16 (2) (1985).

[4] L.D. Schwarz, 'Social class and social geography: the middle classes in London at the end of the eighteenth century', in P. Borsay, *The Eighteenth-century Town 1688–1820* (1990).

[5] G.K. Malmgreen, 'Economy and Culture in an Industrialised Town: Macclesfield, Cheshire' (Unpublished Indiana University Ph.D. thesis., 1981), p. 4.

[6] J.B. Manterfield, 'The Topographical Development of the Pre-Industrial Town of Grantham, Lincolnshire, 1535–1835' (Unpublished Ph.D., University of Exeter, 1981), pp. 267–8.

town as one where there was no spatial manifestation of social class differences. However, he also argues that such manifestations would have been limited by transport technology.[1] Yet Ellis has demonstrated that many of the principal inhabitants of Newcastle-upon-Tyne had moved to more salubrious suburbs on the edge of town as early as the 1730s.[2] Even in Liverpool, where the tendency towards residential segregation in terms of class does not become apparent until the late eighteenth century, this is still earlier than was once thought.[3] These studies not only modify Sjoberg's and Vance's models but they also question the assumption that 'the suburb was quintessentially a Victorian phenomenon'.[4] It is usually said that the more affluent members of urban society fled to the suburbs for a number of reasons, in particular, to avoid adverse living conditions in the town centres and in pursuit of domesticity and privacy, two key Victorian values.[5] Ironically, the middle classes had themselves created the conditions they could no longer tolerate. Not only were they instrumental in the urban renaissance of Georgian towns (See Chapter 6), but equally their growing wealth encouraged the development of slum areas in the town centres, especially as many became rentiers.[6] The evidence that, on the one hand, there was no strict and distinctive pre-industrial and industrial morphological model and, on the other, that residential patterns almost uniquely associated with Victorian urban society can be traced earlier raises the question of how far the eighteenth century had anticipated these developments. Were the conditions and concerns of modern urban living in place before the nineteenth century?

The hearth tax assessments of 1674 show that the Nottinghamshire market towns had a very similar residential pattern to Dublin and Exeter.[7] Assuming that the collectors compiled their lists topographical-

[1] H. Carter, 'Towns and urban systems 1730–1900', in R.A. Dodgshon and R.A. Butlin (ed.), *An Historical Geography of England and Wales* (1978), p. 384.

[2] J. Ellis, 'A dynamic society: social relations in Newcastle-upon-Tyne, 1660–1760', in Clark, *Transformation*, pp. 198–9.

[3] P. Laxton, 'Liverpool in 1801: a manuscript return for the first national census', *Transactions of the Historic Society of Lancashire and Cheshire*, 130 (1981), p. 87.

[4] R.J. Morris and R. Rodger (ed.), *The Victorian City 1820–1914. A reader in British Urban History* (1993), p. 23.

[5] F.M.L. Thompson, *The Rise of Suburbia* (Leicester, 1982); Morris and Rodger, *Victorian City*, introduction.

[6] H.J. Dyos and D.A. Reeder, 'Slums and suburbs' in Dyos and Wolff (ed.), *The Victorian City: Images and Reality* (1973), pp. 359–86.

[7] Langton, 'Residential patterns'.

ly, moving from one house to the next, in none of the towns were houses of eight hearths to be found clearly segregated from those of one or two hearths. Unfortunately, in only two of the towns, Newark and Mansfield, were street names included, which means only a limited analysis of residential patterns can be made. In these two towns, taking the number of hearths as a guide to house size, and this in turn as a indicator of wealth and status, the highest average of hearths per household was to be found in the town centres (Table 5.10). With an average of 4.3 hearths per household, Newark's market place would appear to have accommodated the larger households. The average is distorted by the presence of inns, but the market place also appears to have housed at least some of the town's principal inhabitants, including most of the gentry, the town aldermen and the wealthier traders. William Martin, who lived in the market place in a house with seven hearths, was described as a gentleman and alderman. The inventory taken after his death in 1703 describes a four-storey building with two cellars, a hall, parlour and kitchen with chambers and garratts above.[1] Dennis Cooling, one of two apothecaries known to have lived in the market place in the late seventeenth century, had a house of eight hearths. His inventory was valued at £100 1s. 3d.[2] Of all the names in the hearth tax assessments that can be matched with those of wills and probate inventories, the market place housed at least four aldermen (two of whom were mercers), three mercers, two chandlers or ironmongers, two innholders, two apothecaries, two cordwainers, one haberdasher and one yeoman. Of the 77 market place householders in 1674 36 were accorded the title of Mr or Mrs.

A comparison of Table 5.10 with Fig. 3 suggests that the evidence of the Newark hearth tax assessment demonstrates that the more peripheral streets, such as North Gate and Carter and Balderton Gate, tended to have households with fewer hearths. For North Gate, in particular, this is confirmed in Table 5.11 which shows this street had a relatively high proportion of households with no more than one or two hearths. North Gate runs alongside the river Trent and probably housed the poorer labourers and watermen whose work was closely tied to their location. This was certainly the case in 1841, as will be seen later.

Unlike Newark, Mansfield in 1674 had no clearly defined market place. The centre of the town lay at the junction of the three principal streets, Church Gate, Stockwell Gate and West Gate. Perhaps because of

[1] NAO, PRNW, Martin, Newark, 1703.

[2] NAO, PRNW, Cooling, Newark, 1690.

Table 5.10

Distribution of hearths by street in Newark and Mansfield, 1674

Newark Street Name	*Average hearths per household*	*Mansfield Street Name*	*Average hearths per household*
Market Place	4.3	Church Gate	3.4
Castle Gate	3.2	West Gate	3.3
Mill Gate	3.1	Ratcliffe Gate	3.2
Kirk Gate	3.1	Cockpitt	2.5
Appleton and Barnby Gate	3.0	Stockwell Gate	2.4
Carter and Balderton Gate	2.9	Littleworth	2.1
North Gate	2.2		

this, the distinction between different streets within the town is less marked. The average number of hearths per household was highest in Church Gate, West Gate and Ratcliffe Gate but lower in Stockwell Gate, which led into the town centre (Table 5.10). Living in the first three of these streets in the late seventeenth century was the vicar, two gentlemen, a clerk, a schoolmaster, four maltsters, two mercers and a bodice-maker, two barbers, two cordwainers and a number of other trades including a blacksmith and butcher. As many as 34 of the 136 taxpayers (25 per cent) were given the title of Mr or Mrs, whereas in the other three streets (Stockwell Gate, Cock Pit and Littleworth) the figure was only 15 out of 132 (11.4 per cent). In Mansfield the more peripheral streets, Littleworth and Cockpit, had houses with more than five hearths although Littleworth also had a much higher proportion of houses with only one or two hearths (Table 5.12).

Despite the clear concentration of households with the highest number of hearths in the centres of Newark and, to a lesser extent, Mansfield, these areas also had houses with only one or two hearths. Nearly 12 per cent of households in Newark's market place had only one hearth (Table 5.11). In Mansfield 26 per cent of the households in West Gate had one hearth and, while Ratcliffe Gate had the highest proportion of households with eight or more hearths, it also had a large proportion with only one or two (Table 5.12). Large and smaller houses, even in the town centres, were frequently juxtaposed. As there were more streets in both Newark

Table 5.11

Distribution of hearths by street in Newark

Street	*Percentage of Households with Numbers of Hearths*						
	8+	*6-7*	*5*	*4*	*3*	*2*	*1*
Market Place	15.6	7.8	14.3	13.0	13.0	24.7	11.7
Castle Gate	3.1	9.4	3.1	12.5	31.3	28.1	12.5
Mill Gate	4.2	2.1	6.3	22.9	22.9	20.8	20.8
Kirk Gate	5.3	7.9	2.6	18.4	21.1	23.7	21.1
Appleton and Barnby Gate	4.9	4.9	2.4	17.1	14.6	29.2	26.8
Carter and Balderton Gate	0	8.7	7.2	11.6	26.1	29.0	17.4
North Gate	2.9	5.9	2.9	2.9	8.8	32.3	44.1

and Mansfield than are named in the hearth tax assessment, those listed must have included small houses that did not front the main streets. Wealthier inhabitants occupied the front premises of the main streets, while the less well-off were tucked away to the rear in yards, alleys and lanes. Thus, as Borsay suggests, what zoning there might have been was not so much between areas as within the structure of a street.[1]

For the late seventeenth century, Sjoberg's and Vance's models of the pre-industrial city can be applied here at only the most general level. On the whole these models underplay the degree of social heterogeneity evident in the residential development of these towns. It obscures, rather than reveals, the degree of social heterogeneity in residential patterns for these towns. Although the model is not wholly applicable to the Nottinghamshire towns, it remains an interesting question as to what impact, if any, the development of factories, mills, foundries and maltings had on residential patterns. This has been studied much more thoroughly for the larger Victorian industrial towns than for either the eighteenth century or the smaller town.[2] It has already been established that the introduction of large-scale business forced the development of new plan units, particularly in the larger towns of Newark and Mansfield,

[1] Borsay, *Eighteenth-century Town*, p. 18. This type of development was also true of Ashbourne: A. Henstock (ed.), *A Georgian Country Town. Ashbourne 1725–1825. Vol. II. Architecture* (Nottingham, 1991), p. 20.

[2] Dyos and Wolff, *Victorian City*.

Table 5.12

Distribution of hearths by street in Mansfield, 1674

Street	*Percentage of Households with Numbers of Hearths*						
	8+	*6-7*	*5*	*4*	*3*	*2*	*1*
Church Gate	10.9	5.5	16.4	5.5	14.5	27.3	20.0
Ratcliffe Gate	14.7	0	2.9	11.8	14.7	35.3	20.6
West Gate	8.7	4.3	10.9	10.9	26.1	13.0	26.1
Stockwell Gate	0	5.6	4.2	9.9	25.3	15.5	39.4
Littleworth	0	0	0	8.6	20.0	40.0	31.4
Cockpit	0	0	14.8	3.7	22.2	37.0	22.2

but also, to a lesser degree, in Worksop and East Retford. It remains to be seen if these new developments were accompanied by more clearly defined social zoning.

Residential patterns in the nineteenth century

One of the few studies to examine the residential patterns of a small town is Warnes's study of Chorley (Lancs.). Warnes focused on the impact of the transition from domestic to factory industry between 1780 and 1850.[1] He argues that the growth of industry led to two changes in the built form of the town, the emergence of specialised land-use regions (industrial areas without inhabitants and residential zones devoid of employment) and also 'the rise of socially and morphologically distinct residential areas'. However, Chorley's socially distinct areas were determined by occupation rather than by status and the town's elite were still to be found living in the town centre.[2] Although no allowance is made for the size of Chorley, which had a population of only 12,500 in 1851, this argument has been used to undermine the notion that the

[1] A.M. Warnes, 'Early separation of homes from work-places and the urban structure of Chorley', *Transaction of Historic Society of Lancashire and Cheshire*, 122 (1970).

[2] Ibid., pp. 105, 130–3.

Victorian city was distinctive.[1] With four of the Nottinghamshire market towns experiencing industrial development, together with the evidence for early slum development in the town centres and (as shown in Chapter 3), a growing affluent middle class, we may be in a better position to consider the question of the development of social segregation by 1841.

In an attempt to try to answer the question, each street in the 1841 census was ranked according to the status or employment of the heads of households living within it. The categories of household classification are the same as those adopted for the social groups identified earlier in this chapter. Every household headed by a member of the urban gentry was given six points. At the other extreme, households headed by a labourer were awarded two points and those of the 'poor' just one. A average value for the street was then calculated by dividing the points by the total number of households. Such an exercise has its limitations. It places a lot of emphasis on the occupational and status descriptions recorded in the census and does not allow for those in similar employment but who had very different levels of wealth. Moreover, the census enumerator's appear to have used the term 'independent' loosely, on the one hand, seeming to refer to those of independent wealth and of genteel status, on the other, to those who were less wealthy but who, for some reason, had no identifiable form of income or were to all intents and purposes 'retired'. To try to overcome this difficulty the names of those recorded as independent were checked against directories to see what status they were accorded there.

The exercise can be considered successful inasmuch as it shows how much the residential patterns of the Nottinghamshire market towns changed. Figure 11 shows the results for Newark. The values represented by each different shade in the key relate to the social groups isolated for each of these towns (1 = poor, 2 = unskilled labourers, 3 = artisans/ tradesmen, 4 = retailers/manufacturers, 5 = urban professionals and 6 = gentry). We find no areas exclusive to the gentry. The highest ranked part of the town was South Parade at 5.5 (shown in black on the map). Three out of four of the street's occupants were described in the census as 'independent'. All had at least two servants. Appleton Gate was the next highest ranked street, with an average of 4.4. After these two areas, the town centre still housed many of the town's principal traders and retailers, these could also be found in North Gate running parallel to the river Trent. A slightly lower ranked area lay to the east of the market

[1] D. Ward, 'Victorian Cities: how modern?', *Journal of Historical Geography*, 1 (2) (1975); D. Cannadine, 'Victorian Cities: how different?' in R.J. Morris and R. Rodger (ed.), *The Victorian City*, ch. 4.

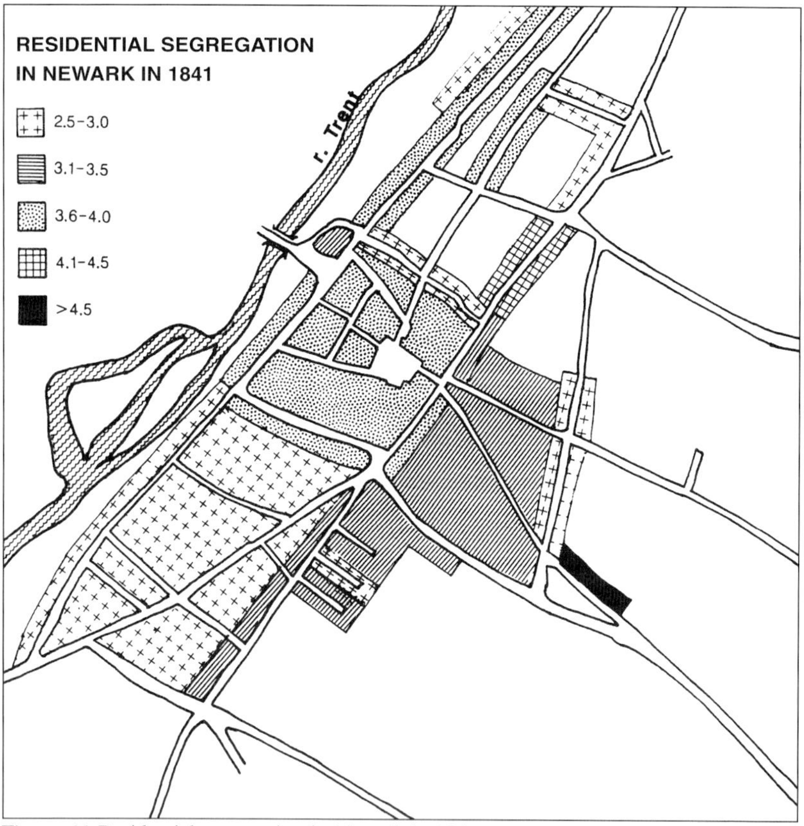

Figure 11 Residential segregation in Newark in 1841.

place (3.1–3.5). The lowest area of all, perhaps not surprisingly, lay to the south of the town, parallel to the river Trent and close to the textile and flour mills (ranked 2.5–3.0). This area was all newly developed in the nineteenth century. Pelham Street was laid out by 1790, followed by Scale's Row in 1820, Parliament Street (1826) and King Street and Queen Street and Union Terrace by 1829. It would seem that by 1841 Newark had developed a small industrial suburb.

A similar pattern emerged for Mansfield and Worksop. In both, the town centre continued to house the gentry, professionals and the more successful retailers and manufacturers. Labourers and poorer tradesmen were found close to the mills and large malting establishments. The general picture, however, tends to oversimplify the residential patterns of these towns, the complexity of which is more clearly demonstrated by a closer look at the distribution of the highest and lowest social groups.

Pigot's *Directory* of 1841 shows what proportion of each town's gentry were living outside the town altogether (Table 5.13). The two smaller towns, East Retford and Bingham, had a much higher proportion of their gentry living in nearby villages. This may be due to the fact that these smaller towns had less to offer in the way of social and cultural facilities, but it is more likely that in both these towns the gentry had come from farming backgrounds and were therefore less likely to be found in the town centres.

Of those members of the urban gentry who actually lived in the town centre in 1832, these individuals, as in 1674, lived in a few specific areas. In Newark, as we have seen, the select areas included Appleton Gate, Lombard Street, Castle Gate and Wilson Street which housed 52 per cent of the town's gentry. The remainder were to be found distributed between thirteen other streets.[1] Not all of these were the old-established principal roads. On the contrary, one gentleman was living in Chatham Street and another in Portland Street, both of which formed part of the new town development south of the town centre. One new street, South Parade, had been built in the early nineteenth century on the outskirts of the town, specifically for wealthier Newark families (this area is shown in black on Fig. 11). It would appear that there was little if any suburban development for the urban elite in Newark by 1841.

In Mansfield 48 per cent of the town-based gentry were living in West Gate, Ratcliffe Gate and Chesterfield Road, with the rest scattered in another 12 streets fairly close to the town centre.[2] Many were probably living in the 'large and handsome villas' built of stone noted in 1832.[3] In Worksop Potter Street, Bridge Street and Park Street remained the favourite locations, all of which were part of the original town centre and well away from the new areas of development north of the town centre and close to the Chesterfield Canal. In East Retford Moorgate, Carol Gate, Grove Street and the Square were the select parts of town. The last three were all close to the town centre, while Moorgate led out of the town. Finally, in Bingham the few gentry who lived in the town could be found in the Market Place and Church Street (leading from it) and in Long Acre, the main road running south of the market place. From this evidence there are no clear signs of residential segregation, although there were obviously preferred areas of living within each of the towns. It is worth noting that in Newark, Mansfield and Worksop, by the

[1] *Pigot's National and Commercial Directory* (1841), pp. 13–14.

[2] Ibid., pp. 7–8.

[3] White, *Directory*, p. 520.

Table 5.13

Gentry residence in 1841

Town	*Gentry resident in the town (%)*	*Non-resident town gentry (%)*
Newark	75	25
Mansfield	67	33
Worksop	77	23
East Retford	54	46
Bingham	24	76

Source: Pigot & Co., *National and Commercial Directory* (London, 1841).

nineteenth century, these were all areas furthest away from industry.[1] The location of urban professionals was slightly more widespread in all the towns. Once again, though, as in the case of the gentry, these individuals seemed to prefer fairly central locations away from industrial areas. Retailers and artisans were scattered randomly all over the towns, although most would be found, as in 1674, facing the market place or a principal thoroughfare.

At the other end of the social scale unskilled labourers and the poor tended to be scattered in different areas. In the town centre they could be found in the alleys and yards tucked behind and in between the main streets. This is where the hawkers, pedlars and washerwomen tended to be found. Others were to be found in areas like Water Lane, Cow Lane and Navigation Side in Newark, behind North Gate and close to the river, inhabited mostly by watermen, labourers and hawkers. In Mansfield factory workers and labourers could be found in most parts of the town, but especially on the outskirts in Pleasley Hill and certain parts of Chesterfield Road or off the main streets in Kay's Buildings and Plantation Row off West Gate. In Worksop Low Town, Abbey Street Marecroft, Bargh's Row, Canal Side and East Gate were characterised by a majority of unskilled labourers. East Gate and Canal Side were close to the Chesterfield Canal while Low Town, Abbey Street and Marecroft lay south-east of the town centre. In 1841 the poorer urban inhabitants were in general to be found still living in peripheral areas or,

[1] This was also found in Ashbourne: Henstock, *Ashbourne*, p. 11–13.

in stark contrast, crowded right in the heart of each town centre. Occupational segregation was specific to very few streets. Spital Row and Scale's Row in Newark were inhabited only by weavers and Water Lane mostly by watermen. In Newark, as in Worksop and East Retford, one would not expect a marked occupational zoning simply because the economies of these towns were highly diversified. Even in the one town to develop a more specialised economy, Mansfield, which by 1841 was predominantly a textile manufacturing town, most of the streets, lanes and alleys accommodated those working in textiles, but no one street housed these people to the exclusion of anyone else.

Even in small market towns it was possible for the inhabitants to have quite different day-to-day experiences of the urban environment according to their wealth and social status. This could be achieved with different social groups living in quite close proximity. As the next chapter will demonstrate, improvement and cleaning in the towns studied here was limited to the main streets and centre, even though these were the areas that probably needed least attention. The numerous alleys and yards that were built on, from the late eighteenth century, did not figure in the minds of contemporary authorities working to improve the environment. All the sample towns remained quite small and compact, and thus the physical distance between different areas was going to be slight. It is, however, possible to argue, as Henstock does for Ashbourne,[1] that the Georgian market town had areas of different social or functional character, but it would be dangerous to interpret these divisions too rigidly. Nonetheless, the urban environment and inhabitants' different experiences of it both reflected and reinforced social divisions, particularly when they lived in close proximity and this they continued to do right up until the end of this period.

Conclusion

The Nottinghamshire market towns, like other provincial centres, saw an expansion of their middle income groups. This development is most noticeable in the four larger towns, but is not confined to them. The evidence of social change supports that of economic change discussed in Chapter 4. Middle income groups also benefited most from economic prosperity, with their homes testifying to their ability and willingness to purchase a growing range of domestic material goods. It is also clear, if

[1] Henstock, *Ashbourne*, p. 20.

we compare the inventory evidence for the sample towns with Earle's study of London, that these groups could amass relatively high levels of wealth. It is more difficult to assess whether the growth in middle income groups was accompanied by a growing body of poor in the sample towns. Periods of depression and hardship were noted in the local papers, but these were periods of general depression for the country at large and it is difficult to identify anything specific to the experience of the Nottinghamshire towns. There was, however, a rising number of waged labourers occasioned by the growth of large textile mills, flour mills and malthouses and in times of economic hardship and unemployment it is possible that these individuals may have been more vulnerable if they were solely reliant on wages. Again, however, there is a lack of hard evidence to test this.

The towns shared in the growth of social, cultural and self-help institutions commonly found in larger towns. We can also see the growth of an elite, polite culture for the wealthier inhabitants, which suggests a growing recognition of status and status differential.

The concept of 'social space' is important, but the fact that individual members of urban society may have become more aware and conscious of distinctions between wealth and status, and felt the need to reinforce these distinctions both in the private and public sphere, does not necessarily mean that this encouraged social disharmony or residential segregation. In fact the awareness and reinforcement of social space, for all levels of society, may have given these urban dwellers a sense of their own place. Moreover, there were times when events in the market towns could not help but touch or impinge on all the inhabitants irrespective of status. In Newark at fair times, for example, the town was transformed. Pavements were cordoned into animal pens, the main streets were filled with shows, 'loud mouthed dealers proclaimed the virtues of their animals', and 'people were accompanied by shoals of itinerant songsters with penny sheets of the latest songs'.[1] How did the gentry, and those aspiring to gentry status, react?

[1] See a series of articles published in the *Newark Advertiser* in 1894 which record the reminiscences of a seventy-year-old of the town in the 1830s (*Newark Advertiser*, 15 Aug. 1894, p. 8).

SIX

Improvement and Refashioning

The process of urbanisation in the 'long eighteenth century' was neither exclusively or even necessarily a demographic or quantitative process but also a qualitative one.[1] This conclusion has been reached from the large amounts of public and private money that was clearly invested in urban fabric from 1660 onwards.[2] The urban landscape was transformed. It included the adoption of classical rather than vernacular architectural styles for both public and private buildings, and the replacement of traditional urban fabrics, such as timber and thatch, by brick, stone and tile.[3] Town streets were widened, cleaned, resurfaced and eventually lit at night. Water supplies were improved and less genteel practices, like the slaughtering of animals in the main streets, were prohibited. Altogether, such measures suggest the rise of a new sensibility towards the urban environment characterised by an increasing effort to make the town a more salubrious and fashionable place. To some extent, the improvements were a necessary adjunct to the sustained demographic, economic and physical growth many towns experienced at this time. More people, trade and traffic meant more dirt, noise, squalor and pressure on urban space, all combining to exacerbate the problems of mass living.[4] Even so, the practical impetus behind town improvement

[1] E.L. Jones and M.E. Falkus, 'Urban improvement and the English economy in the seventeenth and eighteenth centuries', in P. Borsay (ed.), *The Eighteenth-century Town. A Reader in English Urban History 1688–1820* (1990).

[2] It has been estimated that £1.25 million was spent on public buildings in the twelve major towns of the West Riding between 1700 and 1840: K. Grady, 'The provision of public buildings in the West Riding of Yorkshire, *c.*1600–1840' (Unpublished Ph.D. thesis, University of Leeds, 1980). See also Jones and Falkus, 'Urban improvement' and P. Borsay, *The English Urban Renaissance. Culture and Society in the Provincial Town, 1660–1770* (Oxford, 1989).

[3] For the logical foundations of traditional building and the importance of brick as a new urban fabric see H. Bagenal, 'The rationale of traditional building', in C.W. Chalklin and M.A. Havinden (ed.), *Rural change and Urban Growth 1500–1800. Essays in English Regional History in Honour of W.G. Hoskins* (1974), pp. 321–41.

[4] According to Chartres, the number of waggons transporting goods saw almost continuous increase in the period 1681–1775. He also notes that one of the fastest areas of growth in communications between London and the provinces included the East Midlands, J.A. Chartres, 'Road Carrying in England in the Seventeenth Century: Myth and Reality',

was at least matched, if not exceeded, by a growing awareness and concern for the aesthetic appearance of the town. Together, these factors combined to transform the physical appearance and contemporary perception of the urban townscape, no less in the six Nottinghamshire market towns than elsewhere.

This climate of urban improvement from the late seventeenth century is thought to have been stimulated by the rebuilding of London after the Great Fire in 1666, provoked not just by the devastation but also by the need to prevent a recurrence of such a disaster. It was then quickly replicated in the Georgian provincial towns, particularly spa towns like Bath.[1] Modern writers such as Jones and Falkus, Borsay, Corfield and Reed have all identified a widespread movement that saw the improvement and refashioning of many town centres from 1660 onwards.[2] Borsay goes so far as to suggest that what can be seen in the century or so between 1660 and 1770 is an 'urban renaissance', characterised by the social and cultural revival of the larger urban centres and evidenced in the transformation of their townscapes and the growth of an increasingly varied and sophisticated range of leisure facilities.[3] Jones and Falkus have demonstrated that by 1750 many provincial towns had become more 'environmentally commodious, economically efficient and culturally sophisticated'. Corfield suggests that between 1700 and 1800 'a torrent of writing, discussion and analysis ... relating to the understanding and improvement of the urban environment' can be traced.[4] But as Stobart has shown for Liverpool, tensions could arise between the demands for cultural and commercial space.[5]

This 'renaissance' or qualitative urbanisation of the seventeenth and eighteenth centuries was a much wider movement than has been traditionally appreciated. The terminal date of Borsay's thesis is 1770 by when, he concludes, 'the mass of smaller market towns and ports were

Economic History Review, 2nd series, 30 (1977), pp. 73–94.

[1] P. Borsay, *Urban Renaissance*, preface; J. Barrett, 'Spas and seaside resorts 1660–1780', in J. Stevenson, *English Urban History, 1500–1700 (Units 13–16. The Rise of the New Urban Society)* (Milton Keynes, 1977), pp. 37–70.

[2] Jones and Falkus, 'Urban improvement'; Borsay *Urban Renaissance*; P. Corfield, *The Impact of English Towns 1700–1800* (Oxford, 1982); M. Reed, 'The transformation of urban space 1700–1840', in P. Clark (ed.), *The Cambridge Urban History of Britain. Volume II. 1540–1840* (Cambridge, 2000), pp. 615–40.

[3] Borsay, *Urban Renaissance*.

[4] Jones and Falkus, 'Urban Improvement', p. 116; Corfield, *Towns*, p. 168.

[5] J. Stobart, 'Culture versus commerce: societies and spaces for elites in eighteenth-century Liverpool', *Journal of Historical Geography*, 28 (4) (2002), 471–85.

Figure 12 A seventeenth-century house in Mansfield.

much less affected than the regional centres and provincial capitals'.[1] Similarly, Jones and Falkus suggest that urban improvement was felt not so much in the 'industrial towns' of the north but amongst the smaller market and provincial centres of the south.[2] The first of these authors sees the 'urban renaissance' as largely limited to a type of urban settlement (the provincial town), the second pair confine it to a certain geographical region. In neither account is the analysis extended to cover the smaller towns of northern and midland England. It is fair to point out that there is little to suggest such towns experienced much of a renaissance before 1770. After this date, however, a very different picture emerges. From 1770 the Nottinghamshire market towns, together with other settlements of similar status or size in Lincolnshire, Cheshire and Cumbria, all saw extensive urban improvement. In other words, these smaller northern and midland towns appear to have begun their

1 Borsay, *Urban Renaissance*, p. 311.

2 Jones and Falkus, 'Urban improvement', p. 117.

renaissance at exactly the point Borsay stopped looking for it. Their renaissance, like that of the larger centres, was no less founded on economic growth and prosperity (see Chapter 4) but came later. This is probably sufficient to explain the difference in the visual effect. Nevertheless, despite the time-lag, the nature and form of urban improvement—from the new architectural fashions to the cleaning and straightening of streets and even to the vocabulary contemporaries used to describe and appreciate these changes—demonstrates that the urban renaissance of the provincial towns and that of the market towns was clearly one and the same movement. Moreover, the new, entirely fashionable appearance of the Nottinghamshire market town between 1770 and 1840, suggests, yet again, that the distinctive nature of change in the 'long eighteenth century' was not necessarily its newness, but its extent and depth.

In order to appreciate the disjunction in the history of larger and smaller towns, five main aspects of the urban renaissance of the Nottinghamshire market town are explored here. The first concerns physical signs of change in terms of the private and public investment

Figure 13 Handley House, Newark.

in buildings, streets and town centres. Second is the focus on new approaches to environmental improvement. Underpinning both developments was the way these improvements were financed. The incentive to invest in the urban fabric is then discussed in relation to the rise and development of a new urbane sensibility to the market town environment. Finally, the degree to which there were clear limits to urban improvement will be examined.

Buildings and street improvement

As Corfield argued, 'successful towns of whatever size invested their success in smart, brick town houses, new churches, halls and public rooms, street widening schemes and municipal adornment'.[1] These measures were undertaken on both the private and public scale. In some cases, this amounted to no more than the replacement of mullioned with sash or bow windows. At other times the front of a house might be completely refaced in brick and stone. Larger projects included the rebuilding of whole streets and even the market place (as in Mansfield after 1823) which were then often adorned with expensive and prestigious town halls as well as other public buildings. The enthusiasm for new styles of buildings was matched by a growing concern that buildings in the same street should relate to one another architecturally. All these concerns reflect a new perception of the town.[2]

Four of the six towns under examination—Newark, Mansfield, East Retford and Worksop—saw many new public and private buildings erected in the classical style between 1752 and 1840 while existing buildings underwent an architectural facelift to present at least a veneer of fashionable modernity. Streets and market places also saw considerable improvement. In Bingham and Ollerton, in contrast, there was little more activity than the addition of a few Georgian-style buildings. Investment in the urban fabric was expensive and it is not surprising that these smaller and less prosperous communities could make no more than a gesture to the general movement going on around them.

[1] P.J. Corfield, 'Small towns, large implications: social and cultural roles of small towns in eighteenth-century England and Wales', *British Journal of Eighteenth-century Studies*, 10, (1987), p. 128.

[2] Borsay, *Urban Renaissance*, p. 60.

Figure 14 Waverley House, Mansfield.

Private investment in the Georgian town house

The basic building block of the urban architectural renaissance, as Borsay notes, was the town house. That is, above all, houses built for the wealthier members of town society, usually located, as we have seen, in the town centre or fronting its main streets. Among the first signs of an urban renaissance is the appearance of new houses in the larger towns. We can trace these from the mid eighteenth century; there may well have been earlier examples but neither documentary nor physical evidence is available. Similarly, it is likely that many older buildings saw small changes and minor improvements even in the early eighteenth century. The new town houses would have been highly distinctive by virtue of their neat, symmetrical fronts with doors and windows sympathetically set in relation to one another. In contrast to the traditional vernacular town house, floors were no longer jettied one from another. Instead, the new houses were aligned along a straight frontage. Window cases were replaced by sash windows which, when opened, did not protrude from the wall to disrupt the harmony of the buildings. Figs. 12 and 13 show two late seventeenth-century houses in Mansfield and Newark. Both buildings have sash windows which are thought to be later additions, though in neither case do the records survive to verify this. Fig. 14 shows a later building, Waverley House in Mansfield (1754). With its three-storey, symmetrical frontage, consisting of a centrally placed door with Doric columns, rusticated architrave, entablature with trigliphs and dentilled pediments, and five bays of sash windows, Waverley House can be taken as the model mid eighteenth-century Georgian town house.

In Worksop a fine row of late Georgian terraced houses (Fig. 15) still exists and in the centres of East Retford, Bingham and Ollerton there are also a number of examples of eighteenth-century buildings. In Bingham, one of the few references to two or three late Georgian houses built *c.*1830-40 are those recorded by Pevsner.[1]

Like the houses to be found in Nottingham, such buildings served as the tangible evidence of the growing affluence and confidence of at least a few members of the urban community. Those that survive or have been described above were accompanied by many others. Often these were advertised for sale or rent in the local papers. In 1775, for example, *Cresswell's Nottingham and Newark Journal* carried an advertisement for 'a new sashed house in Mansfield' with two 'neatly papered' chambers. In 1777 the *Nottingham Journal* advertised three freehold, three-storey brick houses in East Retford and in 1800 the same paper advertised the letting of a 'modern built house' in Mansfield. Even in Ollerton two new, modern and neatly furnished houses were to be sold by auction in 1829.[2] The evidence from local papers together with the survival of many buildings or plans for new houses shows that the late eighteenth and early nineteenth century was a time of considerable town house building for the middling and wealthier sorts.

Not everybody living in the Nottinghamshire towns felt the need or could afford to build new houses. Many chose the cheaper option of updating their existing homes. Again evidence for this is hard to come

[1] N. Pevsner, *The Building of England. Nottinghamshire* (Harmondsworth, 1979 edn), p. 75.

[2] NAO, DDM 57/18.

Figure 15 Georgian terrace, Worksop.

by. However, one survey of Newark property taken in 1798 demonstrates quite clearly that such improvements were being undertaken by tenants as well as the owners of buildings. We learn that John Newham (silversmith) spent £90 on improving his house, part of which included a new sash door, that John Thorpe and James Dyson paid for new sash windows, and that Thomas Gillson had his shop refronted and new windows added at the cost of £87.[1] These would have been not small sums of money, and the expenditure shows also that the interest in up-dating buildings was not limited to the urban gentry. By 1828 one Worksop historian noted that many of the timber houses within the town had had so many successive alterations that 'little of their first character, and still less of their first materials [were] discernible'. Moreover, the use of bricks and tiles had become so ubiquitous in the town that he described the new houses as being 'literally of earthenware, from the tiles to the floor'.[2]

New town houses and the alteration and improvement of existing

[1] NAO, DC/NK 2/1.

[2] J. Holland, *History of Worksop* (Sheffield, 1828), p. 144.

Figure 16 The new Mansfield Town Hall of 1752.

buildings is evidence of a willingness in the private sector to invest in the urban fabric. The styles and fabrics adopted also suggest that the fashions of London and the provincial centres were well known to these local inhabitants. The Nottinghamshire market town populations had only to look as far as Nottingham, where one contemporary had noted in 1751 that 'many of the Inhabitants have taken to new Fronting their houses after the newest Fashion'.[1] Such private investment was more than matched by public expenditure. This usually covered two aspects, public buildings, and street and general town improvement. Money invested in public buildings, as Borsay notes, was of critical importance in establishing an overall image of the town.[2] This may have been even more

[1] Quoted in Corfield, *Towns*, p. 175.

[2] Borsay, *Urban Renaissance*, p. 101.

important in the smaller towns than in the larger provincial centres. In both cases the town authorities were obviously aware of, and keen to invest in, the 'right' public face.

Public buildings, 1752–1840

One of the key factors underpinning these changes was increased local expenditure on public buildings.[1] In 1752 Lady Oxford financed the building of a new town hall in Mansfield.[2] This was the first in a wave of new public buildings in each of the four larger Nottinghamshire towns, shared, to a limited extent, even by Bingham and Ollerton. The selection of a town hall is a testimony, at least in part, to each town's role as an administrative, religious, commercial, cultural and social centre. Of all the buildings erected or rebuilt at this time, the most important was undoubtedly the town hall. In combining, as it often did, more than one of a town's functions, it also symbolised them: Borsay documented forty examples of halls constructed or modified in the century or so following the Restoration in the larger English provincial centres. Compared with these, Mansfield's new town hall was typical both in function and appearance (Fig. 16). It combined the role of providing shelter for the market traders with 'furnishing the town with a room for discussing public business, and the country gentry with an elegant assembly room'.[3] Three years later, in 1755, East Retford corporation built a new town hall on the site of the old Moot Hall.[4] This too, was funded by a local dignitary. The old hall which had chiefly been built of wood, was replaced by a more imposing stone building bearing the arms of the town. The building housed a large court room for quarter and petty Sessions and a council room. The court room also functioned as an assembly room which was 'elegantly furnished [with] four light fluted pillars of the Ionic order'.[5] The building cost £1,774, less than

[1] C.W. Chalklin, 'The financing of church building in the provincial towns of the eighteenth century', in P. Clark (ed.), *The Transformation of English Provincial Towns* (1984).

[2] S. Lewis, *Topographical Dictionary of England and Wales* (1841), iii. 227.

[3] W. Harrod, *A History of Mansfield*, (1801), p. 6.

[4] W. White, *History, Gazetteer and Directory of Nottinghamshire* (Sheffield, 1832), p. 310.

[5] J.S. Piercy, *History of East Retford* (Retford, 1828), p. 143.

Figure 17 The later Mansfield Town Hall of 1836.

figures quoted by Borsay and Chalklin.[1]

By contrast, Newark's town hall, built in 1773 (Fig. 6.6), cost nearer £17,000.[2] If this figure is accurate Newark corporation spent far more than any other town in Borsay's list. At Newark the money was raised by selling charity lands that had been bequeathed to the town, the sale being justified on the grounds that a new town hall was a necessary requirement for this prospering town. In the 1790s the building was described as 'magnificent',[3] in 1816 as 'sumptuous',[4] and in 1820 it

[1] Borsay quotes costs ranging from £220 to £10,000: *Urban Renaissance*, pp. 105–6 and Appendix 2, and Chalklin £4,300 ('The financing of church building', p. 304).

[2] White, *Directory*, p. 608.

[3] *Universal British Directory of Trade and Commerce* (c.1790–8), i. 57.

[4] W. Dickinson, *The Town of Newark* (1826), p. 135.

was declared that few boroughs 'could boast so enviable an ornament. Its majestic appearance strikes every traveller ... [and] its symmetry would bear the most critical inspection'.[1] To Pevsner this building is 'a proud monument of metropolitan taste'.[2] Palladian in style, it still dominates Newark's market place.

Internally, Newark's town hall was just as impressive. The assembly room was approached by a 'handsome geometrical staircase of stone' and decorated with Corinthian fluted columns.[3] The building also contained a court room, a large committee room, a sub-loggia which functioned as a corn market, and a sub-hall which was used as a butter market.

A second new town hall was built in Mansfield in 1836 to front the new market place (Fig. 17). Estimated to have cost about £6,000, this was financed through the issue of £25 shares, and was described as 'a chaste specimen of the Grecian Doric style'. The ground floor housed a subscription library, news room and sessions hall. The upper floor accommodated 'a handsome assembly room, a card room and a robing chamber'.[4] The assembly room was decorated with crimson chenille curtains, brass chandeliers and nine sash-frame windows.[5]

These buildings reflected the prosperity and new-found confidence of the towns concerned, and also the growing complexity and sophistication of town life. Worksop was the largest of the Nottinghamshire market towns not to build a new town hall, a fact much regretted by the town's historian who in 1828 described the existing hall as 'old and shabby'.[6] Not surprisingly, in 1831 there were said to be plans to replace it with a 'handsome structure, comprising town hall, assembly room, prison and market house'.[7] However, in neither Ollerton nor Bingham were there even any plans. Neither community had the prestige or wealth to warrant such a building, although Bingham did have a theatre by the early nineteenth century, as did many larger towns. Table 6.1 shows the variety of public buildings erected from the mid eighteenth century.

The growth and commercialisation of leisure traced by Plumb as well

[1] R.P. Shilton, *The History of the Town of Newark upon Trent* (1820), ii. 366–8.

[2] Pevsner, *Nottinghamshire*, p. 192.

[3] Ibid.

[4] *Pigot's National and Commercial Directory* (1841), p. 7.

[5] NAO, DD4P 70/50.

[6] Holland, *Worksop*, p. 144.

[7] Lewis, *Topographical Dictionary*, IV (1831), p. 573.

Table 6.1

Public buildings erected, 1752–1840

Building	*Newark*	*Mansfield*	*Worksop*	*East Retford*	*Bingham*	*Ollerton*
Town Hall	1773	1752 & 1836	–	1755	–	–
Theatre	1774	n.d.	1789	1789	n.d.	–
News Room/ Library	1828	1836	1831	1825	–	–
Workhouse	1786	n.d.	1825	1818	n.d.	–
Gas Works	1833	1824	n.d.	1831	–	–
Baptist Church	n.d.	n.d.	–	–	–	–
Catholic Church	1827	–	1782	1830	–	–
Independent Church	1822	1795	1830	1802	n.d.	*c.*1780
Jehovah Jirah	n.d.	–	–	–	–	–
Methodist Church	1828	1824	–	–	n.d.	–
Quakers	–	1792	–	–	–	–
Unitarian	–	n.d.	–	–	–	–
Wesleyan	1787	1812	1813	1823	–	–

Note: n.d. signifies that a record of the building exists, but no construction date is available.

as Borsay played its part, too, in the transformation of the townscape.[1] Church and chapel building was also an important source of investment in the physical fabric of the town. Chalklin has argued that the building of chapels increased from the 1790s in the larger provincial towns with the growth of General and Particular Baptists, Congregationalists and Methodists.[2] This was equally true of the market towns which often became centres of Dissent.[3] To these buildings can be added charity and private schools as well as almshouses and workhouses for the poor. In Mansfield, Clerkson's charity school was built in 1731 and Thompson's and Brunt's in 1786.[4] In 1813, National schools for boys and girls were

[1] J.H. Plumb, 'The commercialisation of leisure in eighteenth-century England', in N. McKendrick, J. Brewer and J.H. Plumb, *The Birth of a Consumer Society. The Commercialisation of Eighteenth century England* (1982), pp. 265–85.

[2] Chalklin, 'The financing of church building', p. 286.

[3] R.W. Unwin, 'Tradition and transition: market towns of the Vale of York, 1660–1830', *Northern History*, 17 (1981), p. 88.

[4] White, *Directory*, p. 527.

opened in Worksop.[1] In Ollerton a Church of England school was built by public subscription in 1842.[2]

Public money was also invested in improving existing public buildings. In 1775 a joiner, painter and mason were employed to repair and improve Mansfield's town hall.[3] In 1778 and 1801 Newark's Beaumont Cross was repaired and ornamented.[4] In 1789, East Retford's theatre was 'improved and decorated … entitling it to rank in the second class of county theatres'.[5] In 1818 East Retford corporation paid for the painting of the interior of the town hall and for the clock dials to be gilded.[6] In 1826 John Saddler was employed to survey Newark's town hall and estimate the cost of repairs.[7] In 1831 Mansfield's moot hall was rechiselled, 'cleansed and beautified', as was the parish church,[8] and in 1840 East Retford corporation obtained tenders for the painting of the town hall and newsroom.[9] From all this evidence of the time and money invested in the building and up-keep of public buildings, it is clear they were considered important by the local authorities. As we will see later, much of the funding for such projects came from local gentry or aristocracy rather than from the rates. This would suggest that wealthy individuals also felt it worthwhile (or even necessary) to invest in the local town fabric. A similar enthusiasm was also directed, more generally, to the urban environment through street and sanitary improvement.

Road and street improvement

In Nottinghamshire, as elsewhere, early road improvement concentrated on turnpiking the main roads in and out of towns which formed part of the national network. Thus in 1726 the Great North Road was turnpiked between Spittal Hill in Grantham and Little Drayton in Nottinghamshire, part of which ran through Newark. This was followed by a further 54

1 Ibid., p. 456.
2 *VCH Notts.*, i. 260.
3 NAO, DD4P 70/51.
4 Pevsner, *Nottinghamshire*, p. 190.
5 Piercy, *Retford*, pp. 146–7.
6 NAO, DDHO 4/8, 30 July 1818.
7 Newark Town Hall, Corporation Minutes, 24 April 1826.
8 White, *Directory*, pp. 520, 524.
9 NAO, DDHO 4/10, 11 May 1840.

turnpike Acts for Nottinghamshire. By 1826 all the main roads in the county were turnpiked.[1] The results were impressive. The time taken to travel from Doncaster to Newark had been reduced between 1760 and 1820 from one day to less than four hours.[2] By 1832 all the main roads in Nottinghamshire were considered to have been 'greatly improved'.[3]

Not until the late eighteenth century did attention turn to the streets in each town centre. For the larger provincial towns, Borsay has argued that streets were remodelled as a result of two complementary pressures, first the desire to integrate separate buildings and second the need to improve the quality and quantity of space within them.[4] This would have been as much for practical as for aesthetic reasons. Attention focused on the paving, widening, resurfacing and lighting of main streets. We can discern something of the process. Usually, but not always, the streets were paved first.[5] In 1772 the new pavements in the streets of Newark were almost complete.[6] In 177 East Retford corporation spent £790 on paving the town's main streets, and a further £140 was spent in 1792.[7] In May 1823 the auditors and treasurers of the corporation were empowered to force property owners on the east side of the market place to 'flag their causeways', the corporation meeting half the expense.[8] Even Bingham had had its streets paved by the third decade of the nineteenth century, when it was described as 'well paved and remarkably neat and clean',[9] as were East Retford, Mansfield and Worksop.[10]

The physical and administrative process of paving the town streets involved fewer problems than that of widening them, which could become a slow, arduous and expensive business. Often widening involved the purchasing of a number of buildings or parts of buildings belonging to different people, all of whom had to be persuaded to sell. In Wolverhampton, for example, the town's expansion was made difficult because of the reluctance of property owners to sell freeholds or grant

1 A. Cossons, *The Turnpike Roads of Nottinghamshire* (1934).

2 G.H. West, *The Great North Road in Nottinghamshire* (n.d. [1956]), p. 3.

3 White, *Directory*, p. 54.

4 Borsay, *Urban Renaissance,* p. 60.

5 S. and B. Webb, *English Local Government. Vol. 4. Statutory Authorities for Special Purposes* (1922), p. 316.

6 *Cresswell's Nottingham and Newark Mercury*, 6 June 1772, p. 3.

7 *Report of the Royal Commission on Municipal Corporations* (Parl. Papers, 1835 (116), XXV), iv. 1865.

8 NAO, DDHO 4/10, 23 May 1823.

9 *Pigot's National and Commercial Directory* (1829), p. 626.

10 Ibid., pp. 2, 7, 54, 62.

long leases.[1]

Quite clearly the status of the property owner was reflected in who the local authorities entrusted to discuss the purchasing of their property. Thus we find in 1773 Newark Corporation discussing how three prominent alderman should approach and discuss with a Mrs Clark the purchasing of part of her yard to enable the further widening of a turnpike road.[2] In contrast, when the corporation wanted to buy the Prince of Wales public house to make a more 'convenient avenue to the church' from Dickinson Rastell (a prominent local minister), it was none other than the mayor who was asked to do the negotiating.[3] Street improvement continued with the rebuilding and widening of Newark's Trent Bridge in 1775 at the expense of the duke of Newcastle. Once completed, tolls were exacted for its maintenance.[4] In 1782 a bill was sought for the widening of one of the main roads leading out of Newark. In 1798 plans were made for two new streets to be laid through the market place, one 20 feet wide, the other 12 feet.[5] In 1822 it was announced that Dry Bridge, a narrow street which led into Newark market place, was to be completely rebuilt and widened. However, it took six years to get the project underway and the new street (named Bridge Street) was not completed until 1830. In 1823 when a vestry meeting was held to consider the widening of North Gate, it was decided to purchase part of an old nursery for this purpose.[6] In 1826 a further meeting was called to discuss the lowering of the gradient on Beacon Hill, leading out of the town to the east.[7] In 1836, Appleton Close was widened after the sale of Crown lands.[8]

In Mansfield the improvement commissioners set up in 1823 had even bigger plans. That year they set about buying 'various buildings and rights' for widening the town's main streets and market place,[9] offering a total of £3,135 to seven individuals for various pieces of property in the main streets and market place. In 1824 a plan was ordered for a new

[1] J. Smith, 'Industrialisation and social change: Wolverhampton transformed, 1700–1840', in J. Stobart and N. Raven, *Towns, Regions and Industries. Urban and Industrial Change in the Midlands, c.1700–1840* (Manchester, 2005), p. 139.

[2] Newark Town Hall, Corporation Minutes, 11 Sept. 1773.

[3] Ibid., 17 May 1794.

[4] White, *Directory*, p. 605.

[5] Shilton, *Newark*, ii. 363.

[6] *Lincoln and Stamford Mercury*, 2 Feb. 1823, p. 3.

[7] *Nottingham and Newark Mercury,* 10 Feb. 1827, p. 3.

[8] Reminiscences of a Septuagenarian, *Newark Advertiser*, 20 June 1894.

[9] NAO, DC/M/1/2/1, 1 Aug. 1823.

road from the market place to Cockpit, but this was rejected. In November 1829 Queen Street was to be levelled and improved. By 1831 the London Road had been widened and the market place considerably enlarged.[1] The improvement commissioners seem to have had much more success than was often the case elsewhere, where their actions were compromised by lack of money.[2]

In both Worksop and East Retford similar measures were taken. In 1775 a notice was placed on Worksop's church door for the consideration of further repairs to Newgate Street[3] and in 1777 East Retford corporation began a project to repair all the town's streets. The bridge crossing the river Idle was 'partly rebuilt and considerably widened' in 1795.[4] In the early nineteenth century Norfolk Street was planned along a straight axis, with a neat row of terraced houses either side. Once widened many of the main streets were resurfaced. In 1827 West Gate in Newark was 'Mc Adamised', and in 1834 Bridge Street, also in Newark, was covered in asphalt, and East Retford corporation decided to 'Macadamise' the market place.

From the 1790s these improvements were accompanied by street lighting. On 10 October 1792, in a ceremonial opening, Newark was lit 'with upwards of 300 lamps, which made a very brilliant appearance'.[5] At first the lamps ran on oil but by the early nineteenth century most were using gas. In 1825 the Mansfield improvement commissioners ordered the placing of street lamps along each of that town's principal streets, not more than 100 yards apart. Detailed calculations were made as to the amount of gas each lamp would consume. They were first lit in 1825, but by 1840 one local inhabitant had decided they achieved no more than making the 'darkness more visible'.[6] By 1831 Worksop, East Retford and Bingham all had street lighting.[7]

Not only were streets widened but, as Borsay argues, there was increasing concern that the buildings along them should be integrated and rise at right angles from the street. Newark's improvement Act (1776) included a clause that the commissioners would set out all building lines for new buildings, and in 1822 Dry Bridge (the narrow

1 Lewis, *Topographical Dictionary*, p. 247.

2 Smith, 'Wolverhampton transformed', p. 141.

3 NAO, PR 23,988, 14 June 1775.

4 White, *Directory*, pp. 310-11.

5 *Nottingham Journal,* 13 Oct. 1792, p. 3.

6 *Nottingham and Newark Journal,* 18 Sept. 1840, p. 301.

7 Lewis, *Topographical Dictionary*.

street leading into Newark's market place) was one of the first to be refashioned in this way. The street had been flanked by timber-framed buildings with jettied upper storeys. In 1828 it was announced that the whole of the south side of these streets was to be pulled down and replaced by 'a handsome row of buildings' in order to transform a 'narrow and dangerous road into a spacious and elegant street'. These new houses would 'gratify the lovers of uniformity'.[1] Similarly, in 1823 East Retford corporation announced that if the purchaser of a plot of land in Carolgate wanted to build houses then these would have to conform 'to a plan and elevation … laid down by the Corporation'.[2] In Mansfield the improvement Act clearly stated that all new houses were to 'rise perpendicularly from the Foundations: and no part of the Front of any ancient or new house … is to be brought forward beyond the old foundations without the consent of the commissioners'.[3]

The concern for the town streets was matched by concern for the town centres, which were supposed to be neat, square and spacious. The market place was the hub of the commercial, administrative and, increasingly, the social and cultural life of the community. Among the prospering Nottinghamshire towns, market and fair days would see the transformation of these places as they were crammed with stalls and penthouses and bustling with people and carriages. However, by the mid eighteenth century, such time-honoured scenes were increasingly attacked, particularly when they took place in the main streets and town centres. There was a new growing concern to free such places from obstructions and nuisances. This went hand in hand with endeavours to tidy up the appearance of the buildings within them.

In 1816 Dickinson bemoaned the fact that Newark's market place was 'much inferior in size' to what it had formerly been. The reason for this, he believed, was the gradual encroachment of buildings on to the market place which projected into and destroyed the 'uniformity of the square'.[4] Similar complaints were frequently printed in the local newspapers until, in 1827 it was announced that it was the intention of Newark Corporation to 'purchase the houses projecting on the north side of the market place [to be demolished] … and make the market place square'.[5] This, the paper suggested, would be a considerable improvement to the town

[1] *Nottingham and Newark Mercury*, 15 Jan. 1828, p. 3.

[2] NAO, DDHO 4/8, 23 May 1823.

[3] NAO, DCM 1/15/1, p. 29.

[4] Dickinson, *Newark*, pp. 139, 140.

[5] *Nottingham and Newark Mercury*, 10 Feb. 1827.

and add much to the spaciousness and uniformity of the market place. In January 1828 the *Nottingham Journal* reported that an order had been given to pull down all the buildings in the middle of the square.[1]

In Mansfield there was great excitement over the planning of the new market place. On 9 August 1825 George Rooth was paid £10 for part of his house which projected beyond the general line of the other buildings. This was demolished to improve the space within the market place. The improvement commissioners then bought property in Church Gate and Stockwell Gate to clear for the new market place where, in their place, 'excellent buildings uniform with each other are to be built [so that] Mansfield will soon boast of an excellent, spacious market place, which will ... undoubtedly add to the appearance of the town'.[2] In 1840, with the new market place nearly completed, the *Nottingham and Newark Mercury* challenged anyone who had been away from Mansfield 'for twenty years' now to visit it 'and witness what the so properly called "Improvement Act" has done'.[3] Similarly, East Retford's contemporary historian believed that 'no town of the same magnitude in England [could] boast of a more spacious square and market place'.[4] Neither newspapers nor antiquaries could be expected to be the most objective commentators on local improvement but it is clear that fashionable, neat buildings and wide, regular streets were deemed to be just as important a reflection on the status of these towns as their larger contemporaries. Moreover, from the vocabulary used this suggests that the market town, like its provincial neighbour, was now perceived as a total environment: buildings were to be uniform with each other while a spacious, regularly laid out market place added to the appearance of the entire town. There is no doubt, too, that the growing number of public buildings, and the social and cultural services they provided, helped to reinforce both a sense of community identity and a wider perception of the urban environment. On the other hand, it is possible to play down the significance of such a new perspective as being forced on the local authorities and inhabitants by the sheer increase in urban growth and by the sheer scale of problems such as sanitation.

[1] *Nottingham Journal*, 5 Jan. 1828, p. 3.

[2] *Nottingham and Newark Journal*, 31 Jan. 1840, p. 7.

[3] *Nottingham and Newark Mercury*, 26 June 1840, p. 4.

[4] Piercy, *Retford*, p. 140.

The rise of improvement commissions

In terms of the urban fabric and the style of building adopted in the market towns of Nottinghamshire from the late eighteenth century onwards, we can suggest that these towns gained a more modern appearance. Equally, it could be argued that the evolution of new bodies (usually improvement commissioners), and a growing realisation of the need for central provision of basic urban amenities, signified the beginnings of a more modern approach and conceptualisation of town living. Jones and Falkus have argued that the establishment of commissions to deal with specific urban problems, together with the introduction of new schemes of rating, marks a significant advance in urban improvement.[1] The Webbs found that 'the establishment between 1748 and 1835, in nearly every urban centre, under one designation or another, of a new statutory body ... was in fact, the starting point of the great modern development of town government'.[2]

Prior to the eighteenth century, the provision of such basic services as road sweeping, the removal of refuse and even the provision of fresh water could not be guaranteed in many towns. Where such services were provided they were often of a very limited nature. Like most other towns, those studied here relied on a system of by-laws to keep public streets and sewers clean and free from obstructions, and it was the manorial or borough courts, with the church vestries, which supervised larger projects of improvement like the paving of town centres or the widening of roads. There was no special body of individuals with the specific task of providing basic amenities or ensuring the upkeep of the town. Traditionally, the responsibility for most street cleansing and sometimes even repair fell on each resident. Those who had property along a public road, pavement or sewer were expected to ensure that these were regularly cleaned, kept free from obstructions, and that minor repairs were undertaken. When it came to the up-keep of larger public areas like the market place, the responsibility was often held by the toll collector or a street scavenger was employed, but their duties rarely extended beyond the town centres and a few of the principal streets. When the need arose to flag or pave a town's streets and market places, the borough or manorial officials usually applied for a local Act of Parliament. As early as 1585 Newark had obtained an Act for paving its

[1] Jones and Falkus, 'Urban improvement', p. 131.

[2] Webb, *English Local Government*, p. 235.

main streets and market place.[1] The acquisition of such an Act was often time-consuming and costly, but one that local authorities were prepared to accept because it gave them the right to levy a local rate to cover the costs of a project.

What little we know about the by-laws in existence at this time, comes from those who failed to follow them and, as a result, found themselves before manorial or borough courts. In 1687 the Worksop court leet and great court baron fined Thomas Sykes for 'making a dung heap in Newgate Street'; a year later they fined Ralph Leadbeake for not 'scouring his common sewer';[2] and in 1737 John Greathead was fined for the same offence.[3] The role of the manorial and borough courts in prosecuting those who broke the common law continued throughout the period studied here. As late as 1783 the Newark borough courts was still prosecuting individuals for such offences as 'placing and leaving Dung, Human Excrements and other filth' in the streets.[4] Increasingly, however, we find first a growing awareness that certain basic sanitary services should be provided and controlled by local authorities and gradually the establishment of new committees and commissioners specifically to deal with such matters.

The reasons behind such a change in attitude were probably first and foremost practical ones. Significant increases in population and an expansion between 1770 and 1840 of trade and industry created new pressures for collective services that would ensure at least the basic amenities for mass living. Local authorities must have been forced to re-evaluate the effectiveness of their provision. Moreover (as will be discussed below), from 1770 onward, there was a rising demand for a better quality of life among many inhabitants. A system of by-laws that relied on devolving responsibility to each inhabitant had evidently become increasingly unworkable and virtually unenforceable, at least in the larger towns.

Local pressure for change may well have been pre-empted or encouraged by national legislation. In 1715 legislation (confirmed in 1736) empowered justices of the peace to appoint scavengers to clean the streets in cities and market towns where this was not already being done.[5] This meant local authorities could initiate and charge for such a

[1] Dickinson, *Newark,* p. 134.

[2] Sheffield Archives, ACM W8, 16 Oct. 1687 and 1688.

[3] Sheffield Archives, ACM W17, 13 Oct. 1737.

[4] NAO, QSNK 1, 1783.

[5] Corfield, *Towns*, p. 177.

service without a local Act. In 1726 Newark justices agreed to levy 1d. in the pound for street repairs.[1] In October 1727 they appointed George Marshall as street scavenger and agreed that 2d. in the pound should be levied for his wages.[2] By 1745 William Rose was to be paid £40 a year to take away all the 'Dirt, Filth and Rubbish' that had been swept into heaps by the local inhabitants once a week.[3]

The appointment of a scavenger and the establishment of a rate specifically for street repair were two small but nonetheless important signs that at least one town was beginning to accept responsibility for providing a basic service. Mansfield followed suit much later in 1823 by contracting with a scavenger, who was to be paid £50 a year.[4] By then, the concept of paying an individual to undertake a certain task was increasingly commonplace. In 1779 Sam Peveral was paid £15 a year to care for Mansfield's town hall.[5] East Retford had its own surveyor of the highways in 1834.[6] By 1835 two policemen and one chief constable were employed by Newark Corporation, while a night watch was supported by public subscription.[7] In December 1837 a permanent day watch was instigated in East Retford,[8] by when the town also had two constables, paid £40–£50 a year by the corporation.[9]

Paid officials were accompanied by the growth of commissions set up to undertake specific tasks. This was another new and important step. The simplest way to establish a commission with effective powers was to apply for an improvement Act. Although Newark's first bill, prepared in 1776, never reached the House of Commons, many of its recommendations were included in a second bill which was passed in 1798. This allowed the Newark authorities to set up a special improvement commission which, like other similar bodies in the larger towns, derived its power not from tradition but from statute.[10] This meant they had independent powers to levy local rates for the provision of special

[1] NAO, QSNK 1/1, 1726.

[2] Ibid., Oct. 1727.

[3] Ibid., 23 May 1745.

[4] NAO, DC/M/1/2/1, 1 Aug. 1823.

[5] Newark Town Hall, Corporation Minutes, 27 Dec. 1779.

[6] NAO, DDHO 4/10, 27 Nov. 1834.

[7] *Report of the Royal Commission on Municipal Corporations* (Parl. Papers, 1835 (116), XXV), pp. 1937–8.

[8] NAO, DDHO 4/10, 7 Dec. 1837.

[9] NAO, DDHO 4/11.

[10] Corfield, *Towns,* p. 157.

services, the hiring of contractors and the equivalent of what we would today call compulsory purchase powers, enabling them to force local inhabitants to sell property which was often demolished for the widening of a road or the rebuilding of a town centre. Newark's improvement Act (1798) was followed by two Acts for Mansfield in 1823 and 1825, one for East Retford in 1836 and another for Newark in 1839.[1] The number of such Acts applied for by larger towns rose dramatically in the eighteenth century. Jones and Falkus calculated that 160 improvement commissions were set up between 1725 and 1799 and by the end of the eighteenth century there were commissions in most large towns.[2] By 1840 Newark, Mansfield and East Retford each had their own.

In 1776, when Newark prepared its first bill, the corporation requested that commissioners should be permitted to erect 'Water Works, Engines, Reservoirs, Water Houses and Pipes and Conduits for conveying water from the River Trent'. This was the first time a special body had been proposed to organise the town's water supply. In 1829 a committee was established to ensure that streets and yards were kept in a 'wholesome state'.[3] In 1831 the *Nottingham and Newark Mercury* announced the appointment of a new committee 'to superintend the cleansing of streets and yards',[4] while in 1836 another committee was appointed for 'restraining nuisances from drains and water courses and to organise the removal of privies and manure'.[5] Commissions were also set up in Mansfield and East Retford. In Mansfield 43 commissioners were appointed in 1823.[6] In 1839 a watch and stallage committee was set up in East Retford.[7]

In 1823 Mansfield's improvement commissioners were empowered to build public drains and to force the owners of private ones to ensure their upkeep. They introduced a £200 fine for anyone caught dumping waste into the rivers and streams, while the Act stipulated that the main streets were to be regularly watered and adequate provision was to be made for the draining of rain water from roof tops. On 8 August 1823 the commissioners ordered all inhabitants to place 'a spout the whole length of the front [of their buildings, if facing a public street], with a

1 Lewis, *Topographical Dictionary*, p. 247.

2 Jones and Falkus, 'Urban improvement', p. 139.

3 *Nottingham and Newark Mercury*, 12 Nov. 1829, p. 3.

4 Ibid., 12 Nov. 1831, p. 8.

5 *Nottingham Journal*, 23 May 1836.

6 NAO, DCM 1/15/1.

7 NAO, DDHO 4/10, 1839.

pipe to conduct the water ... from the roof, under the foot pavement and into the common sewer'.[1] In 1825 plans were ordered for the building of new public drains and two years later it was decided that 'a suitable place for procuring water and a proper water cart' were to be found.[2]

In East Retford the corporation published a new set of by-laws in 1818 which required all houses to have proper spouts for water drainage.[3] They, too, instigated new, harsher, fines for the dumping of rubbish in the streets. On 27 August 1827 the corporation auditors were to superintend 'the putting down and cost of iron pumps in the market place' and to ensure the wells were cleaned and sunk to additional depths if needed.[4] In 1830 the town applied for an improvement Act for the paving and widening of the streets and for improving drainage within the town. The corporation agreed to subscribe £200 towards the improvements.[5] In August 1832 a plan was approved for the cleaning and draining of the town, but nothing was mentioned for a further seven years until in November 1839 the corporation resolved that the town's drainage system would be improved as soon as the resources became available.[6] In 1840 £10 was granted towards 'drainage and improvement'.[7]

There is no doubt that the growth of salaried officials and commissions was an important step in improving the environment of the larger Nottinghamshire towns, although few such measures were to be found in Worksop. The efforts made by local authorities suggest that they were increasingly aware of the need to ensure basic public services were provided for centrally, with paid employees to undertake them. This marked, as the Webbs noted, an important step in the evolution of specialised municipal bodies. Such developments were not to be found in the smaller towns of Bingham and Ollerton. Their need for such services was presumably less, while the finances for such measures may have been lacking. The rise of commissions and the growth of salaried staff was a necessary requisite for these expanding urban communities, but one they had to be able to finance.

[1] NAO, DCM 1/2/1, 8 Aug. 1823.

[2] Ibid., 22 April 1825, 18 May 1827.

[3] NAO, DDHO 4/8, 5 Jan. 1818.

[4] Ibid., 27 Aug. 1827.

[5] *Nottingham and Newark Mercury*, 16 Oct. 1830.

[6] NAO, DDHO 4/10, 9 Nov. 1839.

[7] Ibid., 11 May 1840.

Financing improvement

Improvement could consume large amounts of money, either in a market town or a larger centre. In Borsay's view 'the investment required for many of these projects must have been substantial'. The cost of his urban renaissance was far from cheap; bills for the upper assembly rooms at Bath (1769–71) alone amounted to £20,000.[1] In Nottinghamshire, as already noted, Newark's town hall was believed to have cost about £17,000. How did towns fund their projects?

The levying of rates, especially for poor relief, was well established by the end of the seventeenth century, but it was not until the eighteenth century that rates specifically for urban improvement became widespread. From the establishment of Newark's highway rate in 1726 (the first new rate established in our period), it is possible to trace a growing number of levies exacted for paving, lighting, improving or watching of the towns, in addition to the traditional poor rate. In Mansfield three different new rates were established between 1824 and 1827 alone. Such rates were crucial to urban improvement in both the long and short term. In the long term they established a principle of each householder paying for centrally provided services and are therefore the precursor of the modern rating system. In the short term they raised money to spend on projects. However, while the importance of a principle of rating is hard to deny, in terms of the actual resources raised by rates their importance can be overstated. There was a limit to how much individuals could pay and collection was often slow. In fact, much of the improvement described in this chapter would not have taken place if reliance had been placed solely on rates. On 2 November 1791 the *Newark Herald* welcomed plans to light the town, using money raised by voluntary subscription. As it commented: 'by such means no additional burden is laid on the lower ranks of people, who are already obliged to contribute from their scanty pittances in parochial and other taxes more than they can afford to spare . . . '.

The rates exacted a heavy toll. For example, in 1832 Mansfield, like the other Nottinghamshire towns, was described as having risen to the 'rank of a clean and commodious town well paved and lighted with gas [with] its principal streets widened and other such improvements undertaken', but it was believed the cost had been so considerable that many of the town's 'best houses' were unoccupied because of the heavy

[1] Borsay, *Urban Renaissance,* p. 158.

tax placed on the local inhabitants to fund these improvements.[1] The Mansfield commission's minutes illustrate just how much improvement could cost. Admittedly, most market town commissioners did not attempt to set out to build a completely new market place, but regardless of the ambitious nature of the project, all improvements had to be financed. In Mansfield the costs were such that, within a year of their establishment, the commissioners were forced to borrow £2,000 'on credit of rates and assessments'.[2] Five months later they had to borrow a further £2,300, followed by another £1,400 two weeks later and £6,200 the next year.[3] Loans secured on rates were not difficult to obtain in view of the security offered and often a Act of Parliament was sought to sanction the borrowing.[4] In Newark the improvement Act stipulated that the commissioners were permitted to borrow up to £500. In Mansfield the establishment of rates was as important as a source for raising funds as it was for producing them. There were also instances where local authorities had to curtail the provision of basic services, often because of their cost. In 1830 East Retford corporation resolved to discontinue its expenditure for lighting the town.[5]

Town improvement thus had to be subsidised by sources other than the rates alone. Frequently, corporation or charity funds were used. Charitable donations in terms of money, property or land, remained a vital source of income for local authorities throughout this period. In Newark it was noted that the town was lucky to possess 'very considerable estates which enable the inhabitants to carry on splendid public works'.[6] Indeed, the funding of the new town hall in 1773 had largely come from donations made by the town's three main charities and later the land bequeathed to these charities was sold off to fund further improvement. Similar charities existed in each of these market towns. In East Retford the corporation subsidised several schemes from the income it derived in rents from properties left to the town. In 1835 the gross annual income of the corporation was believed to be £1,070 'raised from rents on various estates and houses'.[7] Since an average of £303 came

[1] White, *Directory*, p. 519.

[2] NAO, DC/M 1/2/1, 23 March 1824.

[3] Ibid., 25 Aug., 8 Sept. 1824, 6 May, 28 June 1825.

[4] Chalklin, 'Financing church building', p. 295; Jones and Falkus 'Urban improvement', p. 137.

[5] NAO, DDHO 4/8, 1 March 1830.

[6] Dickinson, *Newark*, p. 43.

[7] *Report of the Royal Commission on Municipal Corporations* (Parl. Papers, 1835 (116), XXV), iv. 1865.

from the market stalls and stallage, it is perhaps not surprising that the Mansfield improvement commissioners were keen to lease or buy the market rights from the duke of Portland.[1]

Private benefactions helped subsidise a number of projects and, significantly, many of these were the more expensive ones. Donations made by wealthy local inhabitants were another important local source of income. This usually took one of two forms. Either an outright gift of a piece of land or a sum of money was made by one individual or, to spread the expense over a number of people or a period of time, a subscription scheme might be introduced. In 1752 Lady Oxford paid for Mansfield's new moot hall. In Worksop the duke of Norfolk financed and endowed a Roman Catholic church.[2] In Bingham the earl of Chesterfield donated an acre of land for a new day and Sunday school. Often a donation and a subscription scheme were combined. Thus, in Ollerton a new school was built by subscription and then extended at the expense of Earl Manvers. The sums of money may appear small when we consider the vast estates and income these individuals had, but this does not devalue the importance of their contributions to a local community, especially those like Bingham or Ollerton, which were too small to generate money from other sources.

The motives for such donations varied. Lady Oxford probably financed Mansfield's town hall out of a sense of public and social duty. The duke of Norfolk, a leading Roman Catholic, may have felt it his duty to fund the building of a church. Just as important, however, especially in Newark and East Retford, were political motives. When it came to raising private donations of money or land, the right to elect members of parliament was a marketable privilege, especially when the local aristocracy were politically active. Here, it could be argued, urban status was important. So we find the duke of Newcastle funding various projects in both East Retford and Newark, including the building of East Retford's town hall, the rebuilding of Newark's Trent Bridge, and the rebuilding of one street of houses, for which 'to his Grace the Town [of Newark] and Public are mainly indebted'.[3] Likewise, Lord Middleton, another gentleman interested in politics, furnished the community of Newark (or at least its elite members) with a new library.[4] In a town

[1] NAO, DC/M 1/2/1, 13 July 1827.

[2] *Pigot's National and Commercial Directory* (1841), p. 62.

[3] *Lincoln and Stamford Mercury*, 11 July 1829, p. 3.

[4] *Pigot's Directory*, p. 13.

which was renowned for closely contested elections,[1] such donations were probably considered a worthwhile investment.

Sometimes, once a large initial donation had been made by a local worthy, additional money was raised by subscription or the sale of shares. This was increasingly common in Nottinghamshire from the late eighteenth century. When Mansfield's Act for lighting the town was passed in 1823, £5,000 had been subscribed for the project.[2] A large list of subscribers was published which included the town's local gentry, its professionals and main merchants, traders and shopkeepers—what we might broadly term the 'middling ranks'. In this instance the money was used to set up a joint-stock company. On 19 June 1830 the *Nottingham and Newark Mercury* announced the opening of an Independent Chapel in Worksop which 'the [town] inhabitants have contributed liberally towards [and] the site of which was kindly given by the Duke of Norfolk'. In Newark a nightly watch was funded by private subscription and the lighting of the town with gas was similarly funded.[3] In Ollerton the school was built by subscription.[4] In Mansfield the town hall built in 1836 was funded by the selling of £25 shares.[5] Clearly, local authorities expected to raise the required sums of money by such schemes and, equally, enough individuals had to have the disposable income to subscribe. Their donations and the range of subscription schemes are testimony to the wealth and prosperity of these local communities and the importance of having wealthy middling and gentry individuals living within the town centres. Both Borsay and Jones and Falkus explain the extent of urban improvement in terms of renewed prosperity based largely on the growth of inland trade. This, however, was the indirect source: it had to be channelled, often through private individuals, into improvement schemes.

While it would be wrong to play down the importance of the concept of rate paying to provide centrally organised public services, it is equally inaccurate to overstate their contribution to urban improvement. Rates were important in that they provided a steady source of income both to spend and borrow upon, but they did not generate enough to cover all expenses. By 1840 a system of general rating was only in its infancy and

1 R.A. Preston, 'The last days of a rotten borough', *Transactions of the Thoroton Society*, 78 (1974); M.J. Smith, 'Politics in Newark in the 1790s', Ibid., 84 (1980).

2 NAO, DCM 1/15/1.

3 *Report of the Royal Commission on Municipal Corporations* (Parl. Papers, 1835 (116), XXV), iv. 1938.

4 *VCH Notts.*, i. 260.

5 *Pigot's Directory* (1841), p. 7.

towns still relied on private investment for public and charitable projects. For this, it was essential that the population had both the means and the incentive to invest.

The rise of a new urban sensibility in the market town

Why did so many individuals contribute private funds to urban improvement? The renaissance of the market town extended beyond its physical transformation and beyond a growing concern for urban improvement, to include a new attitude towards the town environment. Above all, this involved a much greater sensitivity towards the pedestrian public. This is clearly evident in the changing attitudes of those in authority, as well as among a more discerning urban public. The emerging role of these towns as social and cultural centres encouraged this trend, and the local newspapers are a useful source for charting it. This new sensibility challenged many established practices, such as the holding of fairs, traditionally found in market towns, and banished from public view anything newly felt to be offensive.

Such public concern seems to have emerged in the late eighteenth century, although the problem is to decide to what extent the increased awareness is no more than a reflection of the local newspapers taking a more active concern in local issues. The first evidence of change comes after the completion of Newark's town hall in 1773. This auspicious date marks the beginnings of a long battle between the borough officials and local butchers. The new town hall included purpose-built butchers' shambles behind it so that the butchers could be moved out of the market place and away from public view. The butchers, however, did not feel obliged to go. In 1776 the corportation minutes recorded how 'greatly incommoded and annoyed [the town inhabitants were] by the exposing of Butcher's meat to sale ... before houses situate in the Market Place or in Common Public Streets, and by the killing of such meat [there]'. In 1778 the corporation considered whether they had the power to force the butchers into the new shambles,[1] but this was obviously not the case, because in 1784 it was suggested the town clerk should approach the duke of Newcastle for a copy of his grant of the manor of Newark to see whether a clause could be made to oblige the butchers to move.[2] In fact, it was not until 1798 and the passing of Newark's improvement Act that

[1] Newark Town Hall, Corporation Minutes, 13 Feb. 1778.

[2] Ibid., 22 May 1784.

the butchers actually moved, 25 years after the completion of the town hall.

Butchers were also moved out of the town centres and into enclosed market halls in both Mansfield and East Retford in 1755 and 1836 respectively, but there is no evidence to suggest that this caused the same problems as in Newark. With some of the more 'unsightly' aspects of town life banished from the streets, the authorities turned to matters such as pedestrian access and mobility around the town. If individuals were to be encouraged out into the streets, it was important that the pavements and causeways were free from obstructions. This certainly seems to have been a new consideration, and a direct consequence of the rising social and cultural life of these towns. From the records we have, it appears that prior to the late eighteenth century the key concern of local authorities was trade. On market days and at fair times streets and pavements were transformed into stalls, animal pens and the like. If this was still the case by 1840 it usually sparked a series of complaints. At no time were the local newspapers more full of complaints about the state of streets and the problems of mobility than during or after a fair. Sometimes it was just the sheer increase in people and traffic that provoked complaint, at other times it was the fact that these events tended to take over and dominate the town.

One Newark inhabitant remembered how animal pens would be erected along all the main streets at fair times, impeding movement and generating 'dirt galore'. Those who did not want the pavements outside their houses transformed into animal pens had to erect cordons of posts and chains.[1] Such events did not pass without comment. In 1816 one of Newark's historians wrote of the 'odious singularity which attends the fairs here, to the great inconvenience and interruption of passengers, and the annoyance of the inhabitants themselves'.[2] In 1834 the *Nottingham and Newark Journal* was pleased to announce that the Mansfield town authorities were 'making proper arrangements to compel owners of stalls &c. to stand in a convenient place in the new market place' and thereby free the carriage and causeways 'from annoyance and danger'.[3] A year later the *Nottingham Journal* drew the attention of the Newark magistrates to the continued 'nuisance of the stalls &c. being allowed to be set out in Stodman Street and others more frequented on market days ... '.[4]

[1] Reminiscences of a Septuagenarian, *Newark Advertiser*, 15 Aug. 1894, p. 8.

[2] Dickinson, *Newark*, p. 139.

[3] *Nottingham and Newark Journal*, 24 July 1834.

[4] *Nottingham Journal*, 9 Oct. 1835.

Then in 1840 complaints were made that while a flock of sheep had been driven through Mansfield the roads had been so 'choked by farmers and factors' that the sheep had forced their way over some earthenware. The complaint went on to state that it was 'scandalous that the highway should be impeded either by persons, stalls or otherwise'.[1]

The busy, thriving market centres these towns had become did create problems, particularly in relation to the movement of both traffic and individuals in and around the town. At the same time the traditional precedence given to trade was being superseded by other concerns and this was clearly evident in many of the new regulations introduced to govern town life. Stalls, sheds and animal pens were only some of the nuisances attacked. In 1776 Newark's improvement bill had proposed that all signs projecting onto the streets should be removed, wheelbarrows were no longer to be pushed on the pavements, large dogs were not to wander the streets, and unlighted windows were not to be left open after dark. Whether or nor these recommendations were implemented is not known. Similarly, in 1818 East Retford corporation ordered that no trucks or wheelbarrows were to be used on footpaths, no signs, signposts or foot scrapers were to project from house walls, and in times of frost the making of slides on footpaths was prohibited.[2] In Mansfield the improvement commission took things even further. From 1823 all doors and gates were to open inwards, 'ferocious dogs' were to be muzzled, and riding on shafts of waggons was banned, as was the letting off of guns and pistols, the lighting of bonfires, the playing of football or the baiting of animals in the main streets.[3] Subsequent measures saw the commission order the removal of penthouses, sheds, signposts, projecting shutters, and even barbers' poles and butchers' balks from the town's streets. In November 1824 the use of wheelbarrows on pavements was banned.

Behind all the measures outlined here was an attempt to pedestrianise and socialise each town centre. The Webbs linked such concerns to the elaboration of a detailed municipal code for the suppression of nuisances.[4] Essentially, each of the larger towns was tidied up and tighter controls were placed over many of the trades and practices traditionally associated with them. Some of the measures, for instance the removal of shops signs and barbers poles from the main streets and market places,

1 *Nottingham and Newark Journal*, 17 July 1840.

2 NAO, DDHO 4/8, 5 Jan. 1818.

3 NAO, DCM 1/15/1, p. 36.

4 S. and B. Webb, *Statutory Authorities*, p. 333.

must have altered the appearance of these towns considerably. And for some town inhabitants, especially the butchers, the rationale behind these changes must have been difficult to understand. But these towns were no longer just trading centres: they had developed a social and cultural life which was frequently at odds with the older traditions and roles of the market town. They were also increasingly populated by a middle class of 'polite and commercial people', many of whom became local commissioners and funded or subscribed to improvement projects. It was the aspirations of these people which found vocal expression in this new sensibility, and visual expression in straightened, resurfaced streets, lined with classically styled buildings. These people were still to be located living both their private and social lives in and around the town centres, and this no doubt explains the limitations of urban improvement to precisely those areas. The Webbs argued that this advance was due in part to the rise to power of the 'well-to-do shopkeeping and manufacturing class' who were permanently resident within the towns and constantly 'traversing the streets by foot'.[1]

The limits of improvement

While it is probable that the market town environment was more ordered and clean by 1840, with a greater range of public services offered than ever before, it would be wrong to over-eulogise the achievements of these Georgian improvers. Their aim (and this applies to both large and small town alike) was to provide a veneer of clean, fashionable modernity. Much like the new fashionable façades placed in front of old buildings to give a new public face, so once one looked behind or beyond the town main streets and market centres, another story was often revealed.[2] In Mansfield the town scavenger first appointed in 1823 was given strict instructions as to where he was to sweep. This included only the principal streets and none of the 'several shorter streets ... with many courts, lanes and alleys'.[3] The cleaner, improved town environment did not really extend beyond the town centre and its principal streets. This was equally true of other towns. The Webbs made the same point, arguing that whatever improvement had taken place was confined almost

[1] Webb, *Statutory Authorities*, p. 333.

[2] J. Innes and N. Rogers, 'Politics and government 1700–1840', in P. Clark (ed.), *The Cambridge Urban History of Britain. Volume II* (Cambridge, 2000), p. 542.

[3] White, *Directory*, p. 519.

entirely to the main streets, 'in which the traffic was greatest, and to which the principal inhabitants commonly resorted … private streets … narrow courts and alleys' were left wholly untouched.[1] Behind these and hidden from public view were a growing number of alleys, lanes and yards where small, cramped and poorly ventilated houses were being built. Often houses would be juxtaposed with dung yards, pig sties and slaughter houses but 'out of sight' meant 'out of mind', until the outbreak of disease in these less salubrious quarters spread to the wealthier areas of town and reinforced the physical proximity of squalor in the minds of the towns' principal inhabitants.[2]

Chapter 3 examined the physical expansion of the market towns and in particular the growth of small tenement houses from the late eighteenth century. Much of the urban expansion for this period took the form of infilling vacant plots of land in the town centres. These houses were constructed fairly rapidly and were not subject to any building regulations other than the need to ensure their frontages did not protrude from one another or from existing buildings. Some of these places developed into slums. In Newark, Cross Guns Yard was nicknamed Botany Bay, because as one inhabitant explained 'such a human dustbin did it become that, like the colony over the sea, it was used as a receptacle for the refuse of British humanity'. The people living there were 'herded together' in a very confined space. Not surprisingly, this area, together with parts of Mill Gate (which saw rapid development along the river bank at Newark) and Water Lane (an area of small tenement buildings), were memorable for the outbreaks of cholera and smallpox there.[3] These diseases were not, of course, confined to such places. In 1827 a outbreak of smallpox was described as 'extremely fatal within the last week or two at Newark'.[4] In 1834 it was reported that 'the small pox was never known to rage with such fury in the neighbourhood as at the present time'.[5] Typhus was the other main disease. In 1840 the *Nottingham and Newark Journal* was glad to report 'the fever which had somewhat prevailed in Mansfield had abated'.[6] In East Retford in 1848 the evenings were 'filled … with a dense fog' and numerous diseases drove

[1] Webb, *Statutory Authorities*, p. 344.

[2] NAO, DC/NK 2/1/1.

[3] Reminiscences of a Septuagenarian, *Newark Advertiser*, 20 June 1894.

[4] *Nottingham & Newark Mercury*, 24 March 1827.

[5] Ibid., 11 Jan. 1834.

[6] *Nottingham & Newark Journal*, 4 Dec. 1840.

'men to become dejected and the women hysterical'.[1]

The continued outbreaks and spread of disease, which usually sparked a series of letters complaining of sanitary conditions in the newspapers, together with the regular appearance of individuals at the manorial and borough courts for failing to comply with local by-laws regarding the upkeep of the streets, suggests the authorities had not succeeded in making these places healthy and clean. The 'improvers' did, however, face a number of problems. The initial enthusiasm for improvement might wane, in expanding towns it was difficulty to keep up with the pace of change, and problems of poverty and crime could often prove intractable.[2] The Webbs argued that we would fail to understand the efforts of the improvement commissioners (and other local authorities) 'unless we realise the contemporary perception of their function', rather than that of our own. Whereas we might consider public health to be of prime importance in the work of municipal government, this never occurred to the improvement commissioners. Not until the cholera epidemic of 1831–2 did the Webbs find any 'suggestion than any work of town improvement should be undertaken on the grounds that it would improve public health'.[3] The work of the commissions was limited because they worked to a different agenda. Of utmost importance to these individuals was that the town centre and its main streets looked clean, respectable and fashionable, and in this, if we are to rely upon contemporary descriptions, they were highly successful. Other bodies, like East Retford's corporation, faced different problems. As the sanitary inspector pointed out in 1870, the borough in our period actually straddled four parishes, three of which were predominantly rural, and as a result ratepayers were reluctant to subsidise the improvement of the town itself.[4] In 1849 a public health report on East Retford described the town as a 'wealthy, elegant and aristocratic place', although the commissioner was aware that its 'defective sanitary condition [was] not to be looked for in the principal thoroughfares'.[5] This, as the commissioner noted, was the same in all towns.

[1] *Report to the General Board of Health on a Preliminary Inquiry into the Sewerage, Draining and the Sanitary Condition of the Inhabitants of the Borough and Parish of East Retford and the Parishes of West Retford, Clarborough and Ordsall* (1849), p. 20.

[2] Innes and Rogers, 'Politics and government', pp. 542–3.

[3] Webb, *Statutory Authorities*, p. 274.

[4] National Archives, MH 13/67, p. 29, letter of A. Taylor, sanitary inspector, to the Home Secretary, 3 Dec. 1870.

[5] *Report to the General Board.*

Conclusion: wider implications

The renaissance of the Nottinghamshire market towns between 1770 and 1840 is evidence of both the wealth and prosperity of these towns and certain members of their population, while clearly showing that urban improvement was far from limited to the provincial centres of Georgian England. Neither was it limited to Nottinghamshire market towns. Studies of small towns in Shropshire, Cumbria, Yorkshire and Lincolnshire show similar developments in other northern and midland towns. Ludlow and Bridgnorth in Shropshire, Hawkshead, Brampton, Penrith, Cockermouth, Kendal and Carlisle in Cumbria, Grantham in Lincolnshire and Macclesfield in Cheshire all saw considerable public and private building.[1] Several of these towns had populations barely in excess of 2,000 by 1801. After describing the establishment of libraries, newsrooms and other public buildings in Brampton (population 1,682 in 1801), Marshall states that 'one could make this kind of recitation for almost any moderately sized market town in Cumbria'.[2] He goes on to note that 'it seems reasonably clear that the coincidence of timing within broad but significant periods, in all of the main towns is not accidental ... they did indeed represent a fashion of the age, but they also coincided with the general transformation of these towns into more than trading centres'.[3] The same can be applied to the Nottinghamshire market towns. The qualitative urbanisation of eighteenth and early nineteenth century England was a broad movement that did nor defer to the size or status of a settlement, although these factors did influence the extent to which a renaissance was possible.

[1] See J.D. Marshall, 'The Rise and Transformation of the Cumbrian Market Town, 1660–1900', *Northern History*, 19 (1993); D.J.W. Mawson, 'Brampton in the 1790s', *Trans. Cumberland and Westmorland Ant. and Arch. Soc.*, 72 (1973); R. Millward, 'The Cumbrian town between 1600 and 1800', in Chalklin and Havinden, *Rural Change*; S.A. Lewis, 'An Historical and Geographical Study of the Small Towns in Shropshire, 1600–1800' (Unpublished Ph.D., Leicester University, 1990); J.B. Manterfield, 'The Topographical Development of the Pre-Industrial Town of Grantham, Lincolnshire, 1535–1835' (Unpublished Ph.D., University of Leicester, 1981); G.K. Malmgreen, 'Economy and Culture in an Industrialised Town: Macclesfield, Cheshire' (Unpublished Ph.D., Indiana University, 1980).

[2] Marshall, 'Cumbrian market town', p. 159.

[3] Ibid., pp. 177–8.

SEVEN

Conclusion

The six Nottinghamshire market towns examined here exhibited both important similarities and critical differences in their economic and social history between 1680 and 1840. By 1840 Newark, Mansfield, Worksop and, to a lesser extent, East Retford had experienced a renaissance in their economic, social and cultural development. Between 1674 and 1841 Mansfield's population increased at least fivefold, Newark's and Worksop's quadrupled, Ollerton's and Bingham's trebled, and East Retford's nearly doubled. Population growth was accompanied from the late seventeenth century by diversification in the range of trades and occupations each town supported. This process continued through the eighteenth century and from about 1770 further diversification came with the introduction of large-scale agricultural processing and textile industries. By the nineteenth century, the Nottinghamshire market town was no longer purely a traditional centre of exchange. Newark and Mansfield in particular had developed regional, national and even international markets for their locally produced goods.

The prosperity enjoyed by these towns, and what was probably a minority of their populations, can be seen in a number of ways. First, the towns expanded physically and increased in density of housing and commercial development. Second, the public face of the towns was transformed by the adoption of classical architecture, the use of brick and tile, and the building of prestigious public and private buildings. With this came a much more varied and sophisticated cultural life—assemblies, plays, coffee clubs and newsrooms. Such developments served to indicate enthusiasm for urban life and this carried over into schemes for improvement which often involved the personal expenditure and time of leading townspeople; indeed, the most active members of these urban communities were their middle and upper social groups. This period witnessed the growing affluence and influence of the middling sort—the retailers, dealers, manufacturers and professionals—who seemed to do so well out of economic development. Probate inventories show that many of the Nottinghamshire middling sorts had wealth well in excess of their London contemporaries. As a result they were able to invest in public and domestic improvement, and in their houses we can detect signs of growing consumerism. These men and women had a critical role to play in the four larger towns during the long eighteenth century.

None of these developments was specific to Nottinghamshire; indeed, what this study suggests is that the key changes associated with the emergence of a more modern urban society—sustained population and economic development, consumerism, the rise of the middle classes and an urban renaissance—could clearly be found in smaller as well as larger towns. Although the focus here has been on Nottinghamshire towns, they were by no means the only such settlements to experience these developments. Clark has shown that the population growth of small towns nationally was greater than was once presumed.[1] Both Reed and Corfield have demonstrated the cultural vitality of small towns in the eighteenth century.[2] Their evidence is amply confirmed here. In particular, the case of Nottinghamshire suggests that we should look to the period from 1770 to 1840 as especially significant for the development of small towns. This in turn implies a time-lag in the occurrence of change between the larger and the smaller towns. Borsay may have placed the urban renaissance between 1660 and 1770 for provincial centres but in the smaller towns the process had only just begun by 1770.

The mantle of growth, however, did not fall evenly on all towns. Bingham and Ollerton did not experience the degree of development evident in the four larger towns; indeed, during the eighteenth century the gap between large and small grew wider. Both Bingham and Ollerton struggled to maintain a semblance of urbanity. Their populations certainly grew but their economies did not diversify or develop quickly. Neither saw any significant commercial or industrial development. The wealth which furnished new public buildings, improvements to streets and roads and a more varied social and cultural life in the larger towns, was conspicuous by its absence. On the other hand, these towns did not face stagnation or absolute decline. Their markets, which ceased to function for part of the eighteenth century, were re-established later in the century; a theatre and two new streets were built in Bingham and a school in Ollerton. These might seem small changes but both towns continued to operate as central places and service centres with a wider range of facilities than surrounding villages.

The limited evidence we have for Bingham and Ollerton goes some

1 See his chapter on population in P. Clark (ed.), *Small Towns in Early Modern Europe* (Cambridge, 1995), pp. 90–120.

2 P.J. Corfield, 'Small towns, large implications: social and cultural roles of small towns in eighteenth-century England and Wales', *British Journal of Eighteenth Century Studies*, 10 (1987), pp. 125–38; M. Reed, 'The cultural role of small towns 1600-1800', in Clark (ed.), *Small Towns*.

way to supporting Corfield's, Finberg's and Sweet's arguments for a rationalisation of the market network, but the evidence for the other four towns suggests their argument is too general. Growth clearly varied between different towns in the long eighteenth century, but not to the degree that has often been assumed. Corfield, in discussing the rationalisation of the market network between 1700 and 1800, argues that it 'did not defer to antiquity or novelty of foundation, or to the nature of a market grant' and that by 1700 it was no longer possible to equate possession of a market grant with urban status.[1] This is true but neither was there automatic decline among many of the market towns that Corfield excludes from her analysis simply because they had populations below 2,500. Why was this?

Very few towns, irrespective of size and including large provincial centres like Nottingham, had been entirely transformed by 1840. There was no wholesale shift to industrial production and, as in Nottinghamshire, the development of steam-powered mills did not necessarily undermine traditional domestic industry. Hudson argues that the economic history of this period has remained hamstrung by a 'type of modernisation theory' that divides the eighteenth century into its more 'traditional (domestic production)' and 'modern (industrial production)' constituent parts. She suggests that this contrast arises more from 'functional differences between labour saving and labour using development than out of a chronological sequence of growth'.[2] If we accept that the more traditional sectors of the eighteenth-century economy were a dynamic part of its development, then just because many small towns relied on domestic production we should not necessarily expect them to face economic decline. Furthermore, Berg has demonstrated that domestic production really began to decline only from the second third of the nineteenth century,[3] and it is therefore not surprising that the smaller towns which did not develop industrial concerns seem to have faced a more difficult future from the 1830s and 1840s. As Ellis suggests, 'on the whole the key factors at work in the changing pattern of urban development were the rapid growth of industrial production and the shift of industry towards the major coalfields'. All the fastest growing centres of the early nineteenth century depended directly or indirectly on manufacturing industry. The 1820s and 1830s in particular saw a sharp

[1] P. Corfield, *The Impact of Towns 1700-1800* (Oxford, 1982), p. 21.

[2] P. Hudson, *Regions and Industries: a Perspective on the Industrial Revolution in Britain* (Cambridge, 1989), p. 9.

[3] M. Berg, *The Age of Manufactures 1700-1820. Industry, Innovation and Work in Britain* (1994), p. 205.

readjustment in the traditional perspectives of economic activity as steam-based technology encouraged industrial production to concentrate in urban and suburban locations.[1]

Similarly, the assumption is made that with improving communications the sphere of influence of larger towns extended and as a result smaller towns found it harder to compete. In reality, the exact opposite seems to have happened for those strategically sited along a main traffic route. These towns, whether small or large, benefitted from the improvements that came with turnpiking. Canals too, tended to reinforce rather than undermine traditional communication networks and markets. Freeman has demonstrated how canals often enhanced regional economic systems by facilitating the movement of goods over short distances between existing markets.[2] By contrast, the growth of railways threatened radically to change the existing transport infrastructure. Moyes has shown how investment in roads, rivers and canals almost came to a halt in the railway age.[3] The local Nottinghamshire newspapers reveal how concerned contemporaries were about the impact of the developing railway network. Bearing in mind that for many small towns, including East Retford and even Newark, road and river transport provided vital income, this must also help to explain why the 1840s was such a critical decade for these places. Perhaps the 1840s is a better decade for dating the start of the real rationalisation of the market network.

The nature of change in the eighteenth century was neither so radical nor so fundamental as to undermine more traditional aspects of the market town economy. Wrigley, for example, describes eighteenth- and early nineteenth-century society as having been in an advanced stage of an organic economy, an economy that had experienced considerable growth and development but one that as yet was still limited by the use of inanimate sources of energy and inorganic sources of raw materials.[4] Not until the use of coal became widespread was the economy able to advance and revolutionise its scale of production and output, and this did not occur until the mid nineteenth century. Prior to that time advances in agricultural productivity, urbanisation and the deployment of labour

[1] J. Ellis, 'Regional and county centres 1700–1840', in P. Clark (ed.), *The Cambridge Urban History of Britain. Volume II* (Cambridge, 2000), p. 682.

[2] D.H. Aldcroft and M. Freeman, *Transport in the Industrial Revolution* (Manchester, 1983), ch. 1.

[3] A. Moyes, 'Transport 1730–1900', in R.A. Dodgson and R.A. Butlin (ed.), *An Historical Geography of England and Wales* (1987), pp. 401–29.

[4] E.A. Wrigley, *Continuity, Chance and Change: The Character of the Industrial Revolution in England* (Cambridge, 1989), p. 51.

were largely accompanied by a growth in traditional small-scale industries catering chiefly for the domestic market. There were exceptions to this general picture, in particular, the production of cotton and the malting and brewing industries, but this is as true for Newark and Mansfield as for larger towns such as Manchester and Leeds. It might be suggested, therefore, that the organic economy Wrigley describes produced an environment that was conducive to a much more general expansion of economic opportunities among a range of urban and indeed rural settlements.

For the sample towns the period from 1680 to 1840 was one of significant change, not just because of economic and social developments, but also in terms of how they were perceived. Newark, Mansfield, Worksop and East Retford were subject to serious attempts to control and improve their public image and physical appearance. In this sense they too enjoyed an urban renaissance, while the publication of town histories is further testimony to a growing sense of local pride. Yet it would be wrong to over-emphasise the extent of change. Both in 1680 and in 1840 there was an inequitable distribution of wealth among town inhabitants. Formal associations and institutions remained exclusive and elitist. An aspect not examined here is the nature of town government and of, more specifically, local politics. These factors may have been increasingly influenced by the rise of the 'middling sort' but this part of urban life remained limited to those with wealth and property. It is worth remembering that the majority of the urban population, the labourers, servants, washerwomen and hawkers, remained excluded from urban political life just as they do from many of the primary sources used here.

Finally, although this study suggests that the period 1770 to 1840 saw a renaissance in Nottinghamshire market towns, and that the examination of this process can help to throw light on both the degree and nature of local development in the long eighteenth century, a regional perspective remains important. As Hudson, Langton and Morris, and Stobart have shown, the regional pattern of resources such as water and coal were crucial to local development, as were regional sources of capital for industrial and commercial development at least up to the 1830s and 1840s. The wide variations in the way people thought about and organised their work, even social and economic protest, have also been shown to have had a regional dimension.[1] In addition, Clark has pointed

[1] J. Langton, 'The industrial revolution and the regional geography of England', *Trans. Inst. British Geographers*, 9 (1984); J. Langton and R.J. Morris (ed.), *Atlas of Industrialising Britain 1780-1914* (1986); J. Stobart (ed.), *Towns, Regions and Industries. Urban and Industrial Change in the Midlands,* c.*1700–1840* (Manchester, 2005).

to the way regional disparities among small towns had become more acute during the eighteenth century.[1] The point is that 'the industrial region of the late eighteenth and early nineteenth centuries had a dynamic and operative function and not just a descriptive meaning',[2] and although this study shows that the degree of change in the long eighteenth century may have been more widespread than has hitherto been appreciated, further regional and local studies (particularly for the South and East Anglia) are needed before the full pattern of economic, social and political change in this period can emerge. While the economic and cultural renaissance of provincial towns might be easier to trace, this book has demonstrated that the experience was not exclusively theirs.

[1] P. Clark (ed.), *The Cambridge Urban History of Britain. Volume II. 1540–1840* (Cambridge, 2000), p. 763.

[2] Hudson, *Regions and Industries*, p. 23.

Bibliography

Manuscript Sources

Bassetlaw Museum, East Retford
East Retford Parish Church Vestry Book (1809–72)
Retford Election Returns (1835)
Retford Borough Accounts (1839)
Retford Public Health Report (1849)

Highclere Castle
Carnarvon Papers, HMC 199

Newark Town Hall
Minutes of the Corporation of Newark

Nottinghamshire Archives
AT: Tithe Records for Bingham, East Retford, Mansfield, Newark, Ollerton, and Worksop
CA: Miscellaneous Acts of Parliament
CP: Miscellaneous Letters, Acts, Sale Details, Rentals, Accounts
CS 11/1: Survey of Sewers in Newark and Bingham 1733
DCM: Mansfield Improvement Commissioners Records
DC/NK 2/1/1-17: Valuations and Plans for Newark 1798
DD: Miscellaneous Deeds
DDP, DD2P, DD3P, DD4P: Muniments of the Dukes of Portland
DDFM 61: Deeds and Valuations for Newark
DDH: Miscellaneous Depositions, Rate Books, Charity Commissioner's Report, Inventories, Plans.
DDHO: Corporation Records and Ledgers
DDME: Miscellaneous Ledgers
DDMG: Notes re Paving of Newark 1772-4
DDS 8/2-3: Accounts re Newark Theatre
DDT: Miscellaneous Indentures, Petitions, Catalogues and Letters
M 367-8: Mansfield Rate Books 1801-2
M1874 Plans and Surveys of the Earl of Chesterfield's Estates 1776
MD 2S, 5-6L: Maps and Plans of Mansfield
NE 1L-10S Maps and Plans of Newark 1790-1825
PR: Poor Relief and Enclosure Records for Newark, Mansfield and Worksop
PRNM: Probate Records for Mansfield 1680-1840
PRNW: Probate Records for Bingham, East Retford, Newark, Ollerton, Worksop 1680-1840
QDC 3: Papers re Friendly Society Membership, 1794–5
QDD/1/11: Royal Navy List of Inhabited Houses for Bingham, 1796
QDE: Freeholders Lists 1739, 1780; land tax assessments, 1780-1832

QDJ: Freemen's Lists, 1780-1805
QDU: Turnpike Trusts Accounts, 1823-43
QFR: Bingham Overseers of Parish Poor Return, 1836
QSNK: Newark Borough Quarter Sessions Minutes and Rolls, 1780–1812, 1812–31
TT: Miscellaneous Turnpike Records
WS: Maps and Plans of Worksop
XBC 26S: Miscellaneous Plans

Nottingham University Manuscripts Department
Newcastle Collection
Portland Collection

National Archives
HO 107: Census Enumerators' Books (1841)
IR 18: Tithe Apportionments, Maps and Files
LRRO 1/1108-10: Maps of Nottinghamshire and Town Plan of Newark
MH 13: Local Government Act Office correspondence
MR 1/1132: Plan of Newark, 1804

Sheffield Archives
ACM: Arundel Castle Manuscripts

Printed Primary Sources
Journals of the House of Commons.
Report of the Royal Commission on Municipal Corporations, iv (Parl. Papers, 1835 (116), XXV).
Report to the General Board of Health on a Preliminary Inquiry into the Sewerage, Draining and the Sanitary Condition of the Inhabitants of the Borough and Parish of East Retford and the Parishes of West Retford, Clarborough and Ordsall (1849).
S.L. Ollard and P.C. Walker (ed.), *Archbishop Herring's Visitation Returns, Vol. 4, 1743* (Wakefield, 1930).

Newspapers
Nottingham Journal
Nottingham & Newark Mercury
Lincoln & Stamford Mercury
Newark Advertiser

Contemporary Published Works
A Short Tour in the Midland Counties of England performed in the Summer of 1772, together with a similar excursion undertaken in September 1774 (1774).
T. Cox, *Magna Britannia et Hibernia Antiqua and Nova or a New Survey of Great Britain* (1727).
A Complete History of Nottinghamshire (1730).
J. Curtis, *A Topographical History of Nottingham* (1843–4).
W. Dickinson, *The Town of Newark* (1816).

E. Eddison, *The History of Worksop* (Sheffield, 1854).
F.M. Eden, *The State of the Poor: a History of the Labouring Classes in England, with Parochial Reports* (ed. A.G.L. Rogers) (1928).
W. Harrod, *The History of Mansfield and its Environs* (1801).
J. Holland, *History of Worksop* (Sheffield, 1828).
W. Howitt, *The Rural Life of England* (London, 1838).
S. Lewis, *Topographical Dictionary of England and Wales* (1831; 2nd edn 1841).
R. Lowe, *A General View of Agriculture in the County of Nottingham* (1798).
J.S. Piercy, *History of East Retford* (Retford, 1828).
Pigot's National and Commercial Directory (1841 edn).
W. Pinnock, *The History and Topography of Nottinghamshire* (*c*.1823).
R.P. Shilton, *The History of the Town of Newark upon Trent* (1820).
Universal British Directory of Trade and Commerce (*c*.1790–8).
White's History, Gazetteer and Directory of Nottinghamshire (Sheffield, 1832).

Secondary Printed Sources

D.H. Aldcroft and M. Freeman, *Transport in the Industrial Revolution* (Manchester University Press, 1983).
T. Arkell, 'A method for estimating population totals from the Compton Census Returns', in K. Schurer and T. Arkell (ed.), *Surveying the People* (Oxford University Press, 1992).
'Multiplying factors for estimating population totals from the hearth tax', *Local Population Studies*, 28 (1982), 51–7.
T. Arkell, N. Evans and N. Goose, *When Death Do Us Part. Understanding and Interpreting the Probate Records of Early Modern England* (Oxford: Lepoard's Head Press, 2000).
M.W. Barley, *Documents relating to the Manor and Soke of Newark on Trent* (Thoroton Society Record Series, 16, 1956).
'Farmhouses and Cottages, 1550-1725', *Economic History Review,* 2nd series, 7, (1955), 291–306.
'Newark in the Sixteenth Century', *Trans. Thoroton Soc.*, 53 (1949), 15–25.
J. Barry, 'Bourgeois Collectivism? Urban association and the middling sort', in J. Barry and C. Brooks (ed.), *The Middling Sort of People. Culture, Society and Politics in England, 1550-1800* (Macmillan, 1984), 84–112.
J. Barry and C. Brooks (ed.), *The Middling Sort of People. Culture, Society and Politics in England, 1550–1800* (Macmillan, 1984).
J.V. Beckett, *A History of Laxton, England's Last Open-Field Village* (Oxford: Basil Blackwell, 1989).
'Tithe Commutation in Nottinghamshire in the 1830s and 1840s', *Trans. Thoroton Soc.*, 96 (1992), 146–65.
P. Benedict, 'Late medieval and early modern urban history à l'Anglaise. A review article', *Comparative Studies in Society and History*, 28 (1986), 169–80.
M. Berg, *The Age of Manufactures 1700–1820: Industry, Innovation and Work in Britain* (Routledge, 2nd edn, 1994).
M. Berg and P. Hudson, 'Rehabilitating the industrial revolution', *Economic History Review,* 45 (1992), 24–50.

H. Berry, 'Promoting taste in the provincial press: national and local culture in eighteenth-century Newcastle-upon-Tyne', *British Journal for Eighteenth-Century Studies*, 25 (1) (Spring 2002), 1-17.

M.W. Bishop, 'The Origins of East Retford', *Trans. Thoroton Soc.*, 82 (1978), 26–8.

P. Borsay, '"All the town's a stage": urban ritual and ceremony 1660-1800', in P. Clark (ed.), *The Transformation of English Provincial Towns* (Hutchinson, 1984), 228–58.

The English Urban Renaissance: Culture and Society in the Provincial Town, 1660–1760 (Oxford University Press, 1989).

(ed.), *The Eighteenth-century Town 1688–1820. A Reader in English Urban History* (Longman, 1990).

'The London connection: cultural diffusion and the eighteenth-century provincial town', *The London Journal*, 19 (1) (1994), 21-35.

P. Borsay and L. Proudfoot (ed.), *Provincial Towns in Early Modern England and Ireland. Change, Convergence and Divergence* (Proceedings of the British Academy, 108, 2002).

J. Brewer and R. Porter (ed.), *Consumption and the World of Goods* (Routledge, 1993).

A.F.J. Brown, *Essex at Work 1700–1815* (Chelmsford: Tidal Press, 1969).

C. Brown, *A History of Newark* (Newark, 1904).

J. Brown, *The English Market Town* (Marlborough: Crowood, 1986).

S.M. Brown, C.A. Dyhouse, J.D. Marshall, A. Palmer, D.W. Twiss, 'A small town study: an experiment in teamwork', *Urban History Yearbook* (1974), 19–23.

P. Burke, *Popular Culture in Early Modern Europe* (Temple Smith, 1978).

C. Campbell, 'Understanding traditional and modern patterns of consumption in eighteenth-century England: a character-action approach', in J. Brewer and R. Porter (ed.), *Consumption and the World of Goods* (Routledge, 1993), 40–57.

D. Cannadine, 'Victorian cities: how different?', in R.J. Morris and R. Rodger (ed.), *The Victorian City 1820–1914. A Reader in British Urban History* (Longman, 1993), 114–46.

H. Carter, 'Towns and Urban Systems 1730–1900', in R.A. Dodgshon and R.A. Butlin (ed.), *An Historical Geography of England and Wales* (Academic Press, 1987), 167–400.

C.W. Chalklin, 'A Seventeenth-century Market Town: Tonbridge', *Archaeologia Cantiana*, 76 (1961), 152–62.

The Provincial Towns of Georgian England (Edward Arnold, 1974).

'Capital expenditure on building for cultural purposes in provincial England, 1730–1830', *Business History*, 22 (1980), 51–70.

'The financing of church building in the provincial towns of the eighteenth century', in P. Clark (ed.), *The Transformation of English Provincial Towns* (Hutchinson, 1984), 284–310.

C.W. Chalklin and M.A. Havinden (ed.), *Rural Change and Urban Growth 1500–1800. Essays in English Regional History in Honour of W.G. Hoskins* (Longman, 1974).

W.H. Chaloner and J.D. Marshall, 'Major Cartwright and the Revolution Mill, East Retford, Nottinghamshire', in N.B. Harte and K.G. Ponting (ed.), *Textile History and Economic History* (Manchester University Press, 1973), 281–303.

J.D. Chambers, *Nottinghamshire in the Eighteenth Century* (Frank Cass, 2nd edn, 1966).

'Population change in a provincial town—Nottingham 1700–1800', in L.S. Pressnell (ed.), *Studies in the Industrial Revolution* (Athlone Press, 1960), 97–124.

The Vale of Trent, 1670–1800: a regional study of economic change (Economic History Society, 1957).

J.A. Chartres, 'Road carrying in England in the seventeenth century: myth and reality', *Economic History Review*, 2nd series, 30 (1977), 73–94.

S. Checkland, *British Public Policy 1776–1939: an economic, social and political perspective* (Cambridge University Press, 1983).

C.W. Chiltern, '*The Universal British Directory*—a warning', *Local Historian*, 15 (1982), 144–6.

J.H. Clapham, 'Some factory statistics of 1815–1816', *Economic Journal*, 25 (1915), ooo–oo.

J.C.D. Clark, *English Society, 1688–1832: Ideology, Social Structure and Political Practice during the Ancien Regime* (Cambridge University Press, 1985).

P. Clark (ed.), *The Early Modern Town* (Open University Press, 1976).

Country Towns in Pre-Industrial England (Leicester University Press, 1981).

The Transformation of English Provincial Towns (Hutchinson, 1984).

Sociability and Urbanity: Clubs and Societies in the Eighteenth Century City (Victorian Studies Centre, University of Leicester, 1986).

'Small towns in England 1550–1850: national and regional population trends', in P. Clark (ed.), *Small Towns in Early Modern Europe* (Cambridge University Press, 1995), 90–120.

Small Towns in Early Modern Europe (Cambridge University Press, 1995).

P. Clark and J. Hosking, *Population Estimates of English Small Towns 1550–1851* (Centre for Urban History, University of Leicester, Working Paper No 5, 1993).

P. Clark and P. Slack (ed.), *English Towns in Transition 1500–1700* (Oxford University Press, 1976).

M.R.G. Conzen, 'Alnwick, Northumberland. A study in town plan analysis', *Trans. Inst. British Geographers*, 27 (1967).

P.J. Corfield, *The Impact of English Towns 1700–1800* (Oxford University Press, 1982).

'Small towns, large implications: social and cultural roles of small towns in eighteenth-century England and Wales', *British Journal of Eighteenth-century Studies*, 10 (1987), 125–38.

J. Cornwall, 'English country towns in the fifteen twenties', *Economic History Review*, 2nd ser. 15 (1962-3), 54–69.

A. Cossons, *The Turnpike Roads of Nottinghamshire* (Historical Association Pamphlet, No. 97, 1934).

Inland Waterways of Great Britain and Ireland (1960).

N. Cox, 'The distribution of retail tradesmen in north Shropshire, 1660–1750', *Journal of Regional and Local Studies*, 13 (1) (1993), 4–22.

N. Cox and J. Cox, 'Valuations in probate inventories: Part II', *Local Historian*, 17 (2) (1986), 85–100.

N.F.R. Crafts, 'Eighteenth-century local population studies in the context of aggregate estimates for England and Wales', *Local Population Studies*, No 13 (1974), 19–29.

'British Economic Growth, 1700–1831: a review of the evidence', *Economic History Review*, 2nd series, 26 (1983), 177–99.

British Economic Growth During the Industrial Revolution (Oxford University Press, 1985).

M.J. Daunton, 'Towns and economic growth in eighteenth-century England', in P. Abrams and E.A. Wrigley (ed.), *Towns in Societies: Essays in Economic History and Historical Sociology* (Cambridge University Press, 1979), 246–77.

S. D'Cruze, 'The middling sort in eighteenth-century Colchester: independence, social relations and the community broker', in J. Barry and C. Brooks (ed.), *The Middling Sort of People. Culture, Society and Politics in England, 1550–1800* (Macmillan, 1984), 181–207.

A.F. Denholm, 'The impact of the canal system on three Staffordshire market towns 1760–1850', *Midland History*, 13 (1988), 59–75.

J. de Vries, 'Between purchasing power and the world of goods: understanding the household economy in early modern Europe' in J. Brewer and R. Porter (ed.), *Consumption and the World of Goods* (Routledge, 1993), 85–132.

H.T. Dickinson, Review of P. Borsay, *The English Urban Renaissance*, *Social History*, 16 (1991), 98–101.

R.A. Dogshon and R.A. Butlin, *An Historical Geography of England and Wales,* (Academic Press, 1987).

M. Douglas and B. Isherwood, *The World of Goods: Towards an Anthropology of Consumption* (Harmondsworth: Penguin, 1980).

E.P. Duggan, 'Industrialisation and the development of urban business communities: research problems, sources and techniques', *Local Historian*, 11 (8) (1975), 457–65.

A.D. Dyer, 'The Market Towns of Southern England 1500–1700', *Southern History*, 1 (1979), 123–34.

'Small towns in England, 1600–1800', in P. Borsay and L. Proudfoot, *Provincial Towns in Early Modern England and Ireland. Change, Convergence and Divergence* (Proceedings of the British Academy, 108, 2002), 53–67.

H.J. Dyos and M. Wolff (ed.), *The Victorian City: Images and Reality* (Routledge, 1973).

P. Earle, *The Making of the English Middle Classes: Business, Society and Family Life in London, 1660–1730* (Methuen, 1989).

D.G. Edwards (ed.), *Derbyshire hearth tax Assessments 1662–1670* (Derbyshire Record Society, 7, 1982).

K.C. Edwards, *The Land of Britain. The Report of the Land Utilisation Survey of Britain. Part 60. Nottinghamshire* (Geographical Publications, 1944).

J. Ellis, 'A dynamic society: social relations in Newcastle-upon-Tyne 1660–1760', in P. Clark (ed.), *The Transformation of English Provincial Towns* (Hutchinson, 1984), 190–227.

E.J. Evans, *Tithes and the Tithe Commutation Act 1836* (Bedford Square Press, 1978).

A. Everitt, 'Social mobility in early modern England', *Past and Present,* 33 (1966), 56–73.

'The marketing of agricultural produce', in J. Thirsk (ed.), *The Agrarian History of England and Wales. IV. 1500-1640* (Cambridge University Press, 1967), 466–592.

'Urban Growth, 1570–1770', *Local Historian*, 8 (4) (1968), 118–25.

Change in the provinces: the seventeenth century (Leicester University Press, 1969).

Perspectives in English Urban History (Macmillan, 1973).

'The Banburys of England', *Urban History Yearbook*, 1974, 28-38.

D.E.C. Eversley, 'The home market and economic growth in England 1750–80', in E.L. Jones and G.E. Mingay (ed.), *Land, Labour and Population in the Industrial Revolution* (Edward Arnold, 1967), 206–59.

H.P.R. Finberg (ed.), *Approaches to History* (Routledge, 1962).

M.W. Flinn, *The History of the British Coal Industry. Volume 2. 1700–1830: The Industrial Revolution* (Oxford University Press, 1984).

R. Floud and D. McCloskey, *The Economic History of Britain since 1700. Volume 1. 1700-1860* (Cambridge University Press, 2nd edn, 1994).

D. George, *England in Transition* (Harmondsworth: Penguin, 1964 edn).

D.E. Ginter, 'A wealth of problems with the land tax', *Economic History Review*, 2nd ser. 35 (1982), 416–21.

A Measure of Wealth. The English Land Tax in Historical Analysis (McGill-Queens University Press, 1992).

P. Glennie, 'Consumption within historical studies' in D. Miller (ed.), *Acknowledging consumption: a review of new studies* (London: Routledge, 1995), 164–203.

H.E. Goulding, 'Louth: A North Lincolnshire Market Town', *East Midlands Geographer,* 7 (1957), 31–9.

D. Gregory, 'The production of regions in England's Industrial Revolution', *Journal of Historical Geography*, 14 (1) (1988), 50–8.

A. Henstock (ed.), 'House repopulation from the land tax Assessments in a Derbyshire Market Town, 1780–1825', in M. Turner and D. Mills (ed.), *Land and Property: The English land tax 1692-1832* (Cambridge University Press, 1986), 118–35.

A Georgian Country Town. Ashbourne 1725–1825. Vol. 2. Architecture (Ashbourne Local History Group, 1991).

B.D. Herring, *History of Parliament. The Commons 1660–1690* (HMSO, 1983).

D.G. Hey, *The Rural Metalworkers of the Sheffield Region: a study of rural industry before the Industrial Revolution* (Leicester University, Department of English Local History, Occasional Papers, 2nd ser. 5, 1972).

E. Higgs, 'Women, Occupations and Work in the Nineteenth-century Censuses', *History Workshop*, 23 (1987), 59–80.

B. Hill, *Women, Work and Sexual Politics in Eighteenth-century England* (University College Press, 1993).

E.J. Hobsbawm, 'The British standard of living 1790-1850', *Economic History Review*, 2nd ser. 10 (1957), 46–68.

B.A. Holderness, 'Credit in a rural community, 1600–1800: some neglected aspects of probate inventories', *Midland History*, 3 (1975-6), 94–116.

G. Holmes, *Augustan England: Professions, State and Society 1680-1730* (George Allen & Unwin, 1982).

P. Hudson, *Regions and Industries: A Perspective on the Industrial Revolution in Britain* (Cambridge University Press, 1989).

'Land, the Social Structure and Industry in two Yorkshire Townships, *c*.1660–1800' in P. Swan and D. Foster (ed.), *Essays in regional and local history: essays in honour of Eric M. Sigsworth* (Beverley: Cherry Burton, 1992), 27–46.

E.H. Hunt and R.W. Botham, 'Industrialisation and regional inequality: wages in Britain, 1760–1914', *Journal of Economic History*, 46 (4) (1986), 935–66.

'Wages in Britain during the industrial revolution', *Economic History Review*, 40 (1987), 380–99.

J. Innes, 'Not so strange? New views of eighteenth-century England', *History Workshop*, 29 (1990), 179–83.

J.A. Johnson, 'Worcestershire probate inventories 1699–1716', *Midland History*, 4 (1978), 191–211.

E.L. Jones and M.E. Falkus, 'Urban improvement and the English economy in the seventeenth and eighteenth centuries', in P. Borsay (ed.), *The Eighteenth-century Town. A Reader in English Urban History 1688–1820* (Longman, 1990), 116–58.

E.L. Jones and G.E. Mingay (ed.), *Land, Labour and Population in the Industrial Revolution* (Edward Arnold, 1967).

R.J.P. Kain and H.C. Prince, *The Tithe Surveys of England and Wales* (Cambridge University Press, 1985).

D. Keene, 'The Medieval Urban Landscape, AD 900–1540' in P. Waller (ed.), The *English Urban Landscape* (Oxford University Press, 2000), 74–98.

P.J. King, 'Edward Thompson's contribution to eighteenth-century studies. The patrician-plebian model re-examined', *Social History*, 21 (2) (1996), 215–28.

S. King and G. Timmins, *Making Sense of the Industrial Revolution. English Economy and Society 1700–1850* (Manchester University Press, 2001).

D.S. Landes, *The Unbound Prometheus. Technological Change and Industrial Development in Western Europe from 1750 to the Present* (Cambridge University Press, 1969).

P. Lane, N. Raven and K. Snell, *Women, Work and Wages* (Woodbridge: Boydell, 2004).

P. Langford, *A Polite and Commercial People: England 1727–1783* (Oxford University Press, 1989).

'The uses of eighteenth-century politeness', *Trans. Royal Hist. Soc.*, 6th series, 12 (2002), 311–31.

J. Langton, 'Residential patterns in pre-industrial cities: Some case studies from seventeenth-century Britain', *Trans. Inst. British Geographers*, 65 (1975), 1–27.

'The industrial revolution and the regional geography of England', *Trans. Inst. British Geographers*, new series, 9 (1984), 145–67.

'The product of regions in England's Industrial Revolution: a response', *Journal of Historical Geography*, 14 (1988), 170–6.

J. Langton and R.J. Morris (ed.), *Atlas of Industrializing Britain 1788–1914*

(Methuen, 1986).
P. Laslett, 'Mean household size in England since the sixteenth century', in P. Laslett and R. Wall (ed.), *Household and Family in Past Times* (Cambridge University Press, 1972), 125–58.
The World We Have Lost—Further Explored (Oxford University Press, 1984).
C.M. Law, 'Some notes on the urban population of England and Wales in the eighteenth century', *Local Historian*, 10 (1) (1972), 13–26.
R. Lawton, 'Population and society 1730–1900', in R.A. Dogshon and R.A. Butlin (ed.), *An Historical Geography of England and Wales* (Academic Press, 1987), 313–66.
P. Laxton, 'Liverpool in 1801: a manuscript return for the first national census', *Trans. Historic Soc. of Lancashire and Cheshire*, 130 (1981), 73–113.
R.D. Lee and R.S. Schofield, 'British population in the eighteenth century', in R. Floud and D. McCloskey (ed.), *The Economic History of Britain since 1700. Volume 1: 1700-1860* (Cambridge University Press, 2nd edn, 1994), 17–35.
P.H. Lindert, 'English occupations, 1670–1811', *Journal of Economic History*, 40 (1980), 685–712.
P.H. Lindert and J.G. Williamson, 'Revising England's social tables 1688–1812', *Explorations in Economic History*, 19 (1982), 385–408.
'English workers' living standards during the Industrial Revolution: a new look', *Economic History Review*, 36 (1983), 1–25.
R.W. Malcolmson, *Popular Recreations in English Society 1700–1850* (Cambridge University Press, 1973).
D. Marshall, *Industrial England 1776–1851* (Routledge & Kegan Paul, 1973).
J.D. Marshall, *Autobiography of William Stout of Lancaster, 1655–1752* (Manchester University Press, 1967).
'Agrarian wealth and social structure in pre-industrial Cumbria', *Economic History Review,* 33 (1980), 503–21.
'The study of local and regional "Communities": some problems and possibilities', *Northern History*, 17 (1981), 203–30.
'The rise and transformation of the Cumbrian market town 1660-1900', *Northern History*, 19 (1983), 128–209.
'Cumberland and Westmorland Societies in London, 1734–1914', *Trans. Cumberland and Westmorland Antiquarian and Archaeological Soc.*, 84 (1984), 239–54.
'Communities, societies, regions and local history. Perceptions of the locality in High and Low Furness', *Local Historian*, 26 (1) (1996), 36–47.
J.D. Marshall and C.A. Dyhouse, 'Social transition in Kendal and Westmorland, *c.*1760–1860', *Northern History*, 12 (1976), 125–57.
P. Mathias, 'The social structure in the eighteenth century: a calculation by Joseph Massie', *Economic History Review*, 2nd ser. 10 (1957), 30–45.
D.J.W. Mawson, 'Brampton in the 1790s', *Trans. Cumberland and Westmorland Antiquarian and Archaeological Soc.*, 72 (1973), 299–316.
G. McCracken, *Culture and Consumption: New Approaches to the Symbolic Character of Consumer Goods and Activities* (Indiana University Press, 1988).
A. McInnes, *The English Town 1660–1760* (Saffron Waldon, 1980).
N. McKendrick (ed.), *Historical Perspectives: Studies in Thought and Society*

(Europa, 1974).
N. McKendrick, 'Home demand and economic growth: a new view of the role of women and children in the industrial revolution', in N. McKendrick (ed.), *Historical Perspectives: Studies in Thought and Society* (Europa, 1974), 152–210.
N. McKendrick, J. Brewer and J.H. Plumb, *The Birth of a Consumer Society: The Commercialisation of Eighteenth Century England* (Europa, 1982).
R. Millward, 'The Cumbrian town between 1600 and 1800', in C.W. Chalklin (ed.), *Rural Change and Urban Growth, 1500-1800* (1974), 202–28.
J.S. Moore, 'Probate inventories: problems and prospects' in P. Riden (ed.) *Probate Inventories and the Local Community* (Gloucester: Sutton, 1984), 11–28.
R.J. Morris and R. Rodger (ed.), *The Victorian City 1820–1914. A Reader In British Urban History* (Longman, 1993).
A. Moyes, 'Transport 1730–1900', in R.A. Dodgshon and R.A. Butlin (ed.), *An Historical Geography of England and Wales* (Academic Press, 1987), 401–29.
J. Moykr, 'Is there still life in the pessimist case? Consumption during the Industrial Revolution 1790–1850', *Journal of Economic History*, 48 (1988), 69–92.
'Technological change 1700-1830', in R. Floud and D. McCloskey (ed.), *The Economic History of Britain since 1700. Volume 1: 1700–1860* (Cambridge University Press, 2nd edn, 1994), 140–62.
H.C. Mui and L. Mui, *Shops and Shop-keeping in Eighteenth-Century England* (McGill-Queen's University Press, 1989).
C. Mukerji, *From Graven Images: Patterns of Modern Materialism* (New York: Columbia University Press, 1983).
L. Namier and J. Brooke, *History of Parliament. The Commons 1754–1790* (HMSO, 1964).
J.U. Nef, *The Rise of the British Coal Industry* (Routledge, 1932).
M.K. Noble, 'Land tax returns and urban development', *Local Historian*, 15 (2) (1982), 86–92.
'The land tax assessments in the study of the physical development of country towns', in M. Turner and D. Mills (ed.), *Land and Property: The English land tax 1692–1832* (Cambridge University Press, 1986), 93–117.
'Growth and development in a regional urban system: the country towns of eastern Yorkshire, 1700–1850', *Urban History Yearbook* (1987), 1–21.
P. O'Brien and R. Quinault (ed.), *The Industrial Revolution and British Society,* (Cambridge University Press, 1993).
M. Overton, 'Probate inventories and the reconstruction of agrarian landscapes', in M. Reed (ed.), *Discovering Past Landscapes* (Croom Helm, 1984).
M. Overton, J. Whittle, D. Dean and A. Hann, *Production and Consumption in English Households, 1600–1750* (Routledge 2004), 167–94.
D. Page, 'Commercial directories and market towns', *Local Historian*, 11 (2) (1974), 85–8.
W. Page (ed.), *Victoria History of the County of Nottingham* (Constable, 1910).
J. Patten, 'The hearth taxes, 1662–1689', *Local Population Studies*, 1 (1971), 14–25.
'Urban occupations in pre-industrial England', *Trans. Inst. British Geographers*, new series, 2 (1977), 296–313.
English Towns 1500–1700 (Folkstone: Dawson, 1978).

H. Perkins, *Origins of Modern English Society* (Routledge, 1969).
N. Pevsner, *The Buildings of England. Nottinghamshire* (Harmondsworth: Penguin, 2nd edn, 1979).
J.H. Plumb, 'The commercialisation of leisure in eighteenth-century England', in N. McKendrick, J. Brewer and J.H. Plumb (ed.), *The Birth of a Consumer Society: The Commercialisation of Eighteenth-century England* (Europa, 1982).
R. Porter, *English Society in the Eighteenth Century* (Harmondsworth: Penguin, 1982).
N. Powell, 'Do numbers count? Towns in early modern Wales', *Urban History*, 32 (1) (2005), 46–67.
R.A. Preston, 'The last days of a rotten borough: East Retford', *Trans. Thoroton Soc.*, 78 (1974), 94–103.
U. Priestley, '"The fabric of stuffs": The Norwich textile Industry *c.*1650–1750', *Textile History*, 16 (2) (1985), 183–209.
M. Prior, *Fisher Row: Bargemen and Canal Boatmen in Oxford 1500–1900* (Oxford: Clarendon Press, 1982).
N. Raven, 'De-industrialisation and the urban response: the small towns of the North Riding of Yorkshire *c.*1790–1850', in R. Weedon and A. Milne (ed.), *Aspects of English Small Towns in the 18th and 19th Centuries* (Centre for Urban History, University of Leicester, 1993), 46–69.
M. Reed, 'The cultural role of small towns in England 1600–1800', in P. Clark (ed.), *Small Towns in Early Modern Europe* (Oxford University Press, 1995), 121–45.
P. Ripley, 'Village and town: occupations and wealth in the hinterland of Gloucester, 1660–1700', *Agricultural History Review*, 32 (1984), 170–8.
H.B. Rodgers, 'The market area of Preston in the sixteenth and seventeenth centuries', *Geographical Studies*, 3 (1) (1956), 46–55.
N. Rogers, 'Review article. Paul Langford's "Age of Improvement"', *Past and Present*, 130 (1991), 201–9.
D. Rollison, *The Local Origins of Modern Society: Gloucester 1500–1800* (Routledge, 1992).
J. Rule, *Albion's People. English Society 1714–1815* (Longman, 1992).
The Vital Century. England's Developing Economy 1714–1815 (Longman, 1992).
L. Scammell, 'Town versus country: the property of everyday consumption in the late seventeenth and eighteenth centuries', in J. Stobart and A. Owens (ed.), *Urban Fortunes: property and inheritance in the town 1700–1900* (Ashgate, 2000), 26–49.
See also L. Weatherill.
K. Schurer and T. Arkell (ed.), *Surveying the People* (Oxford University Press, 1992).
L.D. Schwartz, 'Social class and social geography: the middle classes in London at the end of the eighteenth century', in P. Borsay, *The Eighteenth-Century Town 1688–1820* (Longman, 1990), 315–37.
R. Sedgewick (ed.), *History of Parliament. The Commons 1715–1754* (HMSO, 1970).
C. Shammas, 'Consumer behaviour in colonial America', *Social Science History*, 6 (1982), 1–24.

The Pre-industrial Consumer in England and America (Oxford University Press, 1990).

'Changes in English and Anglo-American consumption from 1550–1800', in J. Brewer and R. Porter (ed.), *Consumption and the World of Goods* (Routledge, 1993), 177–205.

G. Shaw, *British Directories as Sources in Historical Geography* (Institute of British Geographers, Historical Geography Research Series, No 8, 1982).

G. Shaw and A. Tipper, *British Directories: A Bibliography and Guide to Directories published in England and Wales (1850–1950) and Scotland (1773–1950)* (Leicester University Press, 1989).

G. Sjoberg, *The Pre-industrial City. Past and Present* (Glencoe, Ill., 1960).

D.E. Smith, 'Otley: A study of a market town during the late 17th and 18th centuries', *Yorks. Archaeological Journal*, 52 (1980), 143–56.

M.J. Smith, 'Politics in Newark in the 1790s', *Trans. Thoroton Soc.*, 84 (1980), 59–67.

M. Spufford, 'The limitations of the probate inventory', in J. Chartres and D. Hey (ed.), *English Rural Society: Essays in Honour of Joan Thirsk* (Cambridge University Press, 1990), 139–74.

J. Stevenson, *English Urban History, 1500–1700 (Units 13–16: The Rise of the New Urban Society)* (Milton Keynes: Open University, 1977).

J. Stobart, 'Culture versus commerce: societies and spaces for elites in eighteenth-century Liverpool', *Journal of Historical Geography*, 28 (4) (2002), 471–85.

'Leisure and shopping in the small towns of Georgian England. A regional approach', *Journal of Urban History*, 31 (4) (2005), 479–503.

J. Stobart and A. Owens (ed.), *Urban Fortunes: Property and Inheritance in the Town, 1700–1900* (Ashgate, 2000).

J. Stobart and N. Raven (ed.), *Towns, Regions and Industries. Urban and Industrial Change in the Midlands, c.1700–1840* (Manchester University Press, 2005)

L. Stone and J.C.F. Stone, *An Open Elite? England 1540–1880* (Oxford University Press, 1984).

J. Styles, 'Manufacturing, consumption and design in eighteenth-century England', in J. Brewer and R. Porter (ed.), *Consumption and the World of Goods* (Routledge, 1993), 527–54.

J. Thirsk, *Sources of Information on Population 1500–1760 and Unexplored Sources in Local Records* (Chichester: Phillimore, 1965).

E.P. Thompson, 'Patrician society, plebian culture', *Journal of Social History*, 7 (1974), 382–405.

Customs in Common (Harmondsworth: Penguin, 1993).

F.M.L. Thompson, *The Rise of Suburbia* (Leicester University Press, 1982).

The Cambridge Social History of Britain 1750-1950. Volume 1. Regions and Communities (Cambridge University Press, 1990).

R.G. Thorne (ed.), *History of Parliament. The Commons 1790–1820. II. Constituencies* (HMSO, 1986).

L. Toulmin-Smith (ed.), *The Itinerary of John Leland 1535–1543* ([Publisher], 1907).

B. Travers, 'Trading patterns in the east midlands, 1660–1800', *Midland History*, 15 (1990), 65–82.

G.H. Tupling, 'Lancashire markets in the sixteenth and seventeenth centuries. Part

II', *Trans. Lancashire and Cheshire Antiquarian Soc.*, 59 (1947), 1–34.

D. Turner, 'A lost seventeenth-century demographic crisis? The evidence of two counties', *Local Population Studies*, 21 (1978), 11–18.

M. Turner and D. Mills (ed.), *Land and Property: The English Land Tax 1692–1832* (Cambridge University Press, 1986).

R.W. Unwin, 'Tradition and transition: market towns of the Vale of York, 1660-1830', *Northern History*, 17 (1981), 72–116.

T. Unwin, 'Rural marketing in medieval Nottinghamshire', *Journal of Historical Geography*, 7 (3) (1981), 231–51.

Late Seventeenth-century Taxation and Population: the Nottinghamshire Hearth Taxes and the Compton Census (Inst. British Geographers, Historical Geography Research Series, No 16, 1985).

J.E. Vance, 'Land assignment in pre-capitalist, capitalist and post-capitalist cities', *Economic Geography*, 47 (1971), 101–20.

N. Vickers, *A Yorkshire Town of the Eighteenth Century. The Probate Inventories of Whitby, North Yorkshire 1700–1800* (Studley: Brewin Books, 1986).

A. Vickery, 'Women and the world of goods: a Lancashire consumer and her possessions, 1751–81', in J. Brewer and R. Porter (ed.), *Consumption and the World of Goods* (Routledge, 1993), 274–301.

D. Wahrman, 'National Society, Communal Culture', *Social History*, 17 (1992), 43–72.

J.K. Walton, 'Trades and professions in late 18th-century England: assessing the evidence of directories', *Local Historian*, 17 (6) (1987), 343–50.

D. Ward, 'Victorian cities: how modern?', *Journal of Historical Geography*, 1 (1975), 135–51.

A.M. Warnes, 'Early separation of homes from workplaces and the urban structure of Chorley, 1780 to 1850', *Trans. Historic Society of Lancashire and Cheshire*, 122 (1970), 105–35.

L. Weatherill, *The Pottery and North Staffordshire, 1660–1760* (Manchester University Press, 1971).

Consumer Behaviour and Material Culture in Britain 1660–1760 (Routledge, 1988).

'The meaning of consumer behaviour in late seventeenth- and early eighteenth-century England', in J. Brewer and R. Porter (ed.), *Consumption and the World of Goods* (Routledge, 1993), 206–27.

See also L. Scammell

S. Webb and B. Webb, *English Local Government. Statutory Authorities for Special Purposes* (Longman, 1922).

W.F. Webster (ed.), *Nottinghamshire Hearth Tax 1664–1674* (Thoroton Society Record Series, 37, 1988).

R. Weedon and A. Milne, *Aspects of Small Towns in the 18th and 19th Centuries,* (Centre for Urban History, University of Leicester, 1993).

F.H. West, *The Great North Road in Nottinghamshire* (n.d. [1956]).

A. Whiteman, *The Compton Census of 1676* (Oxford University Press, 1986).

P. Wilde, 'The use of business directories in comparing the industrial structure of towns: an example from the south-west Pennines', *Local Historian*, 12 (3 and 4) (1976), 152-6.

T.S. Willan, *An Eighteenth-century Shopkeeper. Abraham Dent of Kirkby Stephen,* (Manchester University Press, 1970).

A.C. Wood, *A History of Nottinghamshire* (Nottingham: Thoroton Society, 1947).

'The history of trade and transport on the river Trent', *Trans. Thoroton Soc.*, 54 (1950), 1–44.

S.J. Wright, 'Sojourners and lodgers in a provincial town: the evidence from eighteenth-century Ludlow', *Urban History Yearbook*, 17 (1990), 14–35.

E.A. Wrigley. 'A simple model of London's importance in changing English society and economy', *Past and Present*, 37 (1967), 44–70.

'The growth of population in eighteenth-century England: a conundrum resolved', *Past and Present*, 98 (1983), 121–50.

People, Cities and Wealth: the Transformation of Traditional society (Oxford: Basil Blackwell, 1987).

Continuity, Chance and Change: The Character of the Industrial Revolution in England (Cambridge University Press, 1989).

'Urban growth and agricultural change: England and the Continent in the early modern period', in P. Borsay (ed.), *The Eighteenth-century Town, 1688-1820* (Longman, 1990), 39–82.

'"The Great Commerce of Every Civilised Society": Urban Growth in Early Modern Europe', *Scottish Economic and Social History*, 12 (1992), 5–23.

E.A. Wrigley and R.S. Schofield, *The Population History of England 1541–1871: a Reconstruction* (Cambridge University Press, 1989 ed.).

Unpublished Theses

A.J. Barber, 'Change in the Town of Retford, 1801–1901' (M.A., University of Nottingham, 1993).

D. Flemming, 'A Local Market System, 1549–1720' (Ph.D., University of Leicester, 1980).

J. Goodacre, 'Lutterworth in the Sixteenth and Seventeenth Centuries—A Market Town and its area' (Ph.D., University of Leicester, 1977).

K. Grady, 'The provision of public buildings in the West Riding of Yorkshire, *c.*1600–1840' (Ph.D., University of Leeds, 1980).

S.A. Lewis, 'An Historical and Geographical Study of the Small Towns of Shropshire, 1600–1830' (Ph.D., University of Leicester, 1990).

G.K. Malmgreen, 'Economy and Culture in an Industrialising Town. Macclesfield, Cheshire 1750–1835' (Ph.D., Indiana University, 1980).

C.J.M. Moxon, 'Ashby-de-la-Zouch—A Social and Economic Survey of a Market Town: 1570–1720' (D.Phil., University of Oxford, 1983).

M.K. Noble, 'Growth and Development of Country Towns: the Case of Eastern Yorkshire, *c.*1700–1850' (Ph.D., University of Hull, 1982).

P.R. O'Dell, 'A Study of the Development of Urban Spheres of Influence in Leicestershire' (Ph.D., University of Birmingham, 1954).

Index

agricultural processing 73-7
alehouses: *see* licensed trade
Alnwick (Nthld) 42, 47, 49
apothecaries 90
Arkell, T. 35
Ashbourne (Derb.) 47, 49, 50, 67
assemblies 114
associations 113-18
attorneys 90

Baker, John 53
Barley, M.W. 29
Barnard, William 53
Barry, J. 111, 116
Bassetlaw hundred 112
Bath (Som.) 41
beerhouses: *see* licensed trade
Bentinck, Lord William 115
Bentinck (*later* Scott-Bentinck, *afterwards* Cavendish-Scott-Bentinck), William Henry 4th duke of Portland 115
Berg, M. 8, 15, 16, 168
Berry, H. 89
Bingham
  buildings 50, 50-6
  clubs and associations 114-15
  coach services 81
  framework knitting 79, 80
  freemen's lists 113
  geography 11
  hearth tax assessments 92
  household possessions 107
  landownership 110
  licensed trade 82
  manor courts 113
  market 12
  mentioned 3, 9-11
  middle class in 96
  morphology 40-50
  new private building 135, 137
  new public building 140-4
  occupational structure 65-9
  population 1, 9, 26, 40-2, 61-2
  poverty 92
  residential segregation 126-7
  retailing 69-71
  school 157
  servants in 95
  sources 20
  street improvements 145, 147
  textile production 79
  theatre 114, 142
boat building 80

Borsay, P. 3, 39, 44, 51, 87, 90, 96, 112, 113, 116, 118, 123, 132, 134, 136, 139, 140, 141, 143, 145, 147, 155, 158, 167
Brampton (Cumb.) 18, 165
Breen, T.H. 108
Bridgnorth (Salop) 165
Bristol 89
Brodhurst, William 75
bull baiting 117
Burke, P. 118
Burslem (Staffs.) 72
Burton-upon-Trent (Staffs.) 76

Calvert, John 70
Campbell, C. 105
canals 3, 46, 63-4
  see also Chesterfield Canal; Cromford Canal
Carlisle (Cumb.) 18, 165
Carter, H. 119
Cartwright, John 78
census returns and enumerations 23-4, 26, 125-9
Chalklin, C.W. 4, 141, 143
Charlbury (Oxon.) 5
Chesterfield Canal 47-8, 63-4, 75, 80, 83
cholera: *see* infectious diseases
Chorley (Lancs.) 41, 124
church building 143
Clark, J.C.D. 13, 88
  P. 2, 6, 7, 8, 60, 61, 89, 92, 113, 167, 170
  Samuel 79
Clay, John 102
clubs and associations 113-18
coach services 80-3
coal trade 19, 80, 82-3
cock fighting 117
Cockermouth (Cumb.) 165
Compton Census 22-3
consumer goods 102-10
Conzen, M.R.G. 39, 49
Cooling, Dennis 121
Corfield, P.J. 1, 4, 5, 6, 15, 44, 92, 132, 135, 167, 168
corn trade 80
cotton spinning 77-80, 93
Crafts, N.F.R. 13
Cromford Canal 83
Cumberland, Mathias 105
Cumbria, small towns in 7, 18

dancing schools 114
D'Cruze, S. 116
dealers 91
Dickinson, W. 148

directories 25-6
distribution 80-3
doctors 90, 91
domestic possessions 102-10
Dublin (Ireland) 119, 120
Dyer, A. 2, 7, 11, 62, 79-80
Dyson, James 138

Earle, P. 12, 97-8, 104, 107, 116
East Anglia 2, 80
East Retford
 administrative history 11, 112
 assemblies 114
 boat building 80
 buildings 50-6
 and canal 46, 63-4, 80
 clubs and associations 114-15
 coach services 81
 cotton spinning 76-7, 77-80
 framework knitting 79
 geography 11
 improvements 152-3, 153-4, 160
 infectious diseases 163
 landownership 110-11
 licensed trade 82
 local government 152, 156
 malting 75-7
 market place 149
 market tolls 84
 markets 84, 160
 middle class 96, 105, 108
 milling 74
 morphology 40-50, 124
 new private building 55-6, 135-40
 new public building 140-4
 new streets 55-6
 newsroom 115, 116
 occupational structure 65-9
 parliamentary history 112-13
 politics 158
 population 9, 22, 40-2, 61-2
 probate records 37
 residential segregation 126-8
 retailing 69-71
 Revolution Mill 78
 road improvements 63
 road transport services 81-2, 82
 sanitary condition 164
 servants 95
 street improvements 145, 147, 148
 street lighting 147
 theatre 114, 144
 town hall 51, 140-1, 144
Eden, F.M. 78, 92, 93
Ellis, J. 4, 5, 9, 120, 168
esquires 90-1
Everitt, A. 4, 5, 91, 96
Eversley, D.E.C. 103
Exeter (Devon) 119, 120

fairs 130
Falkus, M.E. 132-3, 150, 153, 158
farmers 108
Finberg, H.P.R. 6, 168
Fiennes-Clinton (*later* Pelham-Clinton), Henry 3rd duke of Newcastle 146
food riots 92-3
Fosse Way 3, 9, 63
framework knitting 34, 79
Freeman, M. 169
freemen's lists 25, 96-7, 113
friendly societies 115-16
furniture 104-10

Gainsborough (Lincs.) 9
gentlemen 90-1, 109
George, D. 12
Gillson, Thomas 138
Ginter, D.E. 31, 32
Glennie, P. 35
Goldsmith, Oliver 86
Grantham (Lincs.) 70, 119, 165
graziers 90
Great North Road 3, 9, 18, 63, 71, 81, 82, 144
Greathead, John 151

Halifax (Yorks.) 80
Handley, W.F. & J. 52
Harrod, William 92
Hawkshead (Cumb.) 29, 165
hearth tax assessments 21-2, 27-31, 93, 120-3
Henstock, A.J.M. 31, 49, 129
Heppenstall, Joseph 53
Herring, Thomas, archbishop of York 23, 40
Hey, D.G. 71
Holland, J. 111
Holles, Henrietta Cavendish wife of Edward Harley earl of Oxford and Mortimer 140, 157
hosiery manufacture 77-80
house building 53-6
household goods 102-10
Howard, Bernard, 17th duke of Norfolk 110
 Charles 16th duke of Norfolk 49
Howitt, William 102, 111
Huddersfield (Yorks.) 80
Hudson, P. 2, 8, 15, 16, 71, 168, 170
husbandmen 90, 108

improvement commissions 146-7, 150-4
industrial buildings 51-2
infectious diseases 163-4
inns: *see* licensed trade
inventories: *see* probate records

Jones, E.L. 132-3, 150, 153, 158

Keene, D. 41
Kendal (Cumb.) 165
King, Gregory 27

land agents 90
land tax assessments 31-2, 110
Langford, P. 89, 91, 109, 114
Langton, J. 2, 4, 5, 7, 8, 59, 119, 170
Laslett, P. 87
Law, C.M. 4
Leadbeake, Ralph 151
Leeds (Yorks.) 41, 80
Leevers, William 93
leisure towns 95
licensed trade 82
Lincolnshire 73
Lindley, Charles 77
linen manufacture 78
Liverpool (Lancs.) 120, 132
London 88-9, 97-8, 119
Longtown (Cumb.) 18
Lowe, Robert 75
Ludlow (Salop) 165
Lumley (*later* Lumley-Savile), John 8th earl of Scarborough 110

Macclesfield (Ches.) 119, 165
McCracken, G. 35
McKendrick, N. 34-5, 103
Malmgreen, C.K. 119
malsters 90
Malthus, T. 14
malting 34, 74-7
Manchester (Lancs.) 80
Mandeville, B. 86
Manning, Mary 69
manor courts 113
manservants: *see* servants
Mansfield
    assemblies 114
    Bridge Street in 38
    buildings 50-6
    clubs and associations 114, 114-15
    coach services 80-1
    and coal mining 19
    coffee clubs 115
    cotton spinning 77-80
    framework knitting 79
    freemen's lists 96-7
    geography 11
    hearth tax assessments 37, 92, 121-4
    improvements 38, 152-3, 153-4, 156, 157, 160
    infectious diseases 163
    land tax assessments 32
    landownership 110
    licensed trade 82
    local government 152, 158
    malting 74-5
    market place 148-9
    market tolls 84
    markets 84, 160-1
    mentioned 74, 117
    middle class 96, 108
    morphology 40-50
    new houses 55-6
    new private building 135-40
    new public building 140-4
    new streets 55-6
    occupational structure 65-9, 102
    population 22, 40-2, 61-2
    poverty 92-3
    probate records 36
    rates 155
    residential segregation 126-9
    retailing 69-71
    scavenging 152, 162
    schools 143
    servants in 95
    sources 20
    Stanton's Mill in 52-3
    street improvements 145-7, 148, 148-9
    street lighting 147
    theatre 114
    town halls 50, 139, 140, 141, 142, 144, 157
    Waverley House 136, 137
Mansfield & Pinxton Railway 83
maps and plans 37
market places 148-9
marketing 80-3
markets 84
Marshall, Dorothy 15
    George 152
    J.D. 7, 17, 28, 165
Martin, William 91, 121
Mason, Richard 104-5
Massey, J.H. 52
Massie, Joseph 102
mercers 91
Middleton, Lord: *see* Willoughby, Henry
Mirfin, William 102
Moore, Robert 71
Morris, R.J. 170
Moyes, A. 169
Mui, H.C. and L. 67
Mukerkji, C. 35

navigable rivers: *see* river navigations; Trent, navigation
Need, Lieut.-Gen. 115
Newark
    administrative history 11, 112

assemblies 114
Beaumont Cross 144
borough court 151
buildings 50-6
Clinton Arms 18
clubs and associations 114-15
coach services 80-1
coal trade 82
coffee club 116
cotton spinning 76-7, 77-80, 93
fairs 130
food riots 93
friendly societies 116
geography 11
Green Dragon inn 50
Handley House 134
hearth tax assessments 37, 121-4
household possessions 108
improvements 150, 152-3, 153, 156, 159-61
infectious diseases 163
land tax assessments 32
landownership 110-11
as a 'leisure town' 95
licensed trade 82
linen manufacture 78
local government 152, 156, 158
malting 75-7
market place 148-9
market tolls 84
markets 159-61
mentioned 90, 91
middle class 96, 104-5, 108
milling 73-4
morphology 40-50
new houses 54
new private building 135-40
new public building 140-4
new streets 54, 56, 57
occupational structure 65-9
parish vestry 113
political history 11-12, 158
population 9, 22, 26, 40-2, 61-2
poverty 92-4
probate inventories 99
and railways 18
rates 155
residential segregation 125-9
retailing 69-71
road improvements 63, 144
road transport services 81-2, 82
scavenging 152
servants 95-6
sources 20
street improvements 145-7, 148-9
street lighting 147
theatre 114
town hall 50, 141-2, 144, 159
trade 80
Trent Bridge 146
Wellington iron foundry in 52
wife selling 117
Newcastle, dukes of 12
see also Fiennes-Clinton, Henry
Newcastle-under-Lyme (Staffs.) 72
Newcastle-upon-Tyne (Nthld) 119, 120
Newham, John 138
newsrooms 115, 116
Noble, M. 32
Norfolk, dukes of: *see* Howard, Bernard; Howard, Charles
Northampton 96
Norwich 4, 119
Nottingham 5-6

occupations 64-9
Ollerton
buildings 50, 50-6
carrying services 81
clubs and associations 114-15
framework knitting 79
geography 11
hearth tax assessments 92
household possessions 108
land tax assessments 32
landownership 110
licensed trade 82
manor courts 113
market 12
mentioned 3, 11
middle class 96
morphology 40-50
new building 56
new private building 135, 137
new public building 140-4
occupational structure 65-9
population 1, 9, 40-2, 61-2
poverty 92
retailing 69-71
school 157
schools 144
servants 95
sources 20
textile production 79
Overton, M. 24, 25, 35, 36, 103, 106, 108
Oxford 119
Oxford, Lady: *see* Holles, Henrietta Cavendish

Paine, Tom 117
papermaking 74
Papplewick 77
parish vestries 113
Penrith (Cumb.) 165
Peveral, Sam 152
Pevsner, N. 137, 142

Pinxton (Derb.) 83
plans: *see* maps and plans
Pleasley Hill (Notts.) 128
Plumb, J.H. 142
poll books 25
population history 21-4, 58-62
Porter, R. 12, 87
Priestley, U. 119
Prior, M. 119
probate records 24-5, 26-31, 36-7, 91, 97-102, 121
property ownership 110-12

quarrying 77

railways 18
Rastell, Dickinson 146
rates 155-6
Raven, N. 2, 8, 63
Reed, M. 39, 132, 167
residential segregation 125-9
retailing 69-71
Retford: *see* East Retford
Revolution Mill (East Retford) 78
riots: *see* food riots
Rippon, Thomas 91
river navigations 2, 18
 see also Trent
road transport 18, 80-3
 see also turnpike trusts
Rooth, George 149
Rose, William 152
Rule, J. 12, 85

Saddler, John 144
Scales, George 53, 78
Scammell, L.: *see* Weatherill, L.
Scarborough, earl of: *see* Lumley, John
scavenging 152
school building 143-4
Schwartz, L.D. 7, 95, 119
servants 95-6
Shammas, C. 35, 67, 103, 108
Shardlow (Derb.) 9
Sheffield (Yorks.) 71, 74
shops: *see* retailing
Simpson, Robert 79
 William 79
Sjoberg, G. 118-19, 120, 123
smallpox: *see* infectious diseases
social geography 118-24
social organisations 113-18
social space 118-24
Spufford, M. 24, 28
Stanton's Mill (Mansfield) 52-3
Stevenson, George 53
 Thomas 79
Stobart, J. 2, 8, 63, 67, 70, 98, 132, 170
stocking making: *see* framework knitting
street lighting 147
street names 57
streets, new 53-6
Styles, J. 103-4
Swan, John 95
Swift, John 105
Sykes, Thomas 151
taverns: *see* licensed trade
tax assesments: *see* hearth tax assessments; land tax assessments
textile production 77-80
theatres 114, 142, 144
Thompson, E.P. 88, 118
Thorpe, John 138
tithe apportionments 32-3, 110
Torr, Worksop 70
town halls 50-1
town plans: *see* maps and plans
trade directories: *see* directories
Trent, navigation 3, 9, 46, 63, 70, 73, 80
Trinder, B.S. 74
Turner, John 79
turnpike trusts 3, 63, 144-5
Tuxford 70

Unwin, R.W. 18, 27
urban sensibility 159-62

Vance, J.E. 118-19, 120, 123
vestries 113
Vickery, A. 108, 111
visitation returns 23
Vries, Jan de 103

Wahrman, D. 87
Wanklyn, M.D.G. 62
Warnes, A.M. 124
Watnaugh, Thomas 105
Weatherill (*later* Scammell), L. 35, 103, 104, 107, 108
Webb, S. and B. 150, 161-3, 164
Wedgwood, Josiah 35
Wellington iron foundry (Newark) 52
wife selling 117
Wigton (Cumb.) 18
Willoughby, Henry 5th Baron Middleton 116, 157
wills: *see* probate records
Wilson, Charles 69
Wolverhampton (Staffs.) 47, 111, 145
Wood, William 84
Worksop
 assemblies 114
 boat building 80
 buildings 50-6

bull baiting 117
and canal 46, 47-9, 63-4, 80
clubs and associations 114-15
coach services 81
cotton spinning 76-7, 77-80
framework knitting 79
geography 11
landownership 110
licensed trade 82
malting 75-7
manor court 113, 151
markets 84
middle class 96, 105, 108
milling 74
morphology 40-50, 124
new houses 54
new private building 135-40
new public building 140-4
new streets 54, 56, 57
occupational structure 65-9
population 22, 26, 40-2, 61-2
residential segregation 126-9
retailing 69-71
Roman Catholic church 157
schools 144
servants 95
social structure 111-12
street improvements 145, 147
street lighting 147
theatre 114
Wrigley, E.A. 4, 13, 169, 170

yeomen 90, 108